Design
Research in
Architecture

Design Research in Architecture

Series Editors

Professor Murray Fraser
Bartlett School of Architecture, UCL, UK

Professor Jonathan Hill
Bartlett School of Architecture, UCL, UK

Professor Jane Rendell
Bartlett School of Architecture, UCL, UK

and

Professor Teddy Cruz
Department of Architecture, University of California at San Diego, USA

Bridging a range of positions between practice and academia, this Ashgate series seeks to present the best proponents of architectural design research from around the world. Each author combines innovative historical and theoretical research with creative propositions as a symbiotic interplay. In offering a variety of key exemplars, the book series situates itself at the forefront of design research investigation in architecture.

Other titles in this series

Design Research in Architecture

An Overview

Edited by
Murray Fraser
Bartlett School of Architecture,
University College, London, UK

Published by
Ashgate Publishing Limited
Wey Court East
Union Road
Farnham
Surrey, GU9 7PT
England

Ashgate Publishing Company
110 Cherry Street
Suite 3-1
Burlington, VT 05401-3818
USA

www.ashgate.com

British Library Cataloguing in Publication Data
A catalogue record for this book is available from the British Library

The Library of Congress has cataloged the printed edition as follows:
Design research in architecture : an overview / [edited] by Murray Fraser.
     pages cm. – (Design research in architecture)
   Includes bibliographical references and index.
   ISBN 978-1-4094-6217-0 (pbk. : alk. paper)
 1. Architectural design. I. Fraser, Murray, editor of compilation.

   NA2750.D413 2014
   720.72–dc23

                                                                2013020868

ISBN: 9781409462170 (pbk)

Printed in the United Kingdom by Henry Ling Limited,
at the Dorset Press, Dorchester, DT1 1HD

Contents

List of Illustrations

Plate 12 Large sectional model for the final exhibition by Johan Van Den Berghe, bringing together scaled models of real and imaginary design projects in an attempt to synthesise the main conclusions of his PhD research. Source: Johan Verbeke. Courtesy of Johan Van Den Berghe

Plate 13 Horizontal sections showing the vertical circulation core interlacing with exhibition spaces, gardens, auditorium and viewing platforms for the historical museum project in Amsterdam by studiokav. Source: Leslie Kavanaugh. Courtesy of studiokav.com

Plate 14 Amsterdam historical museum by studiokav at night reflected in the water of the harbour. Source: Leslie Kavanaugh. Courtesy of studiokav.com

Plate 15 Looking at space differently: the interior of the Pantheon in Rome photographed by Richard Coyne on an iPhone using the '360' app by Occipital. Source: Richard Coyne

Plate 16 'Moving Targets' workshop run by the University of Edinburgh to prototype a system for interfacing social media with streamed media content. Source: Richard Coyne

Plate 17 Spaces of conflict and marginality on the US/Mexican border: the Political Equator 3 meeting in June 2011. 2013 Estudio Teddy Cruz

Plate 18 Diagram showing Teddy Cruz's vision of an urbanisation of retrofit linked into community participation. 2013 Estudio Teddy Cruz

Plate 19 Estudio Teddy Cruz, *Casa Familiar: Living Rooms at the Border*, San Ysidro in southern California (2001 onwards). 2013 Estudio Teddy Cruz

Plate 20 Interior photograph of the model by Shigeru Ban for the 'temporary' cardboard cathedral in Christchurch, New Zealand (2012–13). Source: Shigeru Ban Architects. Courtesy of Shigeru Ban Architects

Plate 21 Conceptual drawing by Yara Sharif for stitching the divided landscape of Palestine/Israel. Source: Yara Sharif. Courtesy of Yara Sharif

Plate 22 Clusters of sponge elements to absorb rainfall and ground water in the reoccupied stone quarries in the Palestinian West Bank, as one project for Yara Sharif's PhD by Design at the University of Westminster, London. Source: Yara Sharif. Courtesy of Yara Sharif

Plate 23 Lebbeus Woods, *Manifesto* (1993). Source: Lebbeus Woods/Aleksandra Wagner. Courtesy of Aleksandra Wagner

Plate 24 Lebbeus Woods, *Injection Parasite, Sarajevo* (1992). Source: Lebbeus Woods/Aleksandra Wagner. Courtesy of Aleksandra Wagner

BLACK AND WHITE ILLUSTRATIONS

2   Design Research: The First 500 Years

2.1 Extract page from Francesco Colonna's *Hypnerotomachia Poliphili* (study for a garden). Source: Francesco Colonna, *Hypnerotomachia Poliphili*, 1499. © The British Library Board

3   An 'Artificial Science' of Architecture

4   What if Design Practice Matters?

5   Design Research and Critical Transformations: Situating Thought, Projecting Action

10   Even More than Architecture

Notes on Contributors

Richard Blythe is Professor in Architecture and Dean of the School of Architecture and Design at RMIT University, Melbourne, Australia. In 2010 he led the establishment of the RMIT Creative Practice Research PhD programme in Ghent, Belgium and was also primary author for the EU Marie Curie ITN grant, ADAPT-r. Richard was a founding director of Tasmanian architecture practice TERROIR.

Richard Coyne is Professor of Architectural Computing at the University of Edinburgh, UK. He is an architect who researches and teaches in theories and practices of architecture, design and digital media, on which he has published eight books. At Edinburgh University, he has been Head of the Department of Architecture and Head of the School of Arts, Culture and Environment.

Teddy Cruz is director of Estudio Teddy Cruz and Professor in Public Culture and Urbanism at the University of California San Diego, USA. He co-founded the Center for Urban Ecologies and is internationally renowned for his design research into the Tijuana–San Diego border. Recently, San Diego's mayor appointed him as advisor on civic imagination and urban initiatives for that city.

Murray Fraser is Professor of Architecture and Global Culture at the Bartlett School of Architecture at University College London, UK and Vice Dean of Research. He has published extensively on design, architectural history & theory, urbanism and cultural studies, including the award-winning book *Architecture and the 'Special Relationship'* (2008). He is a founding member of the Palestine Regeneration Team (PART).

Katja Grillner is Professor of Critical Studies in Architecture at the KTH School of Architecture, Stockholm, Sweden. She directs the state-funded research programme, Architecture in Effect (2011–16). She co-founded FATALE, a feminist architecture teaching and research group. Among her books are *Ramble, Linger and Gaze* (2000) and she was lead editor of *01-AKAD: Experimental Research in Architecture and Design* (2005).

Jonathan Hill is Professor of Architecture and Visual Theory at the Bartlett School of Architecture, University College London, UK. In 1995 he co-founded the Bartlett's PhD Architectural Design programme and was himself the first to gain that doctorate. His books include *The Illegal Architect* (1998), *Actions of Architecture* (2003), *Immaterial Architecture* (2006) and *Weather Architecture* (2012).

Leslie Kavanaugh is an architect and philosopher and the founding director of studiokav.com in Amsterdam, The Netherlands. Formerly, she taught and was a Senior Researcher specialising in the philosophy of space and time at the Technical University of Delft. Her publications include

The Architectonic of Philosophy: Plato, Aristotle, Leibniz (2007), *Chrono-topologies* (2010) and *Meditations on Space* (2010).

Shane Murray is Dean of MADA, Monash University Faculty of Art Design and Architecture, in Melbourne, Australia and an award-winning architect who researches into housing and urban design. He joined Monash in 2008 as Foundation Professor of Architecture to establish its architectural programme, having switched from RMIT University. He received the 2012 Neville Quarry Medal for services to architectural education.

Jane Rendell is Professor of Architecture and Art at the Bartlett Faculty of the Built Environment, University College London, UK. She is a frequently quoted writer, art critic and architectural historian/theorist/designer, whose sole authored books include *Site-Writing* (2010), *Art and Architecture: A Place Between* (2006) and *The Pursuit of Pleasure* (2002). See also her website at: http://www.janerendell.co.uk/.

Leon van Schaik is Professor of Architecture (Innovation Chair) at RMIT University, Melbourne, Australia. He has promoted local and international architectural culture through design practice research and commissioning and founded RMIT's design research programme. Sole publications include *Mastering Architecture* (2005), *Design City Melbourne* (2006) and *Spatial Intelligence* (2008) and he also co-authored *Procuring Innovative Architecture* (2010).

Philip Steadman is Emeritus Professor of Urban and Built Form Studies at the Bartlett Faculty of the Built Environment, University College London, UK and a Research Fellow at the UCL Energy Institute. He has researched extensively into the morphology of buildings and cities, especially in relation to energy use. He is completing a book on building types and built forms.

Johan Verbeke is Professor of Research Design at Sint-Lucas School of Architecture, Ghent, Belgium. He also holds an adjunct professorship at RMIT University in Australia. His main interest is digital architecture and more recently in creative practice research in art, design and architecture. He is currently the president of eCAADe and coordinator of the EU Marie Curie ITN network, ADAPT-r.

Acknowledgements

The genesis for this book was a series of conversations held about five years ago between myself and Jonathan Hill and Jane Rendell from the Bartlett School of Architecture, at a time when I was still at my former institution, the University of Westminster. The Bartlett already possessed by then a substantial design doctorate programme – called the PhD Architectural Design – and I was beginning to grow a different Westminster variant. It had become apparent to us that the usual restrictions of publishing were such that students engaged on PhDs by Design stood very little, if any, chance of ever being able to publish their work as a substantive and coherent entity. Jonathan, Jane and I therefore began to investigate ways for how we might remedy this problem. We were also keenly aware of the notable design research doctorates being produced elsewhere around the world, not least by students guided by Leon van Schaik and Richard Blythe (plus colleagues like Martyn Hook and SueAnne Ware) at the Royal Melbourne Institute of Technology in Australia. Leon and Richard have always been extremely helpful to us in our efforts and so it is a real pleasure they have been able to write a joint essay for this book.

Furthermore, we knew that a growing number of practicing architects who often had strong links (and indeed part-time posts) with various universities were producing excellent design research work which was not being disseminated adequately either. An architect whose design research and intellectual approach we had long admired was Teddy Cruz in the USA and so we invited Teddy to join our venture in seeking a publishing deal for a book series, to be called 'Design Research in Architecture'. We approached two leading publishers with a proposal and duly arrived at an agreement with Ashgate. For that welcome result, we should acknowledge the anonymous reviewers who read our application and who offered many useful comments and suggestions. However, more than anything we must give thanks to Val Rose, the commissioning editor for Ashgate's architectural catalogue, for whom we cannot possibly have higher praise. Val has been an inspiration to work with, whether in terms of the clarity of her thought, her loyalty to us as an editorial team, or her sheer enthusiasm for our book series and for architecture in general. As an architectural graduate herself, the service that Val has performed in establishing such a remarkably innovative catalogue at Ashgate and doing so within just a few years, is astonishing. We salute Val for her integral part in the entire process. This gratitude now has to be extended to the rest of her publishing team at Ashgate who are busily preparing a sequence of volumes for the 'Design Research in Architecture' series, with the first due to emerge in late 2013. With regard to this particular book, we are thankful for the sterling work by Emily Ruskell at Ashgate.

In our deliberations, we soon realised it would be extremely useful to invite some leading exponents of design research to write an essay each on the subject, thereby creating a sort of companion volume for the individual books in the series. It fell upon me to edit this book. My gratitude to the contributing authors, as well as to all who gave us permission to use images, goes without saying. For her superb graphic design for the 'Design Research in Architecture' series as a whole, I am indebted to Avni Patel. Many colleagues at the Bartlett School of Architecture ought to be thanked for the help extended to me while producing this particular volume. I cannot possibly hope to mention them all, but should mention, along with Jonathan and Jane, the ongoing support for this particular project from Adrian Forty, Colin Fournier, Stephen Gage, Penelope Haralambidou, Kenny Kinugasa-Tsui, Justin Lau, Guan Lee, C.J. Lim, Yeoryia Manolopoulou, Barbara Penner, Peg Rawes, Luis Rego, Tania Sengupta and Bob Sheil. An excellent Bartlett doctoral student, Danielle Willkens, proved to be an ultra-efficient and invaluable research assistant in the final stages of preparing this book.

Elsewhere, in terms of helping me to develop ideas and approaches for this book, I am especially grateful to Suad Amiry, Pierre d'Avoine, Shigeru Ban, Pete Barber, Trish Belford, Nigel Bertram, Richard Blythe, Hugh Campbell, Prue Childs, Tom Corby, Teddy Cruz, David Cunningham, Maarten Delbeke, Kim Dovey, Matt Gaskin, Nasser Golzari, Jon Goodbun, Nabeel Hamdi, Katharine Heron, Hilde Heynen, Martyn Hook, Louisa Hutton, Eva Jiricna, Amy Kulper, John Macarthur, Niall McLaughlin, Clare Melhuish, Zeynep Mennan, Bill Menking, Ruth Morrow, Marika Neustupny, Sheila O'Donnell, Doina Petrescu, Philippe Rahm, Kester Rattenbury, Adrian Rifkin, Flora Samuel, Leon van Schaik, Yara Sharif, Ben Stringer, Joram Ten Brink, Jeremy Till, John Tuomey, Johan Verbeke, Johan de Walsche, Cindy Walters, SueAnne Ware, Sarah Wigglesworth, the late Lebbeus Woods and many others. On a personal note, I would like once again to express my love for my two sons, Callum Fraser and Liam Fraser and for my partner, Eva Branscome, for her emotional support and lively intelligence.

Murray Fraser

INTRODUCTION

Murray Fraser

What is the role of design research in the types of insight and knowledge that architects create? That is the central question raised by this book. It is of course a huge subject, not least because of philosophical doubts about the concept of knowledge itself.[1] What does knowledge actually consist of? How can we prove that it is new? What is it able to do in the world? How does it relate to our brains and our bodies and our feelings? How does it operate as a collective social process? These kinds of deeper epistemological issues underlie the discussions in the book, which naturally will focus more directly on the subject of design research in architecture. For it is clear that architects have produced, are producing, and will continue to produce a wide spectrum of new insight and knowledge through their design ideas and design practices. Otherwise we cannot adequately explain why buildings vary so greatly, or why they have changed over time in such dramatic fashion. There are many external and internal influences on architectural knowledge, for sure, but what is equally certain is that new forms of insight and knowledge are continually being created. As such, architecture forms a genuine discourse *and* field of practice, even if it is also one in which there are a myriad of opinions, not least about how even to define what architecture is.

The most accepted mechanism for creating new insight and knowledge in any cultural or academic field, or for attempting to understand past or present or future conditions, is through research. There are many different theories and models for architectural research should be, several of which will be discussed by the contributors to this book. One could however just rely on the terminology adopted by official assessments of research quality in universities.

In the UK, the 2014 Research Excellence Framework (REF) defines research as 'a process of investigation leading to new insights, effectively shared', while the equivalent process back in 2008 stated that research 'is to be understood as original investigation undertaken in order to gain knowledge and understanding'.[2] Correspondingly, the Excellence in Research for Australia (ERA) classifies research, based on the 2002 Frascati Manual definition, as 'the creation of new knowledge and/or the use of existing knowledge in a new and creative way so as to generate new concepts, methodologies and understandings. This could include synthesis and analysis of previous research to the extent that it is new and creative.'[3] Some may find these types of definition far too simple for their tastes, but they do have the benefit of permitting a broad and heterogeneous vision of what can be classified as research. Design research in architecture is something which is most definitely included within the REF and ERA agendas, and so there is no reason why this should not apply elsewhere. It is certainly the view also of the Research Charter of the European Association for Architectural Education (EAAE), which openly welcomes design research into its framework: that document came about largely as the result of the efforts of Hilde Heynen and Johan De Walsche, while Johan Verbeke and I, and several others, helped with the drafting.

As a working definition, architectural design research can be described as the processes and outcomes of inquiries and investigations in which architects use the creation of projects, or broader contributions towards design thinking, as the central constituent in a process which also involves the more generalised research activities of thinking, writing, testing, verifying, debating, disseminating, performing, validating and so on. Adrian Forty has shown eloquently that architects have been deploying a combination of these modes of expression for a rather long time in their work.[4] Likewise, design research as able to blend into other more established research methodologies in the arts, humanities and science, with no intrinsic antagonism. It is vital that the design element and these other modes of research activity and research methodology operate together in an interactive and symbiotic manner, with each feeding into the others throughout the whole process from start to finish. In turn this raises an important point about temporality, in that design research should never be something that just happens at the beginning of a project, as a sort of research and development stage, before the architect 'lapses' into more normative and routine productive modes. Indeed, architectural design research, if undertaken properly, is open to the full panoply of means and techniques for designing and making that are available to architects – including sketches, drawings, physical models, digital modelling, precedent analysis, prototyping, digital manufacture, interactive design, materials testing, construction specification, site supervision, building process, user occupation, user modification and such like. Architectural design research does not of course need to use all of these possibilities in every instance, but they indicate the sorts of techniques which ought to be brought into the frame.

Design research in architecture cannot however be conceived as synonymous with the immensely broad subject of architecture, or indeed of architectural practice; rather, it is a significant seam that runs through design work with a particular focus on the creation of new insight and knowledge. Here there is a useful parallel with practice-led research in the fine arts, as Jane Rendell has pointed out.[5] She notes that compartmentalising the four main disciplinary approaches within architecture (building science, social science, humanities and art/design) works directly against what we realise is the multidisciplinary nature of architecture as a whole. Instead, Rendell believes that design research offers a means to bring these disciplinary strands together and also – importantly – for them then to be able to critique their own methodological assumptions. In this regard, architecture can learn a lot from the development of PhDs by Practice in other artistic fields. Yet while accepting that the influence of practice-led research in the fine arts is important, there are of course other approaches within architectural design research which stem from very different impulses, as the contribution here by Richard Blythe and Leon van Schaik makes abundantly clear. There are many types of research in design research, just as one can see there are many types of research in science or social science or history or fine art.

This then leads on to the issue of the methodology of design research. Other forms of research in architecture openly proclaim their methodological approach, for example science (repeatability) or history (transparency), while in social science, for instance, an articulation is made between theory-testing (deductive) and theory-building (inductive) approaches. Yet in each case, research methodology is not just a narrow matter of being rigorous and consistent and diligent. The importance of speculation and imagination to the scientist, or the social scientist, or the historian, is well testified. Hence the only difference with design research in architecture is a matter of degree, since in the latter – while borrowing where appropriate from the other, more established research methodologies – the creative aspect becomes the dominant part of the investigation, and to achieve that it has to introduce its own ideas of testing and evaluating, even in rather lateral or unexpected ways. Hence there is no methodological schism. As several contributors to this book point out, each of the other kinds of architectural research also rely on creative leaps and lateral thinking in their methodological process, if not nearly as much. In other words, the issue of the methodology of design research as a contested site – in that it clearly opens up a new paradigm of research – is one of its real strengths.

This degree of openness – both in the acceptance of design research as a valid activity and in what it involves as a practice – is of course extremely relevant for the focus of this book. We are interested here in how architects, through their design work and professional practice, carry out forms of research that produce their own particular kind of new insight and knowledge. In other words, they are engaged upon a research process that is noticeably different from, yet equal in value to, the kinds of insight and knowledge from natural scientists, social scientists, historians, geographers, humanities scholars and so on. It is essential to hold this catholic and tolerant view of design research, for if there has been a weakness in previous writings on design research in architecture, it was that they were far too defensive. In turn this caused writers to attempt to justify design research in terms of what it was not – mostly in relation to misconstrued or exaggerated notions of objectivity in the natural sciences – rather than trying to say what it actually was.

There will be none of this defensiveness or apologia in this book. This is because there seems no real argument any more that design research in architecture exists, or that it possesses its own rigour and relevance. An elegant dissection of the hitherto false polarisation between 'design' and 'research' has been provided by David Leatherbarrow.[6] He calls instead for a more confident yet more modest view of design research in which both words are seen not as opposites, but as projective undertakings equally rooted in uncertainty and contingency, and thus needing constantly to oscillate between past, present and future conditions. 'Project making in architecture is no more certain of its outcome than research in modern sciences', notes Leatherbarrow, '… [so] when the actual methods of scientific research are kept in mind, and their similarity to project making understood, architecture's membership in the research community ceases to be a question'.[7] Therefore anyone who still continues to doubt the existence or relevance of design research is a Flat Earther. As noted, the value of design research in general has been demonstrated by its ready adoption – along with concomitants such as PhDs by Design or by Practice – in other cultural fields such as the fine arts, design or music, which indeed in many countries are more advanced in terms of the acceptance design research than in architecture. In the UK, for example, there were a number of groundbreaking art schools in the early 1990s where PhDs by Practice were inaugurated: Adrian Rifkin at Leeds University was just one of these founding tutors. Another recent sign of this maturity in other cultural fields is *The Routledge Companion* to *Research in the Arts*, which sets a precedent for architecture to meet.[8] Perhaps this is because these artistic fields are less involved in, and less worried about, living up to ideals of scientific objectivity, or maybe there is just a stronger intellectual and cultural lag in architecture because it is a professionally regulated discipline. Nonetheless, there have been some notable outposts of design research in architecture since the mid-1990s, the best known proponents of which – Jonathan Hill from the Bartlett School of Architecture at University College London, and Leon van Schaik at RMIT University in Melbourne – have willingly contributed chapters to this book. As such, they have already done much to prove the value of the approach, even if, perhaps predictably, they hold different views on the path that design research should take.

Whatever the historical backdrop, what is now crucial is to map out a terrain of what design research in architecture might encompass. This is perhaps the key task for this present book, operating as it does as a companion volume to the Ashgate book series – also entitled 'Design Research in Architecture' – which I am co-editing with Jonathan Hill, Jane Rendell and Teddy Cruz. Over the course of the next few years, the aim of our parallel book series is to provide space for practicing architects/ academics who are engaged in design research to present and discuss their ideas and projects, all in a spirit that is deliberately open geographically, intellectually and aesthetically. There are countless ways to undertake architectural design research, and in that sense this book offers a taster, or sampler, for the Ashgate book series in general.

What, then, can we say design research in architecture should be about? It is not the aim here to be at all didactic or proscriptive, or in any way limiting – not least because it is such a young, emerging field. We need more architects and academics to get involved in ever more intensive ways, and a sense of freedom and opportunity has to be one of the most attractive features of architectural design research. Just as for much of history it would have been unthinkable for architects to wish to become experts in designing working-class housing, or become experts in low-carbon sustainable design, then today the conceptual challenge is for them to become experts in how architecture produces its own insight and knowledge – and its particular forms of practice – through design research. In some senses this is linked to Donald Schön's text on the 'reflective practitioner' as an agent within the creative industries, even if many authors have suggested that we actually need a more dynamic and engaged model of design practice – often signalled by the use of the term 'praxis' as a condition which is far more critically engaged and socially proactive.[9] Hence we need to view design research as something distinct from Schön's 'reflective practitioner', not least because the latter does not fully take into account the vital processes of knowledge creation in architecture. Some rather obvious and crucial questions arise at this point. Is design research in architecture something that is already inherent in architectural practice, and simply needs to be identified and articulated in the public realm? Or is it something that still needs to be created anew, as a kind of step-change in the way in which architects/ academics conceive of and produce their designs? The earliest prognoses for design research in the 1960s and 70s tended to be written by advocates of what were either termed 'design methods', such as Geoffrey Broadbent or John Christopher Jones, or of systems theory and cybernetics, like Gordon Pask or Ranulph Glanville, which often tended to tip over into 'design science'.[10] In retrospect, these efforts tended to lead us into blind alleys, or else towards organisations such as the Design Research Society, which for most architects offers too narrow a focus to be of much relevance to them.[11] More appealing is the now legendary essay by Christopher Frayling on research in arts and design, in which he spoke of research 'for', 'through' or 'into' design.[12] Some of the contributors to this book deal more explicitly with Frayling's essay, so I will refrain from going into it here. Suffice to say that his essay is also notable for being picked up and developed by those who from the 1990s were amongst the first to write in a more concerted fashion about architectural design research – the best known include Bryan Lawson in the UK, Peter Downton in Australia and Halina Dunin-Woyseth in Norway.[13] If there has been a limitation in these texts, however, it is the relative degree of abstraction – even separation – from actual specific design projects and practices through which architects engage in design research as a fully integrative process.

A different problem, which lies at precisely the opposite end of the scale, is when an aesthetic agenda controls the analysis too much, and *the will to form* takes over. In such cases, design research seems more about defending a style, as a kind of aesthetic determinism that gets too close to the limitations of 'design methods' or 'design science'. It is a regrettable tendency which is partly due to the continuing influence of the avant-garde myth of architects as socially detached form-creators and innovative geniuses. The irony recently is that this type of writing on design research is often linked to the use of advanced computer-aided-design techniques such as parametric modelling, of which adherents – such as Michael Hensel or Patrik Schumacher – claim to be using performance-related (and thus self-generating and democratically distributive) parameters to create the formal designs.[14] What results is a new form of technocracy, the new High Tech. Instead, we ought to be getting away from these aesthetically driven revivals of avant-garde myths, and finding our source of speculation and research opportunities in normative social formations and everyday practices. Design research offers an ideal means to do so and indeed this is another theme running through the essays in this book.

In this sense, it seems appropriate to claim that this is an entirely different kind of book about design research in architecture. At the end, there is an Indicative Bibliography which alludes to a long history of architectural books which can be seen as being in the spirit of design research. The list of items is not meant as any way definitive, and indeed is intended to be eclectic. Readers are bound to disagree with many of the choices, and wonder why others were not included instead. Indeed there is always a dilemma in producing such a list, since it looks like one is trying to establish a canon, which is doubly problematic when the history of architecture has not been well balanced in terms of gender or geography or ethnicity, which makes the list look somewhat skewed in face of contemporary social values. I had toyed with the idea of omitting the Indicative Bibliography altogether, but felt there is a good point in asserting that architects have always been producing design research of various kinds, and also showing – in the most recent entries – that the situation is now changing to become more gender and geographically and ethnically balanced. Another obvious point is that in most cases the writers of the items contained in the Indicative Bibliography did not formally conceive of what they were doing as design research, as with figures from 'deep history' like Vitruvius, who nonetheless famously wrote:

> The architect's expertise is enhanced by many disciplines and various sorts of specialized knowledge; all the works executed using these other skills are evaluated by his [sic] seasoned judgement. The expertise is born both of *practice* and *reasoning*. *Practice* is the constant, repeated exercise of the hands by which the work is brought to completion in whatever medium is required for the proposed design. *Reasoning*, however, is what can demonstrate and explain the proportions of completed works skilfully and systematically ... Thus architects who strove to obtain practical manual skills but lacked an education have never been able to achieve an influence equal to the quality of their exertions; on the other hand, those who placed their trust entirely in theory and in writings seem to have chased after a shadow, not something real. But those who have fully mastered both skills, armed, if you will, in full panoply, those architects have reached their goal more quickly and influentially.[15]

Such sentiments were echoed by later architects such as Alberti or Palladio, and down through to Soane and Schinkel. Even the more studious nineteenth-century analysts of the building industries and professions, such as Gottfried Semper, did not promote their inquiries as design research, and possibly the early-modernists – while generally united in their allegiance to research – were too polemically intent on asserting the ideological supremacy of their new approach to have time to start conceiving of design research more creatively. A constricted vision of research as a kind of *a priori* and quasi-scientific process, primarily geared as the preparatory process for designing and manufacturing, simmered through the initial CIAM conferences in Frankfurt in 1929 and Brussels in 1930; these looked in turn at the smallest possible sizes for the 'minimum existence dwelling' and the optimal height of social housing blocks. This essentially rationalist conception of research was transported to Britain in 1933 with the formation of the Modern Architectural Research Group (MARS), and similar attitudes prevailed among other inter-war groups. As the most fecund and most contradictory member of CIAM, it was Le Corbusier who displayed the subtlest understanding of research as a core part of architectural activity. For example, he observed in one of his South American lectures as reprinted in the 1930 book, *Precisions*: 'When for twenty-five years one has carried out research step-by-step, when this research seems at last to lead to a clear, simple, and complete system, it is a relief as well as a risky test to come to justify oneself ...'[16] Yet as far as I am aware, Le Corbusier never made any reference to the specific activity of design research as such, even if he was manifestly doing so through the interplay of his words and buildings.

Rather, in my own chapter here, I make a case for Eliel Saarinen's 1943 book on *The City* as being perhaps the first which explicitly coined the term 'design research' – he mostly referred to it as 'research design', yet it was basically the same principle.[17] It is also evident that he did not quite grasp the full implications of design research as a process of inquiry and investigation in which thinking and writing and designing were integrally interlinked throughout. Yet a more self-conscious approach did emerge, even if gradually, after the Second World War, especially in the USA which now formed the locus of modernist hegemony. By the time it came to Robert Venturi's *Complexity and Contradiction in Architecture* (1966), or Venturi, Scott Brown and Izenour's *Learning from Las Vegas* (1972), or Christopher Alexander's *A Pattern Language* (1977), or then to classic books/projects such as Rem Koolhaas's *Delirious New York* (1978) or Mike Webb's *Temple Island* (1987), we had entered a phase when a more formalised status for design research was plain to see – even if again these authors didn't specifically mention the term.[18] However, when Aldo Rossi sat down in December 1969 to write the preface for the second Italian edition of his seminal work, *The Architecture of the City*, he felt confident enough to observe:

> These two terms, analysis and design, seem to me to be coalescing into one fundamental area of study, in which the study of urban artifacts and of form becomes architecture. The rationality of architecture lies precisely in its capacity to be constructed out of a meditation on artifacts over time, with certain elements playing an integrating role in this construction. For the archaeologist and the artist alike, the ruins of a city constitutes a starting point for invention, but only at the moment when they can be linked with a precise system, one based on lucid hypotheses which acquire and develop their own validity, do they construct something real. The construction of the real is an act mediated by architecture in its relationship with things and the city, with ideas and history.[19]

This emerging self-consciousness about what is involved in design research was pushed forward by other smart practitioners of the time, notably Bernard Tschumi, who observed in *The Manhattan Transcripts* (1981): 'In architecture, concepts can either precede or follow projects or buildings. In other words, a theoretical concept may be either applied to a project or derived from it.'[20] A growing identification with research processes also spread from Rem Koolhaas to ambitious younger Netherlands practices like UN Studio, headed by Ben van Berkel and Caroline Bos, who have made repeated reference to using research techniques such as 'diagrams' or 'design models' as translational devices for creating their buildings.[21] Another research-orientated Dutch practice, MVRDV, even noted (ruefully) of the conditions under which it is possible to undertake design research:

> A more ambitious terrain clearly demands a more research-like approach within architectural practice ... Since research within architectural practice is not as economically acknowledged as in other professions (for example science), it can only survive in an office with flexibility and a collage of collaborations and finances: research commissions, grants, subsidies, educational institutions, design commissions, and industries.[22]

Speaking of the conditions and possibilities which exist today for design research in architecture, these form a mainspring of the essays throughout this present book. Before I introduce each of the chapters in turn, it is worth perhaps spelling out three main questions which seem to recur among the authors, and which perhaps sit at the heart of the next phase of architectural design research:

1. How do we define (and by implication protect) the very different and mixed forms of insight and knowledge that architects produce, without being dominated by scientific objectivity or technocracy? The modes of research involved in design research in architecture are incredibly broad, and can be said to include investigations that might be scientific, technical, historical, theoretical, social anthropological, psychological, philosophical, economic, political, environmental, narrative, etc. With this in mind, design-based and project-led knowledge created by architects is what is able to intersect with many if not all of them.

2. What are the most effective modes or routes though which architectural design research can be pursued? Here a key issue is how we define are what is meant by multidisciplinary, transdisciplinary or interdisciplinary research. Design research can involve all of these, but always needs to be synthesised through its own combinations of drawn, written, verbal and performed work. There are limitations and problems with each of these formulations, as many of the contributors point out.

3. How does design research relate to the work carried out in architectural practices? Is it something which is entirely separate from what professional architects perform, or is it exactly the same, or somewhere in-between? Do the conditions for design research differ between academia and practice, and if so how? Again there are many views on this matter in this book's chapters, which is perhaps only to be expected, with the

difference seeming to be whether the author feels that practice is performing well already and simply needs to be tweaked, or whether they think the entire professional mindset has to be transformed.

In terms of who has written the chapters, initially it was my intention to maintain an equal balance between architects in practice and those in academia. But I moved away from this position once it became clear, after talking to a number of leading practitioners from around the world, that there would not be enough space within a single chapter to present their ideas and projects to any depth. So rather than attempting to include watered down versions of their work, it occurred to me that the accompanying Ashgate book series offers practicing architects the length to get into a more detailed analysis of their design research. Hence in this book there is now more emphasis on academically-located architects and theorists who wish to discuss the more general issues involved in design research, although even in these cases it was my deliberate strategy to invite those who are also engaged in creative practice themselves so that they could bring this other work into their texts. The next point to make is about the geographical spread of contributors. Initially it was planned to include a far more global mix, but again after much discussion with prospective authors, it became clear that most countries around the world do not as yet possess a sufficiently strong culture of architectural design research – nor seemingly the intellectual space and conditions for it to develop on an extensive enough scale as yet. It must be obvious to anyone that, in terms of where advances in architectural design research are taking place, there is a decided geographic grouping in the UK and Australia and a few specific countries in continental Europe (Norway, Sweden, Belgium and the Netherlands). Those are certainly the locations where various academic conferences have been held over the last decade or so to discuss design research in architecture, frequently linked to the issue of design doctorates. Certain of these events will be referred to in the chapters of this book. In regard to continental Europe, this scenario of a concentration of activity within the aforementioned countries is also very much confirmed in a recent essay by Halina Dunin-Woyseth and Fredrik Nilsson.[23] Hence there is a purpose behind the geographical concentration of authors in this book, although the real hope is that the practice and dissemination of architectural design research will become more globally distributed in future.

Whatever the disclaimers, there is a great deal of fertile interaction in design research, and many modes and opportunities are available. Design research in architecture can be seen as forming a place which can equally happen either in practice and academia, or which more likely – and perhaps more productively – spans between professional offices and universities. As mentioned, it is not yet defined in any way, and as such this openness and diversity are things to be celebrated in this book. It is also for this reason that I have not organised the chapters into different sections, or classifications, as I don't want to give the impression of fixed 'camps' being formed within architectural design research. Someone else might well try to do that in due course, but it will not happen here; fluidity is the key and many of the issues and positions are shared across the essays, which will now be briefly introduced.

The first contribution, fittingly, is a piece by Jonathan Hill. He observes the change during the Renaissance when drawings became essential for architectural practice (*disegno*), and then how the idealised design in treatises – Alberti, Colonna, Palladio, and others – was supplanted by contingency, empiricism and subjectivity in the eighteenth-century Picturesque. Soon after, the broader concept of 'design' was abandoned with the advent of industrial capitalism, creating a split between the fine arts and applied arts. Also vital for Hill is the active role of architectural history, beginning with Vasari. He notes that by the post-war era of British Brutalism, an architect like Denys Lasdun was writing about his own work: 'The architect is a historian twice over: as an author of a book and as a designer of a building.' Hill draws out fascinating links between novels and buildings and gardens, including the influence of *Tristram Shandy's* rambling narrative on the Soane House/Museum. Bringing the tale through to the Solar House by the Smithsons, Hill portrays design research as a confluence of architecture, history, storytelling and landscaping. In Hill's view, design research offers a paradox in that it creates 'novel histories'. Its methods are simultaneously objective and subjective, fictional and factual, yet all this feeds into the creation of innovative buildings and gardens.

Following on is an extremely different chapter by Philip Steadman, someone who for decades has pursued the idea of architecture as an 'artificial science' (to borrow a term from Herbert Simon). Steadman examines how a scientific approach might be applied to architectural design, not in the mould of Christopher Alexander or so-called 'design methods' or 'design science', which, as he points out, tend to be overly reductive in conception. Instead,

Steadman calls for an 'artificial science' that can combine architectural history, building science and spatial/morphological analysis. This he believes could reveal hidden structures of knowledge through experimentation and analysis, showing the functions, goals and adaptations of buildings: in this sense, the development of the 'Spacemate' model at TU Delft offers an interesting contemporary approach. Steadman rejects simple determinism or the search for easy rules, or indeed any false beliefs in optimisation. It is an elegant rebuke to those, for instance, who are now touting parametric certainties. Steadman prefers a scientific approach that will leave creative options as open as possible: 'Designers' knowledge is enhanced, but their hands are not forced'.

Following that is a joint contribution by Richard Blythe and Leon van Schaik which lucidly sets out the practitioner-orientated model of design research developed over the decades at RMIT University in Melbourne. Under the aegis of van Schaik, the impact of the RMIT programme on the urban form and architectural discourse of that city has been remarkable, indeed unique in the world. It is a vision of design research which is very much practice led, aiming above all to examine what architects create 'through the medium of design itself'. The gold standard of design research, in this model, are the very buildings realised in practice, with these being treated as *de facto* 'publications' in the professional/intellectual sphere. Blythe is especially keen not to split – either theoretically or temporally – the acts of designing and reflecting upon design. The latter does not follow the former, but happens simultaneously and in a continuous loop. One of the great achievements of Blythe and van Schaik,

and the RMIT model generally, is to visualise (and spatialise) the processes of design research through expressive ideograms, as shown here in this chapter.

Taking a distinct approach in her contribution, Katja Grillner voices the opinion that design research needs to have a direct impact on the outside world while also preserving a place for speculative thinking within the 'ivory tower' of academia. She picks up on Frayling's definitions of research 'for', 'through' and 'into' design, noting that design research is not interested at all in the first category, but is instead a fruitful mixture of the latter two. Grillner expands upon this to stress the importance of interdisciplinary research and an expanded sense of social and political agency. Hers is an explicitly feminist perspective, outlining the writings and events and projects of the FATALE group in Stockholm, which she co-founded. She identifies above all two key aspects to the feminist agenda within architectural design research: firstly, to expose the structural biases against women in society, and secondly, to devise ways to change the situation. Grillner shows how these aims are being pursued in her current project as a cultural researcher and local user of Rosenlund Park in the Sodermalm district of her home city.

Returning to Australia, Shane Murray regards housing as the central issue of design research in architecture. As the mainspring of the university-based Monash Architecture Studio (MAS), he is a passionate advocate of applied research knowledge. An integral part of his approach is the detailed case-study analysis of prior projects by other architects, from which a series of connections can be identified and discussed. These, Murray argues, can be used in a systematic manner to establish a genuine 'knowledge base' for design research, and he urges architects to be more honest and explicit about how they reuse ideas from precedents. While accepting that design research is highly subjective, and can only perhaps be fully understood by the particular architect themselves, nonetheless he feels a duty to provide a clear explanation to others, especially those outside the discipline. Murray claims only this can create a 'body of knowledge' for design research. His projects deliberately merge speculative thinking with the analysis of 'real world' models of suburban development, as epitomised in the tongue-in-cheek proposal by MAS for the 'Manhattanisation' of Melbourne.

Next, Jane Rendell offers a closely argued and detailed analysis of design research as one of the four key research methodologies in architecture (the others being natural science, social science/ humanities and history/theory). Design research, she argues, reverses the traditional order of research methods by generating more questions and not seeking to solve problems. Rendell provides a useful distinction between multidisciplinary and interdisciplinary research, explaining that the latter is the most beneficial for design research as it inherently raises issues of criticality, ethics and politics – but only, that is, if it happens to be that subset of interdisciplinary research which, as Rendell argues, challenges us emotionally and psychically by 'demanding that we exchange what we know for what we do *not* know'. If addressed in this manner, she adds, 'design is a research-led process, while research can also be thought of as a form of design'. Analysing this proposition through the work of muf architecture/art and Diller & Scofidio, Rendell then uses the text-based work of Jennifer Bloomer as a lead into her own creative practice of site-writing. Her approach openly mixes feminism, subjectivity, psychoanalysis and performance to make the powerful argument that 'the architectonics of writing offers a new way of imagining architectural design'.

Next is Johan Verbeke, who starts by analysing the different kinds of knowledge that are available, and indeed necessary, for architects in practice. This activity, he points out, involves a combination of many forms of insight and knowledge working together. As such there has to be an interaction of explicit and implicit knowledge, and, to cite Ranulph Glanville, all research first needs to be designed. Verbeke suggests that the more active term 'knowledge for' be used instead of the more passive 'knowledge of'. As someone from a mathematical/ computational background, he is keen to explain the nature and processes of architectural design research in an eminently rational manner that is understandable to a predominantly positivist-minded European research establishment. In this regard, Verbeke's citation of the aforementioned EAAE Research Charter, along with his fascination with PhDs which are produced through musical performance, as discussed in his chapter, are clearly part of his view of it as a wider mission. Another interesting linkage, which becomes clear in the design doctorates mentioned in this chapter, is Verbeke's role in the Sint-Lucas School's PhD by Practice programme which is now combined with the RMIT model described in a previous chapter.

The following chapter is by Leslie Kavanaugh, an architect based in the Netherlands who holds a long-standing interest in and knowledge of philosophy. As she notes, the fundamental concept

[handwritten marginal note: VERBEKE CHAPTER - READ THIS]

that shapes her designs is the realisation that space and time exist as a fluid relationship, being folded and pleated accordingly, and hence that space should never be regarded as a thing or object. This insight is drawn from Gottfried Leibniz, as well as Eastern philosophy, and for her it is then given more substance through the writings of phenomenologist philosophers like Maurice Merleau-Ponty. Kavanaugh's practice, studiokav, is pursing these ideas of folding and pleating through supple computer-generated architectural forms. Her chapter features their speculative scheme for a new historical museum and bridge/arch connecting North Amsterdam to the main railway station in the city centre, as a combination of grand civic scheme and a vivid expression of space-time relations. Kavanaugh's work is an example of a philosophically and culturally driven version of parametric design, and thus a beneficial counterpoint to the more rationalist (and usually boys with toys) approach to computer aided design work.

In the next chapter, Richard Coyne argues that an interlinking of design research with open and democratic formations of digital technology, such as the internet and social media networks, is the primary new means to expand the field of architecture. The principle of expanding the field, he points out, has been a constant tendency in architecture; it is just that there is now even more chance to increase the open-endedness, heterogeneity and cross-disciplinary nature of the subject through crowd-sourcing and other techniques. Coyne's plea is hence for there to be more than just a narrow conception of architecture, as has tended to prevail hitherto, and for a greater acceptance of differences. He makes a fascinating allusion to a 'cargo cult' process whereby images and texts are now so ubiquitous through the internet that they are 'falling' on more places than ever, engendering a more rapid and hybrid spread of ideas and precedents. If there is a future for design research in architecture, in Coyne's view it will come through the ability of the internet and other digital means to 'make' audiences for its reception that would never have come across it before.

Another vision of democracy is provided by Teddy Cruz. He thinks we are in a deep crisis that is cultural, not just economic and environmental. His hope is to revive the avant-garde project of reconciling artistic experimentation and social responsibility, by imagining counter-spatial possibilities. This, then, becomes the key task of architectural design research to move from critical distance to critical proximity. It should interrogate the conditions that produce conflict and inequality around the world and devise radical experimental architecture to redress these issues. Where might such changes happen? Cruz argues that 'the most relevant practices and projects forwarding socio-economic sustainability will not emerge from sites of economic abundance but sites of scarcity'. Hence we should not look at growth centres in the UAE or China, but at the 'peripheries' and 'margins' of Latin America. The stealth urbanism of informal settlements needs to become the site of an innovative new form of architectural praxis, and as a two-way process it can also revive teaching and research within universities – as Cruz's work demonstrates so well. Hence, architectural design research is seen as the basis for a new urban pedagogy and civic imagination, as well as a means to argue for socio-economic and environmental justice.

My own final chapter shares similar sentiments, and places the contemporary city as the defining figure for design research. In calling for a more socially and politically engaged role for architecture, I argue that it is design research which can really drive new agendas. In reversing typical chronology, I start out by describing some contemporary projects which deal with sites of emergency and despair, such as the work I am doing with colleagues in the Palestine Regeneration Team (PART), or Shigeru Ban's scheme for a 'temporary' cardboard cathedral in Christchurch, New Zealand following its devastating earthquake. This is then traced back to the astonishing politically-charged projects of Lebbeus Woods, who saw in spaces of war and destruction a chance to overcome and undo the power structures which tend to prevent equality in human societies. This process of reading back from the future to the present to the past is paralleled in my analysis of *Delirious New York* as the progenitor of design research in architecture, with Rem Koolhaas portraying himself as the ghostwriter of a tale that explains, in retrospect, how the architectural growth of New York helped it grow into the 'Capital of Capitalism' in the twentieth century. In turn, this discussion is traced back to what I suggest is the first explicit mention of design research, Eliel Saarinen's *The City*, in which he described the process as working essentially in reverse – that is, how the future vision for a city could be used to shape present-day urban planning.

With this truly original view of Saarinen about design research in mind, as a process effectively in a 'two-fold movement', this book draws to a close. My hope is that it will prove a novel and significant contribution to the widening and enrichment of possibilities for design research in architecture. It is evident that there are going to be many fascinating examples of design research in future, as well as many new routes of discovery which cannot as yet be predicted. One fertile avenue for this development will come via the contributions of our accompanying Ashgate book series, and with a good wind that series is going to demonstrate how the aim of enriching design research in architecture can work in practice.

Notes

1   A general account is laid out, for instance, by the contributors in Matthias Steup & Ernest Sosa (eds), *Contemporary Debates in Epistemology* (Malden, Mass/Oxford: Blackwell, 2005).

2   Higher Education Funding Council for England, *Research Assessment Exercise 2008: Guidance on Submissions – REF 03.2005* (Bristol: HEFCE, July 2005), 'Annex B: Definition of Research for the RAE', p. 49, viewable at the HEFCE website, http://www.rae.ac.uk/pubs/2005/03/ (accessed 24 March 2013); Higher Education Funding Council for England, *Research Excellence Framework 2014: Assessment Framework and Guidance on Submissions – REF 02.2011* (Bristol: HEFCE, July 2011), 'Annex C. Definitions of research and impact for the REF', p. 48, viewable at the HEFCE website, http://www.ref.ac.uk/media/ref/content/pub/assessmentframeworkandguidanceonsubmissions/02_11.pdf (accessed 24 March 2013).

3   Australian Research Council, *ERA Indicator Descriptors: ARC 2008:1* (Canberra: Commonwealth of Australia, 2008), p. 1, viewable at the ARC website, http://www.arc.gov.au/pdf/ERA_Indicator_Descriptors.pdf (accessed 24 March 2013).

4   Adrian Forty, *Words and Buildings* (London: Thames & Hudson, 2000), pp. 11–16.

5   Jane Rendell, 'Architectural Research and Disciplinarity', *Architectural Research Quarterly*, vol. 8 no. 2 (2004), pp. 141–7.

6   David Leatherbarrow, 'The Project of Design Research', in Michael U. Hensel (ed.), *Design Innovation for the Built Environment: Research by Design and the Renovation of Practice* (London: Routledge, 2012), pp. 5–13.

7   Ibid., p. 12.

8   Michael Biggs & Henrik Karlsson (eds), *The Routledge Companion to Research in the Arts* (Abingdon: Routledge, 2010).

9   Donald Schön, *The Reflective Practitioner: How Professions Think in Action* (New York/London: Basic Books, 1983); Nishat Awan,

Tatjana Schneider & Jeremy Till, *Spatial Agency: Other Ways of Doing Architecture* (London/New York: Routledge, 2011), pp. 28–9.

10 Geoffrey Broadbent & Anthony Ward (eds) *Design Methods in Architecture* (New York: George Wittenborn, 1969); John Christopher Jones, *Design Methods: Seeds of Human Futures* (New York: Wiley, 1970); Gordon Pask, 'The Architectural Relevance of Cybernetics', *Architectural Design*, vol. 39 no. 9 (1969), pp. 494–6; Ranulph Glanville, 'Why Design Research' (1980), in Robin Jacques & James A. Powell (eds), *Design, Science, Method: Proceedings of the 1980 Design Research Society conference* (Guildford: Westbury House, 1981).

11 Design Research Society webpage, http://www.designresearchsociety.org/joomla/index.php (accessed on 24 March 2013). The involvement of architects within that organisation has remained relatively minimal since it was set up in 1966.

12 Christopher Frayling, 'Research in Art and Design', *Royal College of Art Research Papers*, vol. 1 no. 1 (1993/94), pp. 1–5. See also Christopher Frayling et al, *Practice-based Doctorates in the Creative and Performing Arts and Design* (Lichfield: UK Council for Graduate Education, 1997).

13 Bryan Lawson, *How Designers Think: The Design Process Demystified* (London: Architectural Press, 1980); Bryan Lawson, 'The Subject that Won't Go Away. But Perhaps we are Ahead of the Game. Design as Research', *Architectural Research Quarterly*, vol. 6 no. 2 (2002), pp. 109–14; Bryan Lawson, *What Designers Know* (Oxford: Architectural Press, 2004); Bryan Lawson & Kees Dorst, *Design Expertise* (Oxford: Architectural Press, 2009); Peter Downton, *Design Research* (Melbourne: RMIT Publishing, 2003); Halina Dunin-Woyseth & M.L. Nielsen (eds), *Discussing Transdisciplinarity: Making Professions and the New Mode of Knowledge Production* (Oslo: AHO/The Oslo School of Architecture and Design, 2004); Halina Dunin-Woyseth & Fredrik Nilsson, 'On the Emergence of Research by Design and Practice-based Research Approaches in Architecture and Urban Design', in Hensel (ed.), *Design Innovation for the Built Environment*, pp. 37–52.

14 Michael U. Hensel, 'Research by Design in the Context of the OCEAN Design Research Association', 'Performance Orientated Design as a Framework for Renovating Architectural Practice and Innovating Research by Design', 'The Research Centre for Architecture and Tectonics: Implementing Research Towards Performance-Oriented Architecture', in Hensel (ed.), *Design Innovation for the Built Environment*, pp. 91–106, 121–60; Patrik Schumacher, 'Parametricism: A New Global Style for Architecture and Urban Design', *Architectural Design – Special Issue on Digital Cities*, vol. 79 no. 4 (2009), pp. 14–23; Patrik Schumacher, 'Architecture Schools as Design Research Laboratories', in Zaha Hadid & Patrik Schumacher (eds), *Total Fluidity: Studio Zaha Hadid 2000–2010* (Vienna/New York: University of Applied Arts, Vienna/Springer, 2011), viewable at the Patrik Schumacher website, http://www.patrikschumacher.com/Texts/Architecture%20Schools%20as%20Design%20Research%20Laboratories.htm (accessed 24 March 2013); Patrik Schumacher, *The Autopoesis of Architecture* (2 vols.; London: John Wiley, 2010/12).

15 Marcus Vitruvius Pollo, *The Ten Books on Architecture* (trans. Ingrid Rowland & Thomas N. Hope, Cambridge: Cambridge University Press, 1st century BC/1999), p. 21.

16 Le Corbusier, *Precisions: On the Present State of Architecture and City Planning* (Cambridge, Mass: MIT Press, 1930/91), p. 25.

17 Eliel Saarinen, *The City: Its Growth, its Decay, its Future* (New York: Reinhold Publishing, 1943).

18 Robert Venturi, *Complexity and Contradiction in Architecture* (London/New York: Architectural Press/Museum of Modern Art, 1966/77); Robert Venturi, Denise Scott Brown & Steven Izenour, *Learning from Las Vegas: The Forgotten Symbolism of Architectural Form* (Cambridge, Mass: MIT Press, 1972/77); Christopher Alexander et al, *A Pattern Language* (Oxford/New York: Oxford University Press, 1977); Rem Koolhaas, *Delirious New York: Towards a Retroactive Manifesto for Manhattan* (New York: Monacelli Press, 1978/94); Mike Webb, *Temple Island* (London: AA Publications, 1987).

19 Aldo Rossi, *The Architecture of the City* (New York/Cambridge, Mass: Graham Foundation/MIT Press, 1966/82), Preface to the Second Italian Edition, reprinted on p. 166.

20 Bernard Tschumi, *The Manhattan Transcripts* (London: Academy Editions, 1981/94), p. xix.

21 Ben van Berkel & Caroline Bos, *UN Studio – Design Models: Architecture, Urbanism, Infrastructure* (London: Thames & Hudson, 2006), pp. 17–18.

22 MVRDV, *KM3: Excursions on capacities* (Barcelona: Actar, 2005), pp. 43–4.

23 Halina Dunin-Woyseth & Fredrik Nilsson, 'On the Emergence of Research by Design and Practice-based Research Approaches in Architecture and Urban Design', in Hensel (ed.), *Design Innovation for the Built Environment*, pp. 37–52.

DESIGN RESEARCH: THE FIRST 500 YEARS

Jonathan Hill

DRAWING FORTH

In contemporary discourse and practice it is familiar to discuss design research as if it is new to architecture. But this is to ignore the history of the architect. At the Bartlett School of Architecture, UCL, I direct the architectural design PhD programme. Combining a project and a text that share a research theme and a productive relationship, the design PhD is a comparatively new architectural qualification. But its methods and means are not. Indeed, they have been invaluable to the architect for over 500 years.

Before the fifteenth century the status of the architect, painter and sculptor was low due to their association with manual labour and dispersed authorship. Trained in one of the building crafts, the master mason was but one of many craftsmen and worked alongside them as a construction supervisor. Of little importance to building, the drawing was understood as no more than a flat surface and the shapes upon it were but tokens of tangible objects. The Italian Renaissance introduced a fundamental change in perception, establishing the principle that the drawing truthfully depicts the three-dimensional world. Consequently, for the first time, the drawing became essential to architectural practice.

The history of drawing is interwoven with the history of design. The term 'design' comes from the Italian word *disegno*, meaning drawing, and suggesting both the drawing of a line and the drawing forth of an idea. Classical antiquity established the principle that ideas are immaterial and that intellectual labour is superior to manual labour. Affirming this assumption, *disegno* allowed the three visual arts – architecture, painting and sculpture – to be recognised as liberal arts concerned with ideas, a status they had rarely been accorded previously. *Disegno* is concerned with the immaterial idea of architecture not the material fabric of building. The sixteenth-century painter and architect Giorgio Vasari was crucial to its promotion: 'one may conclude that this design is nothing but a visual expression and clarification of that concept which one has in the intellect, and that which one imagines in the mind'.[1] In 1563 Vasari founded the first art academy, the Accademia del Disegno in Florence, replacing workshop instruction with education in subjects such as drawing and geometry that emphasised the visual arts' association with the intellect. As a model for art and architecture schools ever since, Vasari's academy enabled painters, sculptors and architects to converse independently of the craft guilds.

The command of drawing – not building – unlocked the status of the architect, establishing the principle that architecture results not from the accumulated knowledge of a team of anonymous craftsmen working together on a construction site but the artistic creation of an individual architect in command of drawing who designs a building in a studio. Asserting their intellectual status, architects made drawings with just a few delicate lines and imagined buildings that were equally immaterial. Whether in the studio or on site, they tended to see not matter and mass but proportion and line.

Painting is often a collaborative process but the work of assistants is concealed within the studio and subjugated to the aura of the artist and artwork. Also, a praiseworthy building is usually attributed to one architect even if a number of collaborators are involved. But the intellectual and artistic status of the architect is less certain than that of the painter. In contrast to the architectural drawing, which is seen in relation to other drawings and a building, the painting is unique and need not refer to an external object, thus appearing further removed from the material world and closer to that of ideas. The purpose of the architectural drawing is complex because it depends on two related but distinct concepts, which both depend on the architect's ability to precisely conceive and represent the building. One indicates that drawing is an intellectual, artistic activity distant from the grubby materiality of construction. The other emphasises the architect's mastery of the complex and collaborative building process. Creativity as well as confusion arises from this contradiction.

The architect as we understand the term today was established in Italy in around 1450, in France a century later and in Britain in the early 1600s with Inigo Jones. In the new division of labour, architects acquired additional means to practice architecture that were as important as building, namely drawing but also writing. To affirm their newly acquired status, architects began increasingly to theorise architecture, both for themselves and for their patrons, ensuring that the authored book became more valuable to architects than to painters and sculptors, whose status was more secure and means to acquire commissions less demanding. Written in around 1450 and published in 1485, Leon Battista Alberti's *De Re Aedificatoria* (*On the Art of Building in Ten Books*) was the first thorough investigation of the Renaissance architect as artist and intellectual. Francesco Colonna's *Hypnerotomachia Poliphili* (1499) was the second architectural book by a living writer published in the Renaissance and the first to be printed with illustrations, establishing the multimedia interdependence of text and image that has been essential to architectural books ever since.

The first part of Colonna's title – *Hypnerotomachia* – derives from three Greek words, *hypnos*, *eros* and *mache*, which respectively mean sleep, love and strife, so that they roughly translate as the 'strife of love in a dream'. The second part – *Poliphili* – refers to the principal character, Poliphilo, who has a restless night after being rejected by his love, Polia. The narrative was not new. Continuing the tradition of the *romanzo d'amore* that peaked in the mid-fourteenth century, love is lost and won in a sylvan landscape. But in *Hypnerotomachia Poliphili* the gardens and buildings are not just locations of lust and desire; they are themselves erotic. Some of Colonna's designs may have been invented while others were taken from ancient and Renaissance sites in Italy, Greece and Asia Minor. *Hypnerotomachia Poliphili*'s most impressive structures are composites: a mobile fountain, a grotto concealed in the domed ceiling of a temple, an obelisk mounted on an elephant, and a temple with hollow columns to collect and disperse rainwater. The largest and most impressive building consists of varied forms mounted one on top of the other: a plinth, a pyramid, a stone cube, an obelisk and, finally, a winged statue 'revolving easily at every breath of wind, making such a noise, from the friction of the hollow metal device, as was never heard from the Roman treasury'.[2]

One model for the architectural book, *Hypnerotomachia Poliphili* is a narrative illustrated with pictorial representations. A second and more familiar model is the analytical manifesto justified with examples and illustrated with orthogonal drawings, such as Andrea Palladio's *I Quattro Libri dell' Archittetura* (*The Four Books of Architecture*),

fine di quella floribonda copertura perueni, & riguardando una innume
rosa turba di iuuentude promiscua celebremente festigiante mi apparue,
Cum sonore uoce, & cum melodie di uarii soni, Cum uenusti & ludibon
di tripudii & plausi, Et cum molta & iocundissima lætitia, In una amplis
sima planitie agminatamente solatiantise. Dique per questa tale & grata
nouitate inuaso sopra sedendo admiratiuo, di piu oltra procedere, trapen
soso io steti.

Et ecco una come insigne & festiua Nympha dindi cum la sua arden-

LA SEGVENTE fabrica è appresso la porta di Montagnana Castello del Padoano, e fu edi-
ficata dal Magnifico Signor Francesco Pisani : ilquale passato à miglior uita non la ha potuta finire.
Le stanze maggiori sono lunghe un quadro e tre quarti : i uolti sono à schiffo, alti secondo il secondo
modo delle altezze de' uolti : le mediocri sono quadre, & inuoltate à cadino : I camerini, e l'andito so
no di uguale larghezza : i uolti loro sono alti due quadri : La entrata ha quattro colonne, il quinto più
sottili di quelle di fuori : lequali sostentano il pauimento della Sala, e fanno l'altezza del uolto bella, e
secura. Ne i quattro nicchi, che ui si ueggono sono stati scolpiti i quattro tempi dell'anno da Messer
Alessandro Vittoria Scultore eccellente : il primo ordine delle colonne è Dorico, il secondo Ionico.
Le stanze di sopra sono in solaro : L'altezza della Sala giugne fin sotto il tetto. Ha questa fabrica due
strade da i fianchi, doue sono due porte, sopra le quali ui sono anditi, che conducono in cucina, e
luoghi per seruitori.

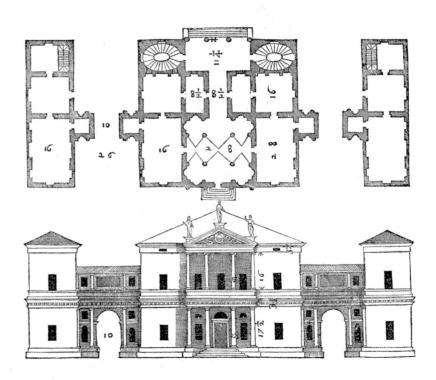

LA FABRICA

2.2　Extract page from Andrea Palladio's
I Quattro Libri dell' Archittetura (plan and
elevation of Villa Pisani, Montagnana)

published in 1570. Historical references appear in both books but for somewhat different purposes. In one they enrich a specific story, while in the other they justify generic architectural solutions. A further literary model, the manual, conveys practical knowledge and is illustrated with diagrams and calculations. But these models are not hermetic and many architectural books refer to more than one, as is the case in Palladio's attention to practical matters..

Often a design does not get built and an architect must be persuasive to see that it does. Sometimes a building is not the best means to explore architectural ideas. Consequently, architects, especially influential ones, tend to talk, write and draw a lot as well as build. Palladio is a notable early exponent of this tradition, and Le Corbusier, Alison Smithson and Rem Koolhaas are more recent ones. The relations between the drawing, text and building are multi-directional. For example, drawing may lead to building. But writing may also lead to drawing, or building may lead to writing and drawing. If everyone reading this text listed all the architectural works that influence them, some would be drawings, some would be texts, and others would be buildings either visited or described in drawings and texts. Studying the history of architecture since the Italian Renaissance, it is evident that researching, testing and questioning the limits of architecture occur through drawing and writing as well as building.

THE PICTURESQUE IMAGINATION

The history of design from the fifteenth to the twenty-first century has not been seamless, and a significant departure occurred in the eighteenth century, when the meaning of an idea and a design changed significantly. The Renaissance imagination was restricted to the universal geometries of ideal forms. But in built architecture, the relations between the immaterial and the material were sometimes considered with great subtlety. Modesty scaled farms in most cases, Palladio's villas recall the relaxed rural life evoked in classical antiquity by Virgil and Pliny, while their elegant but inexact proportions refer to the immaterial and its uncertain presence in the physical world. Emphasising this distinction, the buildings drawn in *The Four Books of Architecture* are each an ideal, not those actually built. Subsequently, the Baroque drew some attention to subjective interpretation; for example, Baroque drama exploited the dialectical potential of allegory, in which meanings are not fixed but endlessly changing and open to appropriation and revision.[3]

In *An Essay Concerning Human Understanding* (1690), the empiricist philosopher John Locke dismissed the search for ultimate truth, accepted that there are limits to what we can know and argued that conclusions must be in proportion to the evidence: 'Our business here is not to know all things, but those which concern our conduct.'[4] Countering the neo-Platonist and Cartesian traditions in which knowledge is acquired by the mind alone, empiricism emphasised that ideas are provisional and dependent upon experience, so that understanding develops through an evolving dialogue between the environment, senses and mind. Describing diverse peoples and beliefs to support his assumption that personality and morality are acquired not innate, Locke concluded that the mind begins as a 'white Paper', an empty cabinet, which experience furnishes with understanding.[5] Locke was very influential. But his empiricist followers soon discarded his assumption that there can be a direct relationship between the observer and the observed, recognising that this ignores the observer's role in shaping that experience. As empirical investigation without prior concepts is impossible, we cannot simply see objects as they are.

Locke required a degree of critical detachment from the natural world, while Anthony Ashley Cooper, third Earl of Shaftesbury, influenced a wider reassessment. Before the late-seventeenth century, uncultivated nature was usually considered to be brutish and deformed. Recuperation in nature was not a new theme but it found enhanced expression in the early-eighteenth century, when nature and moral virtue were linked for the first time. Unlike Locke, Shaftesbury acknowledged an ideal order. However, departing from Plato, he conceived nature not as debased but as a means to contemplate the divine.[6] Sensitivity to one's environment became as necessary as sensitivity to others. In the second volume of *Characteristicks of Men, Manners, Opinions, Times* (1711), Shaftesbury praises nature and weather: 'enliven'd by the Sun, and temper'd by the fresh AIR of fanning *Breezes*! ... I shall no longer resist the Passion growing in me for Things of a *natural* kind'.[7]

Increasingly, the recognition that we make our own reality was exploited for its creative potential, contradicting Locke's moderation and Shaftesbury's elitism. Associating the natural world with subjective experience, and drawing attention to the conditions that inform self-understanding, the eighteenth century transformed the visual arts, its objects, authors and viewers. In Britain, the architect associated with *disegno* was in its infancy when another appeared alongside it, exemplifying a new type of design and a new way of designing

that valued the ideas and emotions evoked through experience. No longer was architecture a cohesive body of knowledge based on universal ideas, forms and proportions. Instead, design could draw forth an idea that was provisional, changeable and dependent on experience at conception, production and reception.

Marking a significant transformation in the role of the architect, the first convincing example of such a design practice occurred in gardens, not buildings, because they were closer to nature and more clearly subject to change. Heightened concern for the fluctuating pleasures of perception and nature found expression in the Picturesque, which is a deceptive term because it emphasises one aspect of the eighteenth-century garden to the detriment of its other qualities, such as the importance of the senses and the seasons to design, experience, understanding and the imagination. Just as the daily weather was part of a larger weather pattern, the eighteenth-century garden was a means to engage the social as well as the subjective. History, politics, love and death were all represented and discussed among garden glades and monuments.

Although the pleasures and liberties of the Picturesque were limited to the educated and prosperous, notable principles were established. The Picturesque gave new emphasis to the environment, exploring human activity in dialogue with an evolving natural world. Rather than a complete and timeless object, a garden building was understood as an incident in an environment with which it conversed, establishing an architectural environmentalism that had a profound influence on subsequent centuries. Valuing the individuality of the designer and the user, the Picturesque acknowledged that beauty is

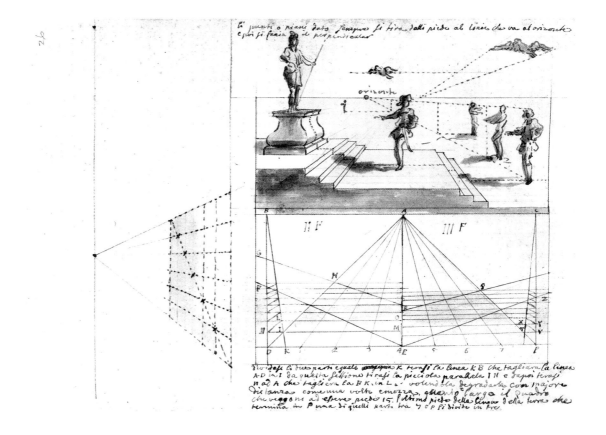

subjective and encouraged varied allegories and diverse interpretations. Rather than being conceived according to the rules of geometry in a distant studio, the garden was designed the way it was experienced, by a figure moving across a landscape and imagining future movements, while special attention was given to drawings that explored the relations between site and experience. William Kent's Italian diary (1714–15) includes accounts of buildings and gardens, small drawings and diagrams in the margins, descriptions of painting practices and delicate illustrations of perspective techniques in line and wash. His drawings for the garden at Rousham (1737–41) are all perspectives, which depict the garden as a set of elaborately inter-related scenes. Their implicit recognition of subjective choices mirrored Kent's willingness to compose and adjust his design in response to the conditions found on site and the advice he received from the steward and head gardener of his client, General James Dormer.

Kent owned several copies of *Hypnerotomachia Poliphili,* as did Dormer, and many of Kent's pyramidal buildings were based on the narrative

illustrations of Colonna, who was not an architect. Kent is considered to be the principal architect of the eighteenth-century Palladian Revival, although his inspirations were varied. Palladio's extensive influence on English architecture was principally due to *The Four Books of Architecture*, and beyond the garden, Kent chose to depict his building designs in orthogonal drawings rather than perspectives. This enduring distinction can also be seen in the letter to Pope Leo X (c. 1519) in which Raphael associates the picture with the painter and the plan with the architect.[8] But the value given to experience in the eighteenth century made it less convincing.

Although Colonna and Palladio influenced Kent's drawings and designs, he adopted Palladio as his principal literary model. Rather than directly refer to the Venetian architect, Kent published *The Designs of Inigo Jones, Consisting of Plans and Elevations for Publick and Private Buildings* (1727) and *Some Designs of Mr. Inigo Jones and Mr. William Kent* (1744). The independent profession of the architectural historian did not then exist and architects wrote architectural histories, although they did not aim to be rigorous and objective in the manner of later historians. The relationship between history and design was central to their treatises.

IDEAS, ARTS AND APPLIANCES

Design as it was first conceived has a number of failings. First, because it suggests that only the architect is creative and fails to recognise the creativity of others involved in the conception, production and experience of architecture, such as the builder or user. Second, because it promotes the superiority of the intellect and denigrates the

2.5 Antinous at the end of the
Long Walk at Rousham

manual, material and experiential. The highly influential concept that ideas are superior to matter is nothing but a prejudice. One option is to dismiss it, concluding that its effect on architecture is only negative because it denies the materiality of architecture and encourages architects to chase after artistic status that they will never fully attain, may not need, and should question. But the original meaning of design – the drawing of a line and the drawing forth of an idea – remains valuable to architectural practice and research as long as its limitations are acknowledged and challenged. It must be tempered by the eighteenth-century attention to ideas that are provisional and dependent on experience at conception, production and reception.

The Picturesque began in the early eighteenth century, while a second reinterpretation of design occurred later in the century and depended upon a reassessment of the arts. The classification of the fine arts – notably poetry, music, painting, sculpture and architecture – in opposition to utility was problematic for architects, and Immanuel Kant concluded that architecture's aesthetic potential was even less than that of a garden.[9] Associated with utility, the design disciplines that proliferated due to industrialisation were categorised as applied arts at best. In the Renaissance a form was synonymous with an idea. But, especially since the late-eighteenth century, a form can be ready for mass production and made without an idea in mind. Painters and sculptors discarded design once it became associated with collective authorship, industrial production and forms without ideas. Among the fine arts, which include the three original visual arts, only in architecture is the term design regularly referred to today. Many people associate design

with the newer design disciplines, which affects how architectural design is understood. But in the discourse of architects, the older meaning of design -drawing ideas – and the newer meaning of design – drawing appliances – are both in evidence.

Today, most architects design and draw on the computer's illuminated screen, which furthers the architect's long fascination with the immaterial. But in bringing drawing closer to building and the ambiguities of architectural authorship to the fore, the conjunction of computer-aided design and computer-aided manufacture (CAD/CAM) questions the history of the architect and division of labour in a manner that refers to the thirteenth century as well as the twenty-first, suggesting a hybrid of intellectual and manual labour and digital and craft techniques.

As architects, when we use the terms 'design' and 'design research' we may refer either to design as in *disegno*, in which a line draws forth an idea, or to design as in the Picturesque, in which ideas are provisional and dependent on experience, or to design as in industrial design, in which the principal aim is not to generate ideas but to solve problems and generate commodities, or to design as in computation and fabrication, in which a designer is also a maker. In actuality, whether we work as academics or as practitioners, we will combine these models because together they reflect the complexities of the architectural discipline.

DESIGN HISTORIES

Just as the eighteenth century transformed the meaning of designs and ideas, it influenced the two model publications formulated in the Renaissance and adjusted their interdependence with building design.

Describing actual events and others of his own invention, Vasari's *Le Vite de' Piu Eccellenti Pittori, Scultori e Architettori* (*The Lives of the Most Eminent Painters, Sculptors and Architects*), published in 1550, was the first significant history of art and architecture, initiating a new discipline. In the sixteenth century, history's purpose was to offer useful lessons; accuracy was not necessary. Significantly due to empiricism's influence, the early-eighteenth century placed greater emphasis on the distinction between fact and fiction, which came to transform historical analysis. By the nineteenth century, history was naively assumed to be a science capable of objective statements, which led to an emphasis on archival research. Science is supported in its claim to objectivity by the presence of its objects of study before the scientist, while history is an understanding of the past written in the present. Any archive, however complete, cannot return the historian to the past and no analysis is more than an interpretation. Any history expresses a particular ideology, as does a scientific statement; they cannot be neutral.

The nineteenth century established the art and architectural historian as an independent practitioner. But the interdependence of design and history remained essential to many architects' treatises. As well as writing and drawing historical arguments, nineteenth-century architects were expected to produce buildings that knowingly reflected on and referred to past styles, while also manifesting the character of their time.

Reacting against eclecticism, modernists advocated an architecture specific to the present. Breaking from previous educational models, Walter Gropius excluded the history of architecture from the Bauhaus syllabus, while in the 'Manifesto of Futurist Architecture' (1914), Antonio Sant'Elia and Filippo Tomasso Marinetti proclaimed: 'This architecture cannot be subject to any law of historical continuity.'[10] But even modernists who denied history's relevance relied on histories to articulate modernism's themes and principles. Books such Nikolaus Pevsner's *Pioneers of the Modern Movement* (1936) and Sigfried Giedion's *Space, Time and Architecture* (1941) identified a modernist prehistory to justify modernism's historical inevitability, rupture from the past and systematic evolution. Once established, modernism was supposed to remain triumphant and history would come to an end, as Pevsner recalls: 'It seemed folly to think that anybody would wish to abandon' modernism.[11] But the newly-established canon was also ripe for reinterpretation and revival, like any earlier architecture.

To some degree, mid-twentieth-century architects merely reaffirmed an appreciation of history that was largely ignored in early modernism but latent in works such as Le Corbusier's *Vers Une Architecture* (1923), published in English in 1927 as *Towards a New Architecture*. But the Second World War was a more scientific war than the First World War, and nuclear devastation undermined confidence in technological progress, which early-modernism had emphasised as a means of social transformation. In the search for stability in the uncertain aftermath from the mid-1940s, modernism's previously dismissive reaction to social norms and cultural memories was itself anachronistic. The consequence was not just to acknowledge early-modernism's classical heritage but also to place a concern for history at the heart

2.6   Denys Lasdun's Royal College of
Physicians, Regent's Park, London (1964)

of architecture once again, affirming the liberal humanist tradition that modernism had once seemed to repudiate. In a BBC radio broadcast in 1966, Pevsner identified 'an anti-Pioneers style' and criticised the Royal College of Physicians, London (1964), even though he had 'the greatest respect for Denys Lasdun', its architect.[12] Pevsner first denigrated the 'over-powering … brutality' of the new style and then, despite his personal distaste, reluctantly recognised 'a successor to my international modern of the 1930s, a postmodern style I would be tempted to call it, but the

legitimate style of the 1950s and 1960s'.[13] To be ancient and modern was no longer a contradiction. Frances Yates – author of *The Art of Memory*, 1966 – described Lasdun's National Theatre (1976), as an 'ancient truth in a new idiom', apparently to Lasdun's 'enormous pleasure'.[14]

Lasdun is not usually described as a postmodernist. His architectural references were multiple – classicist, modernist, the Baroque and the Picturesque – but he did not employ them in the superficial manner that is sometimes associated with architectural postmodernism. Including the postmodern within the modern, and acknowledging the process by which one work questions an earlier one, Jean-François Lyotard writes: 'A work can become modern only if it is first postmodern. Postmodernism thus understood is not modernism at its end but in the nascent state.'[15] In this sense, Lasdun became postmodern to remain modern. But, given that so many of his references were from earlier centuries and without irony, it seems more appropriate to conclude that he became pre-modern to remain modern.

Lasdun's edited volume, *Architecture in an Age of Scepticism* (1984), emphasises the continuing relevance of liberal humanism when it enters into a critical and constructive dialogue with contemporary society. To explain his conception of an evolving historical continuity, Lasdun referred to 'Tradition and the Individual Talent' (1917), an essay in which T.S. Eliot identifies an existing order that influences the present and is subtly altered by it:

> Context is not only topographical and physical, it is also historical … My concern for context is as an agent of architectural transformation. The place you build actually has formative influences on the nature of the building. And when the building is there it has formative influences and effects on the place it is made.[16]

As history is an interpretation of the past formed in the present, each building is a new history. The architect is a historian twice over: as an author of a book and as a designer of a building.

NOVEL DESIGNS

Emphasising activities that led to personal awareness and development, Locke recommended the virtues of preparing a diary. People have written about themselves for millennia but the formation of modern identity is associated with a type of writing that Michel Foucault describes as a 'technology of the self'.[17] As Paul de Man remarks: 'We assume that life *produces* the autobiography as an act produces its consequences, but can we not suggest, with equal justice, that the autobiographical project may itself produce and determine the life'.[18]

The diary's attention to contemporary individualism developed in parallel with a new literary genre. In valuing direct experience, precise description and a sceptical approach to 'facts', which needed to be repeatedly questioned, the empirical method created a fruitful climate in which the everyday realism of the novel prospered as 'factual fictions'.[19] In contrast to the earlier romance, which incorporated classical mythologies, the novel concentrated on eighteenth-century society and the individualism it encouraged. The focused investigation and precise description that empiricism demanded was applied to the novel, which emphasised specific times, peoples and places. Recognising a difference in style as well as content, William Congreve remarked that in contrast to 'the lofty Language, miraculous Contingencies and impossible Performances' of the romance, novels are 'of a more familiar nature' and 'delight us with Accidents and odd Events … which not being so distant from our Belief bring also the pleasure nearer us'.[20] The uncertainties and dilemmas of identity, as in Locke's assertion that '*Socrates* waking and sleeping is not the same Person', were ripe for narrative account.[21] Often described as the first English novel, Daniel Defoe's *Robinson*

Crusoe (1719) is a fictional autobiography, as is his later novel, *Moll Flanders* (1722).

The novel's relationship to the Picturesque garden has not been acknowledged before, even though they were each a response to empiricism and most likely influenced each other. Self-reflection stimulated questions of identity, fractured narratives and digressions in the garden as well as the novel, although the landscape designer emphasised classical mythologies alongside contemporary events. The Picturesque garden was both a romance and a novel. A member of a leading aristocratic Whig family and once a general in the Duke of Marlborough's army, Richard Temple, first Viscount Cobham, conceived Stowe – the grandest eighteenth-century English garden – as a political and cultural statement. In the 1730s he commissioned Kent to design the Elysian Fields, named after the paradise dedicated to the heroes of classical antiquity. But villains were also featured. As a counterpoint to the pristine Temple of Ancient Virtue, the Temple of Modern Virtue was built as a ruin and housed a headless sculpture dedicated to Sir Robert Walpole, the first British Prime Minister, who Cobham opposed. Elsewhere at Stowe, Kent designed a pyramidal monument to celebrate a regular visitor, Congreve, who was best known as a dramatist of human folly. At the edge of the lake, a monkey looks into a mirror, culminating the monument. The carved inscription attests that 'Comedy is the imitation of life and the mirror of society'.

The novel stimulated the Picturesque, and vice versa. Published in nine volumes between 1759 and 1767 as a fictional autobiography, Laurence Sterne's *The Life and Opinions of Tristram Shandy, Gentleman* exploits a Picturesque fascination for fragmentation, incompletion and ruination as a means to engage the reader. With storytelling now part of the story, Sterne's highly self-conscious and meandering narration profoundly influenced the course of literature. The narrator sets out to tell the story of his life but rarely gets beyond his conception, birth and early childhood. As a person is a fluid accumulation of ideas, emotions and experiences, and a life is not necessarily remembered, or even experienced, as a progressive sequence, the story does not develop chronologically but moves back, forward, around and sideways. Sterne remarks: 'Digressions, incontestably, are the sun-shine; —— they are the life, the soul of reading;- - -take them out of this book for instance,- - - you might as well take the book along with them.'[22] Through *Tristram Shandy*'s fractured narrative we actually acquire a more honest, detailed, nuanced and convincing portrait of a person than in a linear narrative. Digressions occur in life as well as literature. Even the attention given to Tristram's formative years is an accurate representation of his concerns.

The influence of the Picturesque and the novel on architecture can be seen in the house, museum and office that John Soane created at 12–14 Lincoln's Inn Fields, London, between 1792 and 1837. In a novelistic essay on the history of his home, Soane imagines that it is first occupied and then allowed to decay. Assumed to be haunted, 12–14 Lincoln's Inn Fields is left empty until a future visitor, on finding it in ruins, attempts to decipher its earlier purpose and character.[23] In his memoirs, Soane refers to 'Padre Giovanni', a 'pious monk' living among the ruins, who is of course Soane himself.[24]

Equivalent to a visual and spatial diary, the process of design – from one drawing to the next iteration and from one project to another – is itself an

2.7   The Dome Area with bust of Sir John
Soane at 12–14 Lincoln's Inn Fields, London

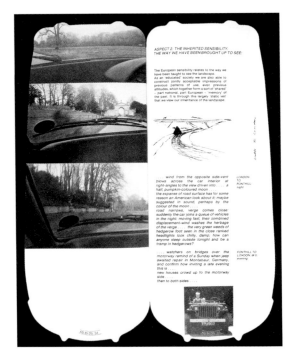

autobiographical 'technology of the self', even when a number of collaborators are involved. Inspired by *Tristram Shandy*, 12–14 Lincoln's Inn Fields is an intensely personal, highly self-conscious and purposively meandering autobiography in which the author edited, narrated and reinvented his life as he reflected upon it.[25] Aware that no art form can fully describe a person and a life, Soane turned an impossible task to creative advantage. 12–14 Lincoln's Inn Fields is an appropriate monument to an era that lauded subjectivity but recognised it to be elusive and uncertain. Equally inspired by Enlightenment buildings and Picturesque gardens, Soane responded to the claim by Nicolas Le Camus de Mézières that a house and a garden can be designed according to similar principles,

by conceiving 12–14 Lincoln's Inn Fields as a garden of architecture, which was intended to engender ideas and emotions, wonder as well as discourse.[26] Avid for acquisition and adjustment, Soane's inquisitive imagination guaranteed seasonal and yearly transformations. Drawings, paintings, windows and mirrors offer vistas and routes punctuated by ruins and monuments. Sculptures and antiquities cover every surface like architectural foliage, recalling the shaggy aesthetic of the late eighteenth-century Picturesque as well as the intricately interconnecting spaces, alternative routes, deceptive dimensions and abundant allegories of Rousham's heavily wooded site.

For the next hundred years, the Picturesque was largely ignored. But in the mid-twentieth century, modernism was associated with the Picturesque and a burgeoning neo-Romanticism, encouraging architects to counter an earlier, didactic and universal modernism by embracing history, landscape and environmentalism. In 1958, as a second home to their one in London, Alison and Peter Smithson bought a small dilapidated cottage on the late-eighteenth century Picturesque estate at Fonthill Gifford, Wiltshire, which they transformed into Upper Lawn Pavilion. Rather than nostalgic, the Smithsons saw the Picturesque as a found condition relevant to the present. Applying the theory of the Picturesque to car travel, *AS in DS: An Eye on the Road* (1983) is Alison Smithson's account of journeys between their urban and rural homes. The book is cut to the plan-shape of the car that made it possible, at 1:18 scale, and a size common to toy cars and architectural guidebooks. Photographs of the Citroën DS in front of Upper Lawn Pavilion pay homage to Le Corbusier's 1921

2.8   Extract pages from Alison Smithson's *AS in DS* book

mass-production '"Citrohan" (not to say Citroën). That is to say, a house like a motor-car', and his habit of photographing a favoured car in front of his houses of that period.[27] But the Smithsons' Citroën was not obsessed with technology. *La Déesse* – the Goddess – 'marks a change in the mythology of cars … it is now more *homely* … conceived as comfort rather than performance', remarked Roland Barthes in 1957.[28] Panoramic windows, pneumatic suspension, front wheel drive, 3125 mm between the front and rear axles and a chassis-cloaking body combine to create a smooth and spacious ride: it was Alison Smithson's 'private room on wheels'.[29] Le Corbusier's appreciation of cars had further relevance. In his analogy of cars to temples in *Vers Une Architecture* there is an echo of Plato's praise for the beauty of 'solids produced on a lathe or with ruler and square', and suggesting a realignment of *disegno* with industrial design.[30] If a car can be a building the Goddess qualifies as both a mobile home and a touring temple.

In his introduction, Peter Smithson describes *AS in DS* as a 'Primer' for the 'sensibility resulting from the moving view of landscape'.[31] Comforted in 'our own-climate-cell', Alison Smithson concludes that observation at a distance and at speed can be detached but engaged.[32] Rather than characterise this sensibility as new, she locates its origins in the eighteenth-century landscape, which was also explored through movement: 'With landscape, we are most encumbered by established English sensibilities; and so deeply involved we have in front of our eyes almost a pre-formed vision, the where-with-all to relive the whole spirit of the English Picturesque.'[33]

AS in DS is about the Picturesque and of the Picturesque: it affords many views literally and in interpretation. In words, drawings, maps and photographs – many produced while travelling in the DS – her diary entries describe nature and weather and refer to travels, peoples and events in the past and present from Thomas Gainsborough to Apollo 13. Each diary entry describes an 'as found' condition in a vivid and immediate manner that is typical of Brutalism and the Picturesque: 'a brush-stroke of duck-egg blue setting-off aggressive grey clouds; a foretaste of the stupendous water-sharp-colours of the view that never fails to please … the sun behind and to the right, shows to perfection massed bare woods and ivy clad trunks'.[34]

Views through side- and rear-view mirrors appear frequently in *AS in DS*, recalling a favoured instrument of the Picturesque. A mirror – often convex, tinted and round or oval – named after the seventeenth-century painter Claude Lorrain, but never used by him, the Claude Glass alters nature according to Picturesque conventions of composition and colour. Praising 'the *general effect*, the *forms of the objects*, and the *beauty of tints*, in one complex view', William Gilpin even described the merits of using the Claude Glass in a fast-moving carriage:' 'We are rapidly carried from one object to another. A succession of high-coloured pictures is continually gliding before the eye. They are like the visions of the imagination; or the brilliant landscapes of a dream.'[35]

The Claude Glass was just one instrument carried by the eighteenth-century Picturesque tourist. Others included pens, pencils, watercolours, sketchbooks, guides, a pedometer, water-flask, telescope and barometer. Together, they equate to the instrumentation available to Alison Smithson in the DS. A car driver looks forward through the windscreen and backwards through mirrors. But a

Claude Glass draws the eye to the reflected landscape not the path ahead. In 1805 a Lakeland traveller who stumbled near the summit of Helvellyn was found with a Claude Glass by his side, becoming 'the first man to die in search of the picturesque'.[36] As a car passenger, Alison Smithson could concentrate on the view and not worry about the drive.

Although she appreciated its compositional possibilities, her concern for the Picturesque was not only visual. As a 'teaching document', Alison Smithson intended *AS in DS* to improve understanding of specific landscape conditions, such as weather, topography, natural history and use, and to encourage designs that respond with thoughtful invention. She notes the delicate adjustments of an old road to site and seasons. In contrast, 'a modern road might lead a passenger to suspect that the road's engineer has no long knowledge of the route, nor the tricks of micro-climate, nor sufficient interest to have travelled "his" route to discover its seasonal weather mutations'.[37] In the subtlety of the old landscape, she identifies a model for building: 'I work with memory, and it allows me to make connections to the past, interpolations of the present and gives foresight – a most valuable facility for an architect – as to a possible future.'[38] As a narrative with pictorial designs and historical references, *AS in DS* follows Colonna's model as well as that of an autobiographical 'technology of the self', which combines design and history as in Kent's diary and Soane's home.

NOVEL HISTORIES

Histories and novels both need to be convincing but in different ways. Although no history is completely objective, to have any validity it must appear truthful to the past. A novel may be believable but not true.

But recognising the overlaps between two literary genres, Malcolm Bradbury notably describes his novel *The History Man* (1975) as 'a total invention with delusory approximations to historical reality, just as is history itself'.[39]

Also associating history-writing with story-telling, Lasdun remarks that each architect must devise his or her 'own creative myth', a set of values, forms and ideas that stimulate the process of design, which should be 'sufficiently objective' and also have 'an element of subjectivity; the myth must be partly an expression of the architect's personality and partly of his time, partly a distillation of permanent truths and partly of the ephemerae of the particular moment'. Lasdun concludes: 'My own myth … engages with history.'[40] Objective as well as subjective, fictional as well as factual, a design is a reinterpretation of the past that is meaningful to the present, transforming both, like a history. Equally, a design is equivalent to a novel, convincing the user to suspend disbelief. Part novelist, part historian, the architect is the history man. We expect a history or a novel to written in words but they can also be cast in concrete or seeded in soil. An architectural book can be a history and a novel, and so can a building and a landscape.

Notes

1   Giorgio Vasari, *Vasari on Technique* (New York: Dover, 1550/1960), p. 205.

2   Francesco Colonna, *Hypnerotomachia Poliphili: The Strife of Love in a Dream* (London: Thames & Hudson, 1499/1999), p. 24.

3   Walter Benjamin, *The Origin of German Tragic Drama* (London: Verso Books, 1977), pp. 159–61. The book was completed but unpublished in 1928.

4   John Locke, *An Essay concerning Human Understanding*, edited by Peter H. Nidditch (Oxford: Oxford University Press, 1689/1975), bk.1 ch.1, p. 46.

5   Locke, *An Essay concerning Human Understanding*, bk. 2 ch. 1, p. 104.

6   Plato, *Timaeus, Critias, Cleitophon, Menexenus, Epistles* (Cambridge, Mass: Harvard University Press, c. 360 BC/1929), p. 121.

7   Anthony Ashley Cooper, Third Earl of Shaftesbury, *Characteristicks of Men, Manner, Opinions, Times* (Oxford: Oxford University Press, 1711/1999), vol. 2, pp. 94–101.

8   Raphael & Baldassare Castiglione, 'The Letter to Leo X, c. 1519', in Vaughan Hart & Peter Hicks, *Palladio's Rome: A Translation of Andrea Palladio's Two Guidebooks to Rome* (New Haven/London: Yale University Press, 2006), p. 188.

9   Immanuel Kant, *Kant's Critique of Judgement* (London: Macmillan, 1790/1931), p. 210.

10 Antonio Sant'Elia & Filippo Tomasso Marinetti, 'Manifesto of Futurist Architecture'. (1914), in Ulrich Conrads (ed.), *Programmes and Manifestoes on 20th Century Architecture* (Cambridge: MIT Press, 1970), p. 35.

11 Nikolaus Pevsner, 'The Anti-Pioneers', (1966), in Stephen Games (ed.), *Pevsner on Art and Architecture: The Radio Talks* (London: Methuen, 2002), p. 295.

12 Pevsner, 'The Anti-Pioneers', pp. 305, 298.

13 Ibid., p. 299.

14 Frances Yates, letter to Denys Lasdun, 17 May 1976; Denys Lasdun, letter to Frances Yates, 21 May 1976 – both letters in Lasdun Archive, RIBA Library Drawings and Archives Collection, Victoria & Albert Museum, London, UK.

15 Jean-François Lyotard, *The Post-Modern Condition: A Report on Knowledge* (Manchester: Manchester University Press, 1986), p. 79.

16 Denys Lasdun, in 'Interview with Denys Lasdun', Agreed Draft, 27 June 1979, p. 4, in the Lasdun Archive, RIBA Library Drawings and Archives Collections; Thomas Stearns Eliot, 'Tradition and the Individual Talent', in *Points of View* (London: Faber & Faber, 1941), pp. 26–7.

17 Michel Foucault, 'On the Genealogy of Ethics: An Overview of Work in Progress', in Paul Rabinow (ed.), *The Foucault Reader* (London: Pantheon, 1984), p. 369.

18 Paul De Man, *The Rhetoric of Romanticism* (New York: Columbia University Press, 1984), p. 69.

19 Lennard J. Davis, *Factual Fictions: The Origins of the English Novel* (Philadelphia: University of Pennsylvania Press, 1996), p. 213; Ian Watt, *The Rise of the Novel: Studies in Defoe, Richardson and Fielding* (London: Hogarth Press, 1987), p. 62.

20 William Congreve, *Incognita: or, Love and Duty Reconcil'd. A Novel* (1692), pp. 5–6. Davis, *Factual Fictions*, pp. 103–4.

21 Locke, *An Essay Concerning Human Understanding*, bk. 2 ch. 27, p. 342.

22 Laurence Sterne, *The Life and Opinions of Tristram Shandy, Gentleman*, edited by Melvyn New and Joan New (London: Penguin, 2003), vol. 1 ch. 28, p. 64.

23 John Soane, 'Crude Hints towards an History of my House in L(incoln's) I(nn) Fields', 1812, in Christopher Woodward, *Visions of Ruin: Architectural Fantasies and Designs for Garden Follies* (London: Sir John Soane's Museum, 1999), p. 73.

24 John Soane, *Memoirs of the Professional Life of an Architect, between the Years 1768 and 1835. Written by Himself* (London, 1835), pp. 65–6.

25 As the Professor of Architecture at the Royal Academy, Soane mentioned Laurence Sterne early in his first lecture in 1809 and again in his two final lectures. Soane, 'Lecture I', 'Lecture XI' and 'Lecture XII', in David Watkin, *Sir John Soane: Enlightenment Thought and the Royal Academy Lectures* (Cambridge: Cambridge University Press, 1996), pp. 491, 647, 653.

26 Nicolas Le Camus de Mézières, *The Genius of Architecture; or, the Analogy of That Art With Our Sensations* (Santa Monica: The Getty Center, 1780/1992), p. 88. The book first published in French as *Le Génie de I'Architecture; ou, l'Analogie de Cet Art avec Nos Sensations.*

27 Le Corbusier, *Towards a New Architecture* (London: Architectural Press, 1946), p. 222.

28 Roland Barthes, *Mythologies* (London: Farrar Straus & Giroux, 1973), p. 89.

29 Alison Smithson, *AS in DS: An Eye on the Road* (Baden: Lars Muller Verlag, 1983/2001), p. 111.

30 Le Corbusier, *Towards a New Architecture*, p. 31; Plato, *Philebus* (Oxford: Oxford University Press, 1975), p. 51.

31 Peter Smithson, in Alison Smithson, *AS in DS*, p. 1; Alison Smithson, *AS in DS*, p. 47.

32 Ibid., pp. 47, 111.

33 Ibid., p. 151.

34 Ibid., p. 39.

35 William Gilpin, *Remarks on Forest Scenery, and other Woodland Views (Relative Chiefly to Picturesque Beauty), Illustrated by the Scenes of New-Forest in Hampshire*, 2 (London: R. Blamire, 1791), p. 225.

36 Richard Hamblyn, *The Invention of Clouds: How an Amateur Meteorologist Forged the Language of the Skies* (London; Picador, 2001), p. 172; H.D. Rawnsley, *Past and Present at the English Lakes* (Glasgow: J. MacLehouse & Sons, 1916), pp. 153–208.

37 Alison Smithson, *AS in DS*, p. 91 – see also p. 11.

38   Alison Smithson, 'Patio and Pavilion, 1956, Reconstructed USA 1990', *Places: A Quarterly Journal of Environmental Design*, vol. 7 no. 3, 1991, p. 11.

39   Malcolm Bradbury, 'Author's Note', *The History Man* (London: Arrow Books, 1975).

40   Denys Lasdun, 'The Architecture of Urban Landscape', in *Architecture in an Age of Scepticism: A Practitioner's Anthology Compiled by Denys Lasdun* (London: Heinemann, 1984), pp. 137, 139.

AN 'ARTIFICIAL SCIENCE' OF ARCHITECTURE

Philip Steadman

In recent decades a number of activities have come under the banner of 'design research' or 'design science'. In architecture there have been studies of the *process* of architectural design: protocol studies of architects at work; the devising of normative methods for design; the creation of exemplary types or models to be followed in design; and cognitive theories of the mental processes of architects. To these one might add the production of *tools* for designers, either printed (guides, standards) or digital computer-aided design (CAD) systems. The work has generated a large literature and has come to support its own specialised journals.

Many of these activities build and elaborate on the work of the 'design methods movement' of the 1960s and 70s, of which John Christopher Jones and Christopher Alexander were leading protagonists – although both later distanced themselves from their earlier positions.[1] The design methodologists in turn looked back to developments in operations research and general systems theory during the Second World War. The 1960s were when computers were first coming into wider use – at least in universities, governments and large corporations – and when work began on computer-aided design in architecture. Some of the very earliest computer-aided design systems were intended to *generate* plans, given a set of 'requirements', and often with the goal of minimising pedestrian movement. In the late 1970s the attention of the growing CAD industry shifted towards tools for the *representation of designs*, that is to say two-dimensional drawing and three-dimensional modelling packages, to replace ink, paper, cardboard and balsa wood. It is only more recently that researchers have returned to generative CAD tools, but without much practical application to date other than in complex curvilinear form making.

The history of design methods is an extensive and complicated one, not to be entered too deeply here. I will make one point in relation to Christopher Alexander's *Notes on the Synthesis of Form* of 1964, one of the most influential of design methods texts (note the emphasis in his title on synthesis, that is, design generation). Alexander diagnosed the failings of current design practice as stemming from the inadequacy of architects' 'mental pictures' of both the forms of buildings and their 'contexts' – the problems that are to be resolved by the forms. His answer was to create 'formal pictures' of these mental pictures of forms and contexts, in which the structure of relationships between the various factors or elements involved in a design task would be clarified using the mathematics of graph theory and automatic classification.

There were, however, deep contradictions in this proposed approach, which were perhaps among the causes of Alexander abandoning the method. I have argued elsewhere that had Alexander truly followed the logic of his own argument, it would have led him in a quite different direction.[2] The way in which greater precision is generally given to our 'mental pictures' of the physical world is of course through scientific research and the development of ever better explanatory theories and models. In the context of building science this would mean for example better predictive models of the energy performance of buildings, or the behaviour of light in architectural interiors, or the movement of people through circulation networks. Such models can be used to increase designers' *knowledge* of the phenomena in question – knowledge that can then be deployed in the design process.

This is the programme for which I argue in this chapter. I want to propose – not for the first time – a kind of scientific research in architecture, with connections to architectural history, but which goes beyond building science as traditionally understood, to address questions of the possible forms and spatial arrangements of buildings.[3] This would have bearings on the design process, but in a less direct way than the techniques put forward by the design methods movement and much current design research. In 1969 the economist and pioneer of artificial intelligence, Herbert Simon, argued for the academic recognition of the 'sciences of the artificial', in parallel with the natural sciences of physics and biology.[4] 'Artificial sciences' would be devoted to the study of man-made objects of all kinds. Simon was thinking mainly about engineering, computing science, and the theory of machines.[5] But sciences of the artificial would also include linguistics and archaeology (whose practitioners study many kinds of artefact, among them of course buildings). I have in mind an 'artificial science of architecture'.

A central premise of the sciences of the artificial is that artefacts – despite the fact that they are made by humans – can embody 'knowledge' or possess properties of which their makers and others are not aware. This is obviously true for the objects retrieved by archaeology, whose makers are long dead and have left no records. But it can also be true for contemporary artefacts. A person can speak a language with no formal understanding of the linguistic structures and constraints on which that performance rests. In craft production and vernacular architecture new tools or buildings are produced by copying old ones, and the craftsman or woman may be unaware of why or how they

function, just that they *do* work in practice. Such craft knowledge as does exist is, much of it, in Simon's phrase, 'intuitive, informal, and cook-booky'.[6] It is arguable that this is even true in some areas of modern engineering. Certain artefacts like cities are constructed collectively through the decisions and actions of many parties, and may come as a result to acquire unknown and unanticipated properties. Large numbers of artefacts, considered *en masse*, may be found to display statistical regularities of which their individual designers would not be conscious.

It follows that in order to retrieve this hidden knowledge and structure, artefacts must be subjected to analysis and experiment, in something of the way that natural scientists treat physical phenomena. One might even venture the proposition that more can be learned about the *process of design* of artefacts by studying those objects directly, than by studying designers in action. After all, when literary critics want to analyse style and composition, they do not watch writers at their desks, or question them as they work: they read texts. It is similar for art critics and paintings. Why, then, should we not learn about how architects design by analysing their buildings?

The distinctive feature of the sciences of the artificial would therefore be their effort to understand – where this is not consciously understood already – how artefacts are organised and how they function. The implication or hope would be, naturally, that any understanding gained by this research could help designers to be more effective in their decision making. Architects would have a clearer picture of the range of strategic possibilities open to them, and the likely performance and properties of each alternative. They would profit, that is to say, by widening their knowledge of options in design, rather than by changing their method of designing.

All of this discussion has perhaps been rather abstract. I will try to illustrate the argument with three pieces of research that seem to me to exemplify the character and potential of an artificial science of architecture. Two were carried out more than 40 years ago, the third very recently. Although the authors worked quite independently, there are connections between the three studies, as we will see. Their research has to do in all cases with the geometry of built form. It treats buildings at a relatively high level of abstraction, and is concerned with simple measurable properties such as volume, surface area, plan depth, floor area and ground coverage. It deals with those basic aspects of performance that can be characterised as 'generic functions' of architecture: the provision of daylight, ventilation and access, the use of land, the spacing of buildings apart for privacy and views. These are matters I believe which an architectural science can address – among others – and about which it can generalise and make predictions, which are the hallmarks of any science. Where the findings have relevance for design, it is in early strategic decisions about the overall form, massing and arrangement of buildings.

RANKO BON AND THE RATIO OF VOLUME TO WALL AREA

My first example comes from the work of Ranko Bon, who was a member in the 1960s of an interdisciplinary seminar at MIT called the 'Philomorphs'. The group was devoted to the comparative study of form in many subjects including biology, geography, crystallography and art. Bon represented architecture. He collected a sample of residential buildings of widely varying sizes, from Neolithic and Egyptian huts to grand hotels and high-rise apartment blocks, taking in mobile homes, modern houses and mansions along the way.[7] In each case he measured the volume, and the total area of the external walls, and compared the two.

Bon's results are plotted in the two graphs shown in Figure 3.1.[8] These are drawn at different scales to show the smaller buildings and the larger buildings. Although there is some scatter, it emerges that there is a fairly consistent ratio of wall area to volume: the points lie along or close to a straight line. Why should this occur? All these are habitations whose rooms are in almost all cases naturally lit and naturally ventilated. As a consequence their plans may be either one room or two rooms deep; but they cannot be three or more rooms deep, since then the interior spaces could have no windows. This effect, together with the fact that 'habitable' rooms in houses and flats tend not to vary very greatly in size, means that the range of possible depths of such buildings in plan is quite tightly constrained.

Most modern houses tend to have plan depths around 7 metres, although of course there is variation around this norm.[9] This is what Bon's results show. Dividing a building's volume by its external wall area gives an approximate measure of its depth in plan: in fact it gives a value that is close to half of the plan depth.[10] The lines in the two graphs correspond to a 'half-depth' of 3.5 m, that is a plan depth of 7 m. The houses in the centre of the size range in Bon's sample come close to this value. The depths of the huts and smaller dwellings are somewhat lower, since many of them are just one room deep.

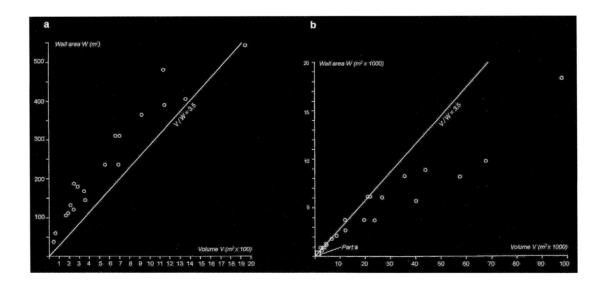

3.1 Measurements by Ranko Bon of the volume and external wall area of 40 residential buildings of different sizes. The two graphs at different scales show (a) the smaller buildings and (b) the larger buildings. The area covered by graph (a) is shown as a small box in graph (b). The sloping lines correspond to a value of 3.5 metres for the ratio of volume to wall area: that is, to a plan depth of around 7 metres

The depths of the hotels and apartment buildings are higher, up to 14 m at a maximum. This is because they can have larger mean room sizes, and may contain internal corridors, bathrooms and even windowless kitchens.

Speaking loosely, we can say that the extent of the walls and their windows is governed by the need to supply the enclosed volume with sufficient illumination and air. This is something of which architects are of course well aware in the individual case; but Bon was the first to show how the relationship holds over many buildings. There are profound consequences for the overall forms of houses and apartments. As residential buildings are made larger, they cannot be made deeper – beyond 14 m or so – and thus they must become elongated in either the vertical or the horizontal direction. They may be stretched vertically into towers or slabs, or stretched horizontally into elongated ranges, branching wings or closed courts. Bon

also showed regularities in another geometrical property of buildings: the length of the circulation system compared with the floor area.[11] Again a reasonably constant ratio of the two quantities is observed in buildings of increasing size, as the network of corridors, lobbies and halls is extended progressively to serve the growing number of rooms.

Bon was interested in such effects as architectural cases of *allometry*, the biological phenomenon whereby organisms change their shapes as they grow larger, in order to preserve certain ratios essential to their physiological functioning.[12] The ratio of surface to volume is important for example in warm-blooded animals, since it affects heat loss or gain through the skin. As a consequence, allometry can be seen in the different body shapes of animals, either individuals of one species as they grow, or diverse species with different body sizes. Going back to buildings,

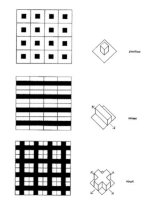

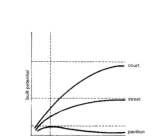

3.2   Three different dispositions of built forms – 'pavilions', 'streets' and 'courts' – considered by Leslie Martin and Lionel March in their work on the use of land by buildings. These arrays should be imagined as continuing indefinitely

3.3   A 'cut-off angle' *(a)* measuring the angle between the ground and a line joining the base of one building façade to the top of the façade opposite

3.4   Floor space index (here referred to as 'built potential') plotted against number of storeys for the three arrays of built forms in Figure 3.2. For 'streets' and 'courts' the value of FSI reaches a maximum, beyond which density does not rise further despite the increase in number of storeys. In the case of 'pavilions', FSI reaches a maximum and then *declines* as more storeys are added

the constraints on plan depth that Bon demonstrated are important for my two further examples in an artificial science of architecture.

THE 'LAND USE AND BUILT FORM STUDIES' OF LESLIE MARTIN AND LIONEL MARCH

While Bon was working in Cambridge (Massachusetts) in the 1960s, over in Cambridge (England) Leslie Martin and Lionel March had become interested in the ways in which different generic forms of building make use of land.[13] They distinguished three simple types of form: 'pavilions' (or what might otherwise be described as freestanding towers), 'streets' and 'courts' (see Figure 3.2).[14] They imagined regular arrays of these forms continuing indefinitely; and they measured the densities of these developments in terms of their floor space indices (FSI). The floor space index is calculated by taking the floor area of the building on all levels, and dividing by the land area. In order to make comparisons on an equivalent basis, Martin and March controlled for three variables: storey height, the depth of each of the forms in plan, and the cut-off angle between forms. The cut-off angle is the angle between the ground plane and a line joining the base of one façade to the top of the façade opposite (Figure 3.3). In effect the assumption was that these were day-lit and naturally ventilated buildings, either residential or offices. So the depth in plan would be limited, in the way that Bon demonstrated. And the cut-off angle would control the spacing apart of the forms, such that lighting and ventilation would be preserved (this was a questionable assumption, to be discussed shortly).

Martin and March then varied the number of storeys in each of their three forms and calculated

the resulting densities as values for the floor space index (Figure 3.4).[15] The cut-off angle is fixed throughout, so as the forms are made higher they are pushed further apart, and use more land. The FSI rises with number of storeys in all three forms as one would expect: but in the case of the 'street' and 'court' forms, density approaches a maximum value, beyond which it cannot rise further. A law of limiting returns sets in. And with the 'pavilion' form, the FSI rises to a maximum value and thereafter declines: as more storeys are added, the density actually *decreases*.

Figure 3.4 shows that when the numbers of storeys are the same, the 'court' forms always provide much more floor area on a given land area than 'streets', which in turn provide much more floor area than 'pavilions'. At the number of storeys for which the FSI for 'street' forms reaches its maximum, the 'streets' fit twice as much floor area on the given area of land as the 'pavilions', and the 'courts' fit three times as much floor area as the 'pavilions'.

These were, and still are, counter-intuitive findings, with major implications for architecture and urban design. It is arguable that even now, more than 40 years later, their lessons have still to be widely understood. The general public and large parts of the architectural and planning professions continue to believe that in order to raise densities it is always necessary to build higher. Martin and March's work shows that this belief needs to be seriously questioned and carefully qualified.

We can perhaps understand their findings better if we consider Martin and March's built form units in a slightly different way. Figure 3.5 shows equally sized square sites on which are placed (a) a 'pavilion' form at the corner, (b) a 'street' form along one edge,

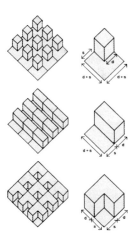

and (c) an L-shaped form along two edges. If these respective units are repeated they recreate Martin and March's arrays, as shown. The L-shaped units join together to make an array of 'courts'. The forms have been drawn such that the distance by which the forms are spaced apart is equal to their depths in plan. This is the specific condition under which the FSI of the 'pavilion' form reaches its maximum. At this point the (L-shaped) 'court' occupies three-quarters of the site, the 'street' occupies half of the site, and the 'pavilion' occupies a quarter of the site. If the buildings were on one storey, their respective FSIs would be 0.75, 0.5 and 0.25. On more storeys, the FSIs would still be in these same ratios, i.e. 3:2:1.

When the spacing apart of the forms is less than or greater than plan depth, the FSI ratios differ, as we can see in the graph in Figure 3.4. But the rank ordering of the three forms in terms of their densities does not change. Speaking loosely (and somewhat misleadingly) we can say that, in a continuous array, each façade of a form obtains its light and air from the area of open space onto which it fronts. For the arrays of 'pavilions' and 'streets', the piece of space between two opposite façades is 'used twice'. But in the array of 'pavilions', there are also spaces diagonally between buildings that are not 'used' in this way at all. For 'court' forms, all four façades face onto the same piece of space, which is thus 'used four times'.

Since Martin and March published their original research, architectural scientists have challenged certain aspects of the argument. Here is should be appreciated that their work predated the general introduction of computers, and Martin and March made all their calculations by hand. They were conscious that their model was 'a gross

simplification in practical terms', adding that 'more elaborate models can be designed'.[16] One point which Martin and March themselves acknowledged was that there are losses in day-lit floor space at the internal corners of courtyards (often used in practice for vertical circulation or service rooms), which do not occur in 'street' or 'pavilion' forms. Indeed an external corner on a 'pavilion' obtains light from two façades.

More serious is the question of whether setting a specific value for the cut-off angle between opposing façades can assure an equal standard of daylighting in the three forms (all other things being equal, such as the sizes of windows, the reflective properties of the walls and so on). The tacit assumption behind the use of the simple two-dimensional cut-off angle to determine this spacing is that daylight only arrives perpendicularly to the façades of buildings; but clearly this is not true. In reality, daylight is received from the whole of the visible part of the sky. More of the sky can be seen from a given position and floor level in 'pavilions' than from equivalent positions in 'street' or 'court' forms, since in the latter two cases the respective solid angles are obstructed to a greater extent by adjacent forms or parts of forms.

Carlo Ratti studied these lighting effects using simulation software to estimate the levels of illumination at the bases of the façades of equivalent arrays of 'pavilions', 'streets' and 'courts' (the reflective properties of surfaces, as well as the relevant dimensions, were all standardised throughout).[17] Ratti found, as one might expect, that daylight levels at these positions are highest for pavilions, lower for streets, lowest for courts. He demonstrated nevertheless that for *equal* lighting levels, the rank

3.5 Martin and March's 'pavilions', 'streets' and 'courts' represented in a slightly different way, as repeating units. The 'courts' are created with repeated L-shapes. All are drawn such that plan depth (*d*) equals the spacing apart of the forms (*s*). Cut-off angles and heights are equal throughout. The areas of the sites of the three units are the same. The L-shaped 'court' unit occupies three-quarters of the site, the 'street' occupies half of the site, and the 'pavilion' occupies a quarter of the site. Their FSI values are therefore in the ratio of 3:2:1

ordering of 'courts'/'streets'/'pavilions' in terms of FSI remains the same, although the differences are not as great as Martin and March calculated. With these reservations in mind, it is worth emphasising that cut-off angles remain a simple and useful geometrical way of expressing the distances by which building façades are spaced apart in relation to their height; distances that can bear upon other aspects of performance besides lighting, such as privacy and natural ventilation.

Let me conclude this account of Martin and March's findings with an illustration of their practical implications. In the 1920s the American architect, Raymond Hood, designer of splendid Art Deco office buildings, published a series of propositions for a 'City of Towers'.[18] Figure 3.6 is by Hood and shows a standard Manhattan block with the existing development replaced by three slender skyscrapers of roughly 50 storeys. Hood's idea was that developers should be given incentives to release more ground area for public use, in return for being permitted to build higher. This would allow for wider streets and help to avoid traffic congestion:

> Whole blocks would soon develop of their own accord, where two or three towers would provide more floor space than there is in the average block of today, and there would be ten times as much street area round about to take care of the traffic.

His drawing in Figure 3.6 shows the results: 'Three operations have completed one block'.[19] 'Average blocks of today' are also visible at right and left.

Given the standard size of the Manhattan block, it is possible to make rough measurements of the plan dimensions of these towers, and calculate the FSI for the whole block, which has the value 5.7 (it is conventional to include half the widths of the surrounding streets in the figure for total ground area). The three towers therefore cover about 11 per cent of the ground.

Now let us compare this with a development on an adjoining block in the form of buildings along the four street-fronts creating a closed court (Figure 3.7). The depth in plan here is 17.5 m throughout, typical for day-lit office buildings, and the height is 13 storeys. The FSI for this development is again 5.7, exactly the same as Hood's towers, but in buildings which are less than one third of their height. Ground coverage is 44 per cent.

This very striking illustration of Martin and March's general comparison of the respective land use performances of 'pavilions' and 'courts' is not entirely fair in their terms: the cut-off angles are different in the two developments.[20] The angles are in fact *steeper* for Hood's towers: that is to say the towers are actually *closer* together in relation to their height than are the court forms (if they were repeated on adjacent blocks).[21]

THE 'SPACEMATE' DIAGRAM OF BERGHAUSER PONT AND HAUPT

In the last decade there has been a revival of interest in issues of density in Holland, a country where land is of course in short supply, and where architects are still much involved in the design of public housing. Two researchers at the Technical University of Delft, Meta Berghauser Pont and Per Haupt, have recently published an ingenious and useful graphical tool called 'Spacemate'.[22] This allows floor space index, the coverage of ground area for buildings, and also their heights, to be compared in a two-dimensional coordinate system (Figure 3.8).

3.6　Illustration by Raymond Hood of
a Manhattan block with three towers of
approximately 40, 50 and 60 storeys

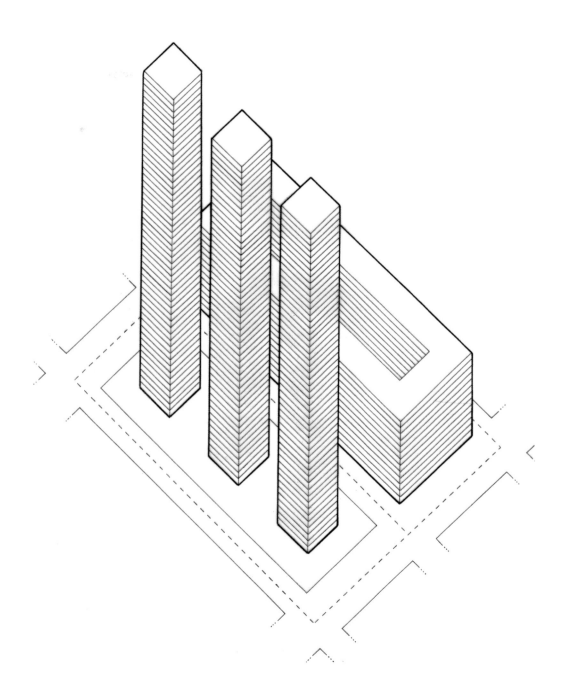

3.7 Three 50-storey towers on a Manhattan block measuring 60 m × 180 m, similar to Hood's scheme in Figure 3.6, compared with a 13-storey court on the same size of block (axonometrics drawn at 1:2500). The FSI is 5.7 in both cases. Ground coverage is 11 per cent and 44 per cent respectively

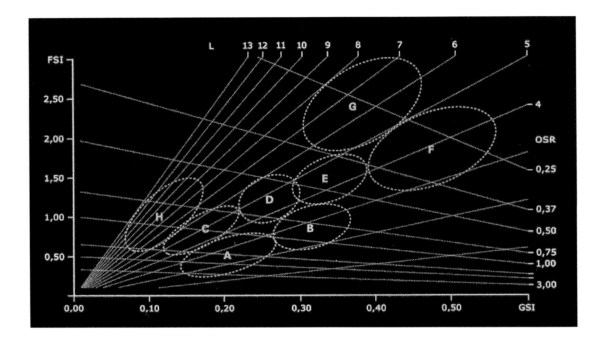

Ground coverage is not expressed here as a percentage, but by what the authors call a 'ground space index' (GSI) calculated by dividing the area covered by buildings by the total ground area. Thus a ground space index of 0.5 would describe the case where 50 per cent of the ground is covered.

In 'Spacemate', the floor space index (FSI) is plotted on the *y*-axis, and ground space index (GSI) on the *x*-axis.[23] The result is for buildings with the same numbers of floors (L) to lie along straight lines radiating from the origin. This is because of the intrinsic relationship between FSI and ground coverage. For a single-storey building the two variables take the same value; they describe the same thing. In a multi-storey building, FSI is equal to ground coverage times the number of storeys. See how, for example, on the 10-storey line that where

ground coverage = 0.1, FSI = 1 (it is assumed that buildings have the same floor area on every storey).

One of the first points made by Berghauser Pont and Haupt is the same as that made about Hood's scheme in Figure 3.7. Developments which have what are clearly very different morphologies – different heights, different spacing of the buildings – can share similar FSI values. Indeed, they illustrate four examples of very diverse housing developments which all have FSIs of around 0.7 (Figure 3.9).[24]

Berghauser Pont and Haupt have measured a large number of residential estates in Amsterdam and Rotterdam, and have plotted values for the relevant variables using 'Spacemate'. The ground areas are gross values throughout, and include associated open spaces, gardens, and the appropriate fractions of road areas. The result is that what to the eye seem to be

3.8   The 'Spacemate' diagram of Meta Berghauser Pont and Per Haupt. The *y*-axis plots Floor Space Index (FSI) and the *x*-axis plots Ground Space Index (GSI) or ground coverage. The diagonal lines (L) correspond to different numbers of storeys. The ellipses enclose groups of Dutch housing developments with distinct morphological characteristics

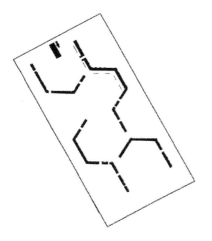

3.9 Four Dutch housing developments with very different heights and morphologies but the same floor space index

similar morphologies become clustered within separate regions of 'Spacemate', as indicated by the zones enclosed by ellipses and marked with letters in Figure 3.8. Berghauser Pont and Haupt name these groups as:

A   Low-rise spacious strip developments
B   Low-rise compact strip developments
C   Mid-rise open building blocks
D   Mid-rise spacious building blocks
E   Mid-rise closed building blocks
F   Mid-rise compact building blocks
G   Mid-rise super blocks
H   High-rise developments

By 'low-rise' the authors mean two or three storeys, and by 'mid-rise' four to seven storeys. The 'high-rise' buildings (H) are typically on ten storeys: notice how these achieve FSIs of around 1, comparable with the 'low-rise' Group B, and lower than most of the 'mid-rise' groups. Berghauser Pont and Haupt arrived at these intriguing findings empirically. But why should their sample of buildings become grouped in these particular patterns? We can provide some theoretical interpretation by examining them in the light of Martin and March's work.

Specifically we can introduce two more variables discussed in the last section: plan depth

45

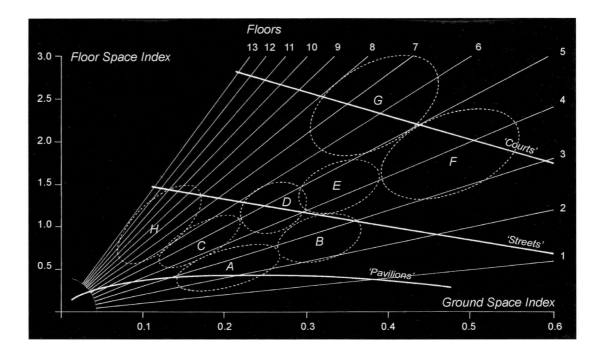

3.10 'Spacemate' with curves plotted for Martin and March's 'pavilion', 'street' and 'court' forms. In every case plan depth = 10 metres, storey height = 3 metres, and cut-off angle = 27°. The zones corresponding to the groups of Dutch housing developments from Figure 3.8 are again enclosed by ellipses and identified by letters

and cut-off angle. The buildings in Figure 3.8 are mostly terraced houses and blocks of flats. On the basis of Bon's work we could expect their depths in plan to vary between about 7 and 14 m. Let us take a central value of 10 m for illustration. We can assume a standard storey height of 3 m. As for cut-off angles, these could obviously vary very widely, between patterns of detached houses with extensive gardens at one extreme, and central city apartments at the other. For the purposes of direct comparison, let us take a value of 27° throughout, corresponding to the spacing of buildings by a distance equal to twice their heights. This value can be changed.

Of course few real buildings conform exactly to Martin and March's schematic types. Depth may vary even in different parts of the same plan,

and the actual cut-off angles on different sides of a building may vary greatly depending on its exact relationship to neighbouring buildings. The Martin and March forms and their associated measures can nevertheless capture some important generalised features of actual built developments, and can serve to characterise broad tendencies and average values.

Once the depth and cut-off angle are fixed for 'pavilions', 'streets' and 'courts', these determine the relationships between height, ground coverage and FSI, as we saw earlier. We can vary number of storeys and plot the results as three lines in 'Spacemate' (Figure 3.10). Consider the lowest line, for 'pavilions'. Reading from right to left, this rises to a maximum FSI (of about 0.4) with increasing number of storeys and then declines, as we would expect from Martin and March's results. All 'pavilion' forms with cut-off angles equal to or less than 27° must fall below this line. The similar happens for the 'street' and 'court' lines. The lines define in effect three bands, in the uppermost of which we could expect to find most of the 'courts', in the middle the 'streets', and in the lowest the 'pavilions' (this assumes that 27° is a reasonable cut-off angle to apply throughout, which is certainly debatable).

Now look at the real Dutch buildings in relation to these bands. Groups B and C are terraces and fall as they should within the 'streets' band. Group H consists mostly of elongated high-rise slabs, which therefore also qualify as 'street' forms and are also found in this band. Groups D, E, F and G are courtyard developments of various types (Berghauser Pont and Haupt refer to courts as 'blocks'). Large parts of all the four groups are indeed found within the 'court' band, although they overlap its upper and lower boundaries. There are no real freestanding or tower buildings in the 'pavilion' band, since the surveys did not include any examples. Had detached and semi-detached houses been covered, these would have been located here, at the lower left of the diagram near the origin.

The actual Dutch buildings, that is to say, are found generally in the bands for the Martin and March built forms to which they approximate. Where they do *not* conform, this must be because the blanket assumptions about plan depth and cut-off angle made for the purposes of Figure 3.10 are not correct. Different values would shift the lines up or down. Better knowledge of actual values in the real buildings would allow homogeneous groups to be distinguished in terms of these variables, and located

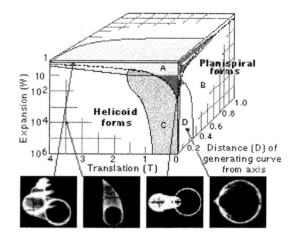

more precisely. For example, there are courtyard buildings in Groups F and G above the 'court' line in Figure 3.10, either because their plans are deeper than 10 m or the cut-off angle is greater than 27°.

POSSIBILITY IN ARCHITECTURAL FORM

The 'Spacemate' diagram is an architectural 'morphospace': a theoretical space of possible forms for buildings. The term morphospace has gained currency in biology to mean a mathematical/ graphical method for representing the ranges of actual and possible forms of animals and plants. It was the University of Chicago palaeontologist David Raup who pioneered such methods. Figure 3.11 shows Raup's three-dimensional morphospace for the shells of snails, limpets and other gastropods.[25] Three parameters that control the geometrical forms of these shells are plotted on the x, y and z-axes, the effect being to separate shells of different helical types – some flatter, some more steeply conical, some more tightly wound – into different zones within the space. Certain zones (such as those

3.11 A three-dimensional morphospace for the shells of gastropods, developed by David Raup. Actual species are found in the zones marked A, B, C and D, but not in the remainder of the space

labelled A, B, C and D) correspond to the shells of actual species. Elsewhere there are zones in which no real species are found, perhaps because such forms, although geometrically possible, are for some reason biologically unviable.

'Spacemate' has the similar effect of segregating groups of morphologically similar buildings into discrete zones within the two-dimensional space of the diagram. If the space was extended we would reach zones where the forms of buildings, if not impossible to imagine, would be highly unlikely to occur in practice. For example, to the upper right of an enlarged 'Spacemate' diagram would be multi-storey buildings approaching a ground coverage of 1, that is to say merging into one continuous structure without gaps. Near to, but not at that limit, would be very deep plan forms, packed close together, which would still be highly improbable. There would be a graded transition, that is to say, between the possible, through the improbable, to the outright impossible. Berghauser Pont and Haupt's data show that residential estates in today's Holland with ground coverage greater than 0.6 and FSIs greater than 3 are rare, if not architecturally out of the question. This must say something about the prevailing standards of building depth and relative spacing thought necessary to preserve acceptable levels of lighting, ventilation, privacy, the provision of gardens and so on.

This is what sciences do: they define the realms of possibility within which actual instances of the phenomena under study are to be found. But what exactly might be meant by 'possibility' in the architectural context? Clearly since buildings are material objects they must obey both the laws of physics and the laws of geometry. It might be argued

on that basis that the scientific study of artefacts must constitute just specialised branches of those disciplines. But as Herbert Simon points out, the distinguishing feature of all useful artefacts is that, because they are produced for human purposes, they 'can be characterised in terms of functions, goals, adaptation'.[26] This fact, he suggests, has consequences for the special way in which sciences of the artificial must operate. Physical sciences can describe the internal structure or mechanism and the external 'environment' of an artefact. What they cannot allow for is the third term that relates these two conditions: that is the artefact's purpose.

The buildings measured by Bon showed the consistent relationship between volume and wall area because of the architectural purposes satisfied in every case: the generic functions of lighting and ventilation. Martin and March's theoretical built forms were not just a random selection of geometrical solids: they were chosen carefully for the way in which they satisfy the same two generic functions, while making use of land in distinctively different ways. Such basic purposes of buildings remain relatively unchanged throughout the history of architecture. But there are other kinds of possibility that change over time: those created for example by advances in building services and construction technology.

A 'Spacemate' diagram of the mid-nineteenth century would not have bothered to show the numbers of storeys much above six, with the effective vertical limit being imposed by people's willingness to climb stairs (although buildings taller than this were not strictly impossible before elevators, and were occasionally constructed). In the contemporary Dutch 'Spacemate' there is a gap immediately above and to the right of the high-rise Group H. This is presumably because lifts are now general in buildings above five or six storeys, and once these are introduced it is more economic to build up to ten storeys or higher. Seven- or eight-storey buildings (with lifts) are in this context less 'probable'. Again, the depths of multi-storey buildings in plan were released from the constraints imposed by the purposes of natural lighting and ventilation by air-conditioning in the 1920s and fluorescent lighting in the 1940s. And so on.

Besides these boundaries broken by technical innovations, there are limits on architectural 'possibility' created by collective decisions – whether tacit or conscious – taken by large parts of the profession. This was the case for example with the *de facto* choice by architects, from the Renaissance through to the early-twentieth century, to give overall bilateral symmetry to the forms of many buildings. This choice was of course self-imposed, and was abandoned by Modernism; but while it lasted it had profound consequences in restricting the morphospaces of designers. I have been making experiments myself with a particular design of architectural morphospace, again concerned with the generic functions of lighting and ventilation as well as circulation.[27] A large class of built forms can be distinguished using binary codes and mapped across a two- or three-dimensional coordinate system. This morphospace is too elaborate to explain in any detail here; but it allows one to plot the positions within this space of examples of building types from different periods, and study the consequences for formal possibility of the decisions made by communities of designers to impose certain general requirements of function

or aesthetics. These delimit the zones in which instances of the types occur.

The forms of the nineteenth-century 'pavilion hospitals', with which the name of Florence Nightingale is associated, were constrained for example to fishbone or comb-like plans, as the result of two decisions. The wards were made the terminal branches on the circulation system in order to discourage cross-infection, and the courtyards between wards were kept open at one end to encourage maximum natural ventilation. The forms of prisons on the model of Philadelphia's Eastern Penitentiary and London's Pentonville were limited to radial plans by the desire for all cell doors to be visible from a central observation point. Once medical or penal policy changed, these constraints disappeared, and were replaced by others. This is where an artificial science of architecture meets with the architectural history of building types. The history can follow the contingent trajectories of types as they pass through the spaces of possibility defined by the science. In sum, then, there can be a variety of meanings of 'possibility' in an architectural science – physical, geometrical, technological, institutional, even aesthetic (think of symmetry) – all of them defined and shaped by the practical and social purposes to which buildings are put.

A CONCLUDING WORD ON BIOLOGICAL ANALOGY

In this chapter I have introduced some techniques for the analysis of form in biology as methodological tools for an architectural science. Ranko Bon sought allometric properties in populations of buildings. 'Spacemate' constitutes a morphospace, as in a different way did the experiments of March and Martin. It is no accident that biology should show the way here, since, of all the natural sciences, biology alone deals – like the artificial sciences – with adaptation of form to function. I have written at length elsewhere about biological analogies in architecture and their potential dangers.[28]

Those dangers lie however in an improper equation of organic evolution with the 'evolution' of artefacts. This has the paradoxical and absurd result of effectively removing teleology, of removing designers and their intentions, from any account of the design process. Artefacts come to be seen merely as 'evolved' products of their 'functional environments'. Evolutionary analogies are conducive in this way to the fallacy of functional determinism, and to the false belief that unique or optimal 'solutions' exist to design 'problems'. Although Christopher Alexander denied any simple analogy from biology in his book *Notes on the Synthesis of Form*, this was nevertheless the trap into which he fell.

Notice that these dangers do *not* lurk in methods borrowed from biology for describing and analysing *form*. The concept of the morphospace in architectural research implies that there are worlds of formal possibility from which designers may choose. Those options may be shown to have different properties of interest, varying levels of performance according to different criteria, leading designers to prefer some above others. Compromises can be reached between conflicting demands of function. Designers' knowledge is enhanced, but their hands are not forced.

Notes

1   John Christopher Jones, *Design Methods: Seeds of Human Futures* (New York: Wiley, 1970); Christopher Alexander, *Notes on the Synthesis of Form* (Cambridge, Mass: Harvard University Press, 1964).

2   Philip Steadman, *The Evolution of Designs: Biological Analogy in Architecture and the Applied Arts* (Cambridge: Cambridge University Press, 1979; Revised edition, London: Routledge, 2008), pp. 190–95.

3   For example, see the editorial by Philip Steadman in *Transactions of the Martin Centre for Architectural and Urban Studies*, vol. 4 (1979), pp. 1–2.

4   Herbert Simon, *The Sciences of the Artificial* (Cambridge, Mass: MIT Press, 1969/81).

5   Ibid. Simon gives examples of functional descriptions of machines, and refers to an 'empirical science of computers' (2nd edition, p. 24). It should be said however that when he comes to discussing 'The Science of Design', (2nd edition, Chapter 5, pp. 129–59), he sets out a series of proposals that are very close to contemporary 'design science' in the sense outlined in my first paragraph. Indeed, Simon had a major influence on the foundations of that field of work.

6   Ibid. (2nd edition), p. 130. Simon was talking here about design knowledge in traditional engineering schools.

7   Ranko Bon, 'Allometry in Micro-Environmental Morphology', Special Papers Series, Paper E, *Harvard Papers in Theoretical Geography*, Laboratory for Computer Graphics and Spatial Analysis, Graduate School of Design, Harvard University, Cambridge, Mass (1972); Ranko Bon, 'Allometry in the Topologic Structure of Architectural Spatial Systems', *Ekistics*, vol. 36 no. 215 (October 1973), pp. 270–76. See also: Philip Steadman, 'Allometry and Built Form: Revisiting Ranko Bon's Work with the Harvard Philomorphs', *Construction Management and Economics*, vol. 24 (July 2006), pp. 755–65.

8   These graphs shown here are mine: Bon plotted his data on logarithmic scales.

9   Frank E. Brown & Phillip Steadman, 'The Morphology of British Housing: An Empirical Basis for Policy and Research. Part 1: Functional And Dimensional Characteristics', *Environment and Planning B: Planning and Design*, vol. 18 (1991), pp. 277–99.

10   Volume divided by external wall area is exactly equal to half of plan depth in an elongated block when only the long walls are counted, and the end walls are ignored. The inclusion of the end walls gives a somewhat different value.

11   Bon, 'Allometry in the Topologic Structure', Figure 1, p. 271.

12   For an accessible and general account of allometry in biology, see Stephen Jay Gould, 'Allometry and Size in Ontogeny and Phylogeny', *Biological Reviews*, vol. 41 (1966), pp. 587–640 – as reprinted in *Ekistics*, vol. 36 no. 215 (October 1973), pp. 253–62.

13   Leslie Martin & Lionel March (eds), *Urban Space and Structures* (Cambridge: Cambridge University Press, 1972). The diagrams as reused here are contained in Chapter 1 (Leslie Martin, 'The Grid as Generator', pp. 6–27); Chapter 2 (Leslie Martin, Lionel March et al.;

'Speculations', including 'Speculation 4', pp. 35-8), and Chapter 3 (Lionel March, 'Elementary Models of Built Forms', including 'Example four', pp. 89-96).

14   Ibid., Figure 2.3, p. 36.

15   Ibid., Figure 2.4, p. 37. March and Martin use the term 'built potential' in place of 'floor space index'.

16   Ibid., p. 95.

17   Carlo Ratti, 'Urban Analysis for Environmental Prediction', Unpublished PhD thesis, Cambridge University, Cambridge, UK (2001).

18   Howard Robertson, 'A City of Towers (Proposals Made by the Well-known American Architect, Raymond Hood, for the Solution of New York's Problem of Overcrowding)', *Architect and Building News*, 21 October 1927, pp. 639-43. Robertson's article quotes at length from Hood himself, but without any reference to the original source of the quotes.

19   Ibid., p. 639.

20   It should be said that the building of Figure 3.7 is not precisely a 'court' in Martin and March's sense. It encloses a courtyard but is freestanding, not part of a continuous array. It is one might say, a 'court' on the inside and a 'pavilion' on the outside. March himself studied built forms of this type. See: Martin & March, *Urban Space and Structures*, 'Example four', pp. 90-91.

21   For Hood's towers the cut-off angles are 80° between the buildings themselves, and 76° and 80° between the buildings and adjacent blocks. For repeated courts, the corresponding angles are 64° inside the courtyards, and 58° and 70° with adjacent blocks.

22   Meta Berghauser Pont & Per Haupt, *Spacemate: FSI·GSI·OSR als instrument voor verdichting en verdunning* (Amsterdam: PERMETA Architecten, 2002); the English edition was published as *Spacemate: The Spatial Logic of Urban Density* (Delft: Delft University Press, 2004). See also Meta Berghauser Pont & Per Haupt, 'The Spacemate: Density and the typomorphology of the urban fabric', *Nordisk Arkitekturforskning*, vol. 4 (2005), pp. 55-68; Meta Berghauser Pont & Per Haupt, 'The Relation Between Urban Form and Density', *Journal of Urban Morphology*, vol. 11 no. 1 (2007), pp. 62-4, and viewable online at Urban Morphology Journal Online website, http://www.urbanform.org/online_public/2007_1.shtml (accessed 21 March 2013).

23   There is a fourth variable plotted in 'Spacemate', called the Open Space Ratio (OSR), which is ignored here, since it is in effect just another way of expressing the same data. It takes the ground area, subtracts the area of the building footprint(s), and divides by total floor area.

24   Berghauser Pont & Haupt, 'Density and the Typomorphology of the Urban Fabric', Figure 3, p. 59.

25   David M. Raup, 'Computer as Aid in Describing Form in Gastropod Shells', *Science*, vol. 138 (1962), pp. 150-52; David M. Raup, 'Geometric Analysis of Shell Coiling: General Problems', *Journal of Paleontology*, vol. 40 (1966), pp. 1178-90. For a recent general discussion of morphospaces in biology, see George R. McGhee, *The Geometry of Evolution: Adaptive Landscapes and Theoretical Morphospaces* (Cambridge: Cambridge University Press, 2007).

26   Simon, *The Sciences of the Artificial* (2nd edition), p. 8.

27   Philip Steadman & Linda Mitchell, 'Architectural Morphospace: Mapping Worlds of Built Forms', *Environment and Planning B: Planning and Design*, vol. 37 (2010), pp.197-220.

28   Steadman, *The Evolution of Designs*.

WHAT IF DESIGN PRACTICE MATTERS?

Richard Blythe and Leon van Schaik

This chapter begins with overview by Leon van Schaik of the 25-year development of the PhD research programme at RMIT University in Melbourne, which focuses on research undertaken in practice. It therefore starts out with a set of questions concerning the veracity of the techniques of research undertaken by designing that inspired the genesis of the programme and have continued to fuel its growth. Following this, Richard Blythe will then propose a dynamic reflection model for creative practice research based on observations of work undertaken at RMIT and in other related practice-based research. Together, the authors provide a model for design research undertaken in the design studio and for the role of the academy in facilitating and collectivising that research. Blythe used the principles outlined in this chapter in drafting the successful documentation for the EU Marie Curie ITN grant entitled *Architecture, Design and Art Practice Training Research* (ADAPT-r), which is being coordinated through the Sint-Lucas School of Architecture in Ghent.[1]

LEON VAN SCHAIK (PART 1)

- What if design practice matters and is researched?
- What would we do?
- How would we do this?
- What would we discover?

These are the questions that confronted me as I initiated the RMIT programme in design practice research some 25 years ago. They are also the questions that confront the team of researchers who now work with me.[2]

They are fairly unexceptional questions, but are pressing nonetheless, and the answers are simple enough. Though simple, they are often confronting to researchers in the adjacent fields of theory and history, though unexceptional to researchers embedded in the practice of other disciplines.

The answers matter to practitioners and to the future development of practice in built environment and creative industry professions: design professions on whose shoulders rest our successful adaptations to a changing world. Can there be a more important focus for research than this? Even as I pose this question, I want to make it very clear that this research needs to be hedged with enquiries that are historical, sociological and scientific. We need the constant probing of actuality that these disciplines provide even as we establish new knowledge about design practice. Why? Here is an example. In his biographies, Giorgio Vasari colours the work of the painter Andrea del Castagno with the suggestion that this work was the product of an angry and jealous disposition. This sets up anger and jealousy as drivers of creativity. Vasari says that the painter stabbed Domenico Veneziano to death because he could not bear being overshadowed by a rival. Recent historical research shows that Andrea only once lost his temper – and that was when a careless youth bumped into the rickety scaffold he was working on. It also shows that Domenico outlived him. And that a vague namesake might perhaps have been linked to a stabbing. We now look at the works of Andrea through a different lens, and confront yet another equable and mainly amiable creator of works.

This is very important because knowledge in our field is expressly narrative, captured in anecdotes, and these stories impact on theories of creativity.[3]

Our anecdotes must be accurate. Historians and sociologists (and environmental scientists) can help us ensure that they are. So we welcome our research into individual design practice being illuminated by research into practice: if only there was more such work going on.[4]

But let me go back to my questions posed at the outset: if design practice matters, and we decide to research it, *what do we do?*

My first response was: bring to the surface evidence about what designers actually do. So it was that as soon as I was appointed Head of Architecture at RMIT in 1986–7, I invited architects with a body of work admired by their peers to enter into the business of 'surfacing the evidence about their already established mastery' within a critical framework that I would curate: a framework consisting of their peers and of invited outsiders from other cities, and open to observers. I recruited an initial research cell of eight practitioners that began completing its research in 1990. The programme has now grown to half a dozen such cells convened concurrently on three continents. They meet twice yearly in practice research symposia (PRS) which are held in both Melbourne and Ghent, and soon to be held in Hanoi.[5] Practitioners engaged in this research make an average of six presentations in these forums before completing their research.

Using the ideogram in Figure 4.1, I am going to do a quick canter through the evolution of the model that we use for this practice-based research at RMIT. This overview demonstrates that as we work with practitioners our understanding of what we are doing (and what they are doing) changes, and the model shifts. This approach to creative practice research began, conceptually at any rate,

when I began to work in Melbourne and saw this really quite remarkable work being produced by architects there – all of whom regarded their work as extremely peripheral, out of the mainstream, always to be ignored, never to be part of the conversation that was going on internationally. This bothered me. It also concerned me that these same architects were enthralled by visits from relatively distinguished architects from the rest of the world, but did not regard themselves as equal partners in the pursuit of architecture. I challenged them and said: 'Look, you are always asking these people here – do you ever get invited to talk about your work in their countries?' They looked a bit dumbfounded at that, because they had not been so invited, and I argued that the problem was that they had not equipped themselves with the ability to talk about what they actually do as architects in such a way that they had the confidence to excite an international audience. I invited them to overturn this Australian 'cultural cringe' and establish a knowledge base in design practice, by saying: 'Let's begin a research into your already proven mastery because the work's there; it's had a degree of acceptance and you've had awards, you've done exhibitions, you've published in a small way: let's look at what you do in the medium in which you already work.' So the first principle that I wanted was to get them to look at what they were actually doing.

There is a terrible tendency for people, as soon as they start talking about their work, to refer to one or another theorist (usually not an architect) and validate what they were doing by saying, 'Well, it's like this' and 'It's like that'. They are not really trying to extract an understanding from what was actually happening when they were doing their work,

4.1   Ideogram of the evolution of the research
       model from early intent to current practice

and therefore not ever understanding or claiming what they were doing and always being in the position of supplicant, regarding themselves as dwarves in the world of intellectual change, always looking up at these giant heroes sitting usually in New York, London or Tokyo, sometimes Paris. So I issued that challenge to them, and perhaps naïvely I knew from the models that existed elsewhere, but not in architecture, that what I had to do was to get them into a framework where they would begin to look at their work *but not stop practising*. And so I had to do something that would bring them together, looking at their work, at the way they work: researching their practices through the medium of design itself (see Figure 4.2, where the work is 'placed' on a stage for examination within a rich context).[6]

I ran with the idea of getting them to present their work to each other and to panels of critics, and so we started meeting twice a year. They would present their work and they would say, 'This is what I think I'm doing', and their peers would say, 'That's not what we think you're doing – we think you are doing this, that or the other'. Slowly this research refined our understanding of design practice. Eventually we had enough accumulated knowledge for me to realise that what we were uncovering was very similar to research being done by other people into creative innovators. Howard Gardner's work on the natural history of innovators (Figure 4.2: see the left face of the cylinder segment in the rear centre of the ideogram) came into my mind because I could see that, in the way my people were working, they were thinking of themselves as if they were the only people who had ever been through the agonies of creating things.[7] I then invited them

to understand their position as creators and to explicate the contextual aspects of that practice. My approach was informed by research into creative innovators in all sorts of different fields. A common impact on these researcher-practitioners was that a great weight dropped from their shoulders. The perception at the beginning amongst some of the architects I was working with (and they were all architects at the beginning) was that creative energy came from getting drunk or being angry and fighting. Most of their little groups who got together to support architecture involved quite a lot of drinking, throwing bottles and fighting, and there was an adversarial culture that asserted: 'I'm trying to do something and all the rest of you are rubbish!' They also felt lonely and peripheral, at the 'arse end of the world'. Gardner's natural history is a story of coming from the margins to the centre and seeking recognition, but also of finding ways to return to the margins to look back at things from the edge. This focus on a common natural history enabled an early emergence into a space of understanding what happens in design practice that aligns with all creative practice.

It was also a puzzle to me that the work that was being produced in Melbourne was invisible in other parts of the world where people would look at it and say, 'Oh, well, that's just West Coast abstractionism, something that's already happened in California, or something that we did years ago' – when in fact I could see that it was in many ways unique to the place in which it had been created. So I began to apply an interest that I have always had in people's spatial intelligence (Figure 4.2: indicated in the bottom left of the ideogram).[8] I am interested in the way that it is developed through their histories in space and how place inflects spatial intelligence just as place inflects language, and how that inflection (usually unconscious) is inevitably part of what happens when people address an idea, even if it is an idea that is being pursued all over the world. Even simply to build in a particular place there are inflections from the local construction culture! I started to get people to look at the development of their spatial intelligence, and this became part of the model, determining how we understand what we are doing as a tension between, if you like, people's formal canon or canons (as defined by different people at different times but of an international nature) and the tacit internalised knowledge that all of us have through the whole business of the unfolding of our spatial intelligence capability in a particular place. So that started to be something that people looked at.

Then, working with the researching practitioners, we developed the early incarnation of the research model: the 'scholarship cone' (Figure 4.1: the cone is located in the middle left). It was the first step in a process that has since undergone significant development. That early version of the model still illuminates the ways in which the research proceeds. The cone model shows that the research you are doing sits on a base of all your existing practice: that you try to understand that practice, and that you think about the practice you are aspiring towards; that you identify the gap between where you are and where you want to be (and who else has tried to fill this gap); that in a tier further up the cone you do some work in which you are trying to fill that gap – in other words, that in a tier above you evaluate that new work and identify how this has changed the nature of the gap. So you look back at what you have

done, look at what you are currently doing and look to what you aspire to do, and you slowly build your way up what we called the 'scholarship cone' until you reach a point at which you can show, through the shifts that have taken place, how being conscious – more conscious – of the way in which you work and of what you really do helps you to do it in a more controlled and a better understood manner. This resulted in what you can see in this conical version of the model: a point at the top of the cone where there is then a sense of having completed this tranche of research. We began to call this 'the PhD moment', this moment where you could look back and say: 'Oh, look: I can tell this story, here it is, here are the shifts, this is what I can communicate.'

Part of what people have to understand was how they differentiate their practice from other practices, and to assist in this research we ask people to do some mapping: 'Who are your mentors, who are your challengers, who are your peers? Where do you seek recognition? Who supports you, and can you map out your community of practice?' This gave some quite good insights into how people differentiate themselves from others. Even though they may share the values of another practice, they may then have slightly different sets of mentors or challengers and this alters the 'mental space' in which they work. I will come back to that in a moment, but the business of 'enchainment' with mentors, peers and challengers led me to find the work of Randall Collins in establishing a sociology of intellectual change.[9] Again there were resonances between his research into the evolution of western and eastern knowledge from a sociological perspective, and what we were observing in communities of architectural practice. The fundamental principle that Collins distils from his research is that intellectual change is most fruitfully supported when there are three strong positions in a field being argued for (Figure 4.3: enchainment in small numbers, or tri-polarity). We were confronting problems of adversarial thinking. People would say: 'How can you work with me when you are working with them? Our work is so different to theirs!' The response was to get people to identify the sets of arguments that they adhere to and also to identify the arguments that they see in other corners of their field. In Melbourne, tri-polarity emerged as soon as people started to articulate their positions, and the phenomenon that Collins noted became absolutely evident in the community of practice that I have been working with, and this was that the adversarial bottle-throwing, beer-swilling culture was no longer the way in which people needed to operate. They could actually observe other positions without feeling threatened and could learn from them; and flowing from the consequential emergence of three poles you have a new flowering of architecture in Melbourne.

The development of our current model, a PhD by project, has been informed by looking at how universities structure their PhDs 'by publication', which gave us clues as to how to deal with practitioners who commence a PhD having already completed substantial (in research terms) works – as all of our invited practitioners at RMIT by definition have. Comparing our process with the 'by publication' processes is a way of clarifying what is happening in this research. We argue that the people who are doing the research have already made major contributions to the field through their number of projects and those projects themselves are the 'publications'.

This has refreshed the way we ask practitioners to indicate the back-stories of their works, of how they came to produce that work. We now ask them to reflect upon the views and critiques that have been made about their work. We ask them to think about what is happening to the work that they are currently doing in the office as they go through this process of reflection, and we ask them late in the process to have themselves interviewed by a valued peer who checks through with them on the validity of their descriptions of what they are doing. Finally they produce an overarching description of their research journey. This means that we can keep the emphasis on the work and their reflections on the work, rather than on extensive verbal justifications in the terms of other disciplines (an unfortunate phenomenon that Richard Blythe has addressed elsewhere).[10] At the end of the process, practitioners are very clear about their mental space, their enchainments, their polar alliances and the ways in which they differentiate their practice from other creative practices – and so are we.

The model is shown also on the poster that we use to describe our programme, and as you can see there is a cube that has served up the natural history of the creative individual on one face, on another face (here on the right of the ideogram) there is Randall Collins' work on the public behaviours that support intellectual change. Across the top of the cube is this other very important concept. Universities are bedevilled by the administrative division between research and practice and for many years we have been using the research done by Ernest Boyer into what actually happens in universities.[11] We use it to challenge that notion that there is this division because his research discovered that in universities

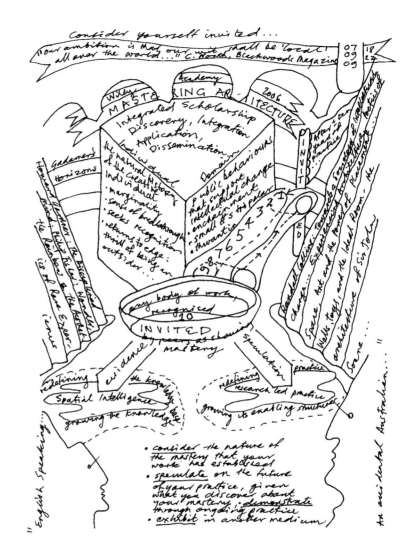

4.2   Poster created in 2009 describing the RMIT PhD: the faces of the cube at the centre of the ideogram delineate the core ideas that underpin the research approach: the shared natural history of creative individuals on the left face, the enchainments and tri-polarities (or 'public behaviours') on the right face, and on the top face the integrated scholarship model

there are four forms of scholarship – one of discovery, one of integration, one of application, one of dissemination – and everybody in the community of learning is engaged in those at different times and in different ways. This concept is crucial because it helps people who are in practice to avoid thinking, as they can sometimes do, that if they are doing research they have to stop practicing, put on the white coat, go into a laboratory and do something entirely different!

This integrated approach to our research has helped us, through working with practitioners, to develop more and more tools that help us to understand how practices differentiate themselves from other people's endeavours, and how they position their creative practice. Figure 4.3 is hence an ideogram about differentiations. The first of these tri-polar 'fans' is the political one: realist/idealist/populist. The others will soon be published.[13] It captures my current understanding of how people, through a series of different shifts, pick their positions in a range of tri-polar 'constellations' (to use Marcelo Stamm's term).[14] In that way they differentiate themselves, generating work which itself builds up and then alters their spatial intelligence.

The question therefore arises, how would we do this? In this work a lot of the input has come from Richard Blythe, whose own research into his practice TERROIR makes him a coalface researcher into design practice, and as such he has provided a new account of how the research is conducted. In essence, what Richard did was to use our theatre-of-practice metaphor to arrive at his own new animated ideogram. On the theatre stage, he placed the runway or conveyer belt on which the works of a practice are

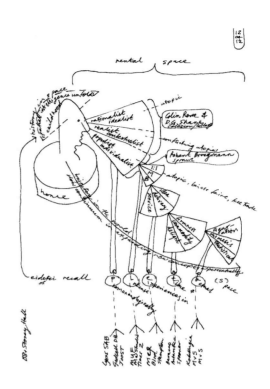

examined. He also inserted a theatre-drop shaped in the profiles of the researching practitioner(s) facing inwards. This he described as 'R-o': reflection on the existing body of work of the practice in question. Behind this he then inserted another flat with the profiles of the practitioners facing inwards: this he called 'R-i': reflection into work of the practice that is going on concurrently with the 'R-o' reflection. This in turn is nested with a further set of drops in the theatre, this set being named 'R-f': reflection triggered by future projects in the practice. Each of these drops looks outwards: on one side, towards a mapping of mentors; on the other, towards a mapping of challengers. In a panorama around the back of the theatre are the peers of the practice.

4.3 The Differentiation Process in five tri-polar shifts[12]

60

Where this new ideogram gathers further force is in the relationship between the projects on the runway. 'R-o' tends to arrange these in a series of linear teleologies relating to current understandings of the nature of the practice. 'R-i' sets the projects in a more dynamic relationship with one another, revealing tensions and opportunities, while 'R-f' completely re-jigs the relationships in the pursuit of new, emerging creative leaps. I will hand over to Richard to explain the ideas in more detail.

RICHARD BLYTHE

In the text above, Leon van Schaik has provided us with a global picture of where the RMIT programme has come from and how it relates to our current approach. I will now explore one of the critical aspects of this sort of research: how reflection works in design research. Leon identified a problem that occurs in some examples of creative practice research when researchers search for authority not in the work itself but rather in the work of researchers from other discipline areas, for example in history, theory and philosophy.[15] In this text I will explore further characteristics and processes of instantiated reflection, in which the authority of the research is established through the observation and explication of designing.

The RMIT practice-based approach to research is a reflective practice model, and it is critical that we are precise about how reflection works in such research because some reflection models, particularly those that seem to misunderstand instantiated aspects of Donald Schön's observations, are problematic in that they oversimplify reflection by dissociating the reflection from its subject.[16] I am pointing here to the kinds of reflection that call on

the production of a reflective journal created after the fact and dissociated from the activity being reflected upon. The point of my argument is not necessarily to devalue that kind reflection, but rather to point to what else is going on in reflective terms in designing.[17] Based on our observations, many practitioners reflect in an instantiated way without necessarily dissociating reflection and designing. So my question is one concerning the nature of reflection that is instantiated within designing in creative practice research.

We should begin by clarifying the different types of reflection at play in designing. Reflecting on an existing body of work is a well-established way of clarifying directions and opportunities. In the RMIT model, practitioners are encouraged to 'tell the back story' of key works in order to begin to explicate key aspects of that practice. This kind of retrospective reflection also occurs at the moment of carrying out a new design. For example, my own practice TERROIR has documented ways in which its practitioners 'recall' aspects of earlier projects.[18] This is at times quite literal: for example, by taking pieces of earlier study models and placing them in the context of an existing design action.[19] As I have noted previously, this has an effect not only of informing the current project, but also of transforming how earlier works are understood – a point that I will elaborate later in this chapter.[20] The Australian architectural practice, Ashton Raggatt McDougall, has also used this technique, for example using the unsuccessful competition entry for Federation Square, Melbourne, to inform their design for the Museum of Australia in Canberra. This sort of reflection we could call reflection 'on' completed work: 'R-o' (Figure 4.4).

 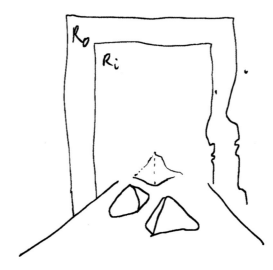

4.4   Reflection 'on': Step 1 of the Reflection Model ideogram explaining core reflection concepts discovered in this kind of research (this ideogram is the first of a sequence of drawings)

4.5   Reflection 'in': Step 2 of the Reflection Model ideogram

While retrospective reflection is important in and of itself, it is, when considered in a contextually and temporally disengaged way, inadequate in terms of describing designing in a holistic way. Leon van Schaik has previously described the inadequacy of this kind of approach by explaining that for the sort of research we do the reflection happens not so much 'on' the work but rather the reflection takes place 'in' the activity of making the next project; that is to say, reflection happens while engaged in the activity of designing (or art making), and this becomes the 'scene' of the reflection: temporally and contextually synthesised.

Here a window to another kind of reflection opens: reflection undertaken during the process of working on a design project, or, if you like, reflecting in the act of actually designing the thing itself in which designing and reflecting are simultaneous. In this kind of reflection the emerging design reflects back to the designer even from its emergent state to inform the next move. We can call this reflection 'R-i', or reflection in designing – identified by Marcelo Stamm as a kind of instantiated reflection (Figure 4.5).

In addition to 'R-o' and 'R-i' reflection, there is also a third reflection that returns to the designer from what we might call emergent future moves. What I mean here is that, while the designer makes moves relevant to the project at hand, other as yet non-specific moves also appear. These moves are potential future designs waiting, if you like, for their appropriate project, and even in their nascent state they are nonetheless capable of reflecting back into the project at hand. Let us call this 'R-f': reflection for (Figure 4.6). 'R-f' has been described a number of times during the PRS presentations. For example, the painter Lucas Devriendt explains in his proposal for his completion catalogue (this being part of the

required PhD documentation) that he would like to show on the page his paintings arranged not as being flat, but shown as if in perspective and facing each other to illustrate how he has seen a second painting emerge while working on the first.

So we could then take all three reflective frames ('R-o', 'R-i', 'R-f') and instead of presenting them in separated terms, in particularised ways, we can represent what we see actually going on reflectively in the act of designing: a kind of synthesised, synthetic space in which these three moves of reflection are happening in a simultaneous way in something that we might begin to think about as a synthesised reflection model.

The work undertaken by creative practitioners (researchers) in the PRS programme reveals that when people are in the process of designing the work itself they are also reflecting in another way. They remember earlier instances while working on a current project. This remembering involves a re-membering or re-constructing of a version of an earlier instance – a process that is substantially different from simply recalling, in the sense that what emerges are all sorts of possibilities for creating a new construction of that earlier instance, perhaps not unlike the Nietzschean notion of *Historia Abscondita*: 'Every great human being exerts a retroactive force: for his sake all of history is placed in the balance again, and a thousand secrets of the past crawl out of their hiding places – into *his* sunshine. There is no way of telling what may yet become a part of history. Perhaps the past is still essentially undiscovered! So many retroactive forces are still needed!'[21]

Of course these re-membered projects usually exist as a cluster or family of previous projects rather than as individual, isolated instances: a group of past projects that sit on what we might describe as a runway of projects, a runway in the sense that these projects come and land in this space of the practice.

So far my discussion of reflection has been as if from inside the eyes of the designer – a kind of lonely, almost psychological, pursuit. It is useful then to also take a different, more social view of reflection and to introduce a notion of social reflection that has parallels, for example, in the work of Lev Vygotsky. He identified that learning occurs in non-hierarchical and multiple iterations and exchanges that take place between body, world and language, and by social means.[22] Leon van Schaik has explained that reflection does not happen simply as an inward reflection, but within a wider contextual picture, and he referred to our challengers and our mentors. So this process of reflection takes place within what might be described as a social theatre,

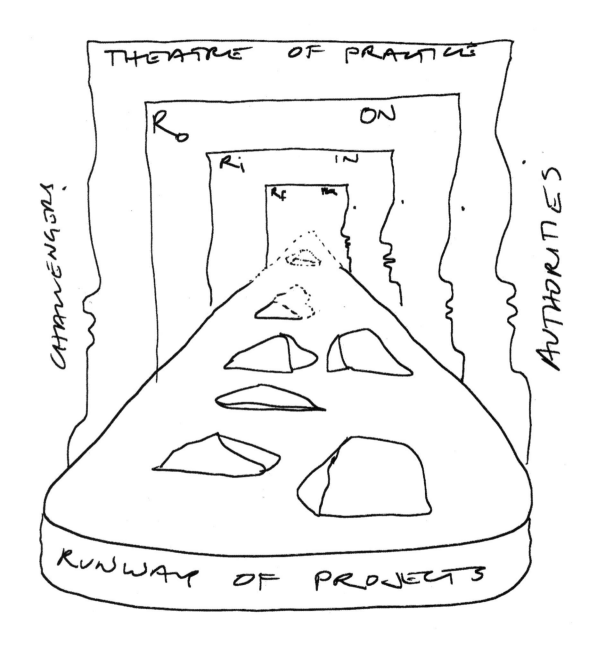

THEATRE OF PRACTICE

Ro
ON
Ri
IN
Rf

CHALLENGERS

AUTHORITIES

RUNWAY OF PROJECTS

4.7   Theatre of Practice: Step 4 of the
      Reflection Model ideogram

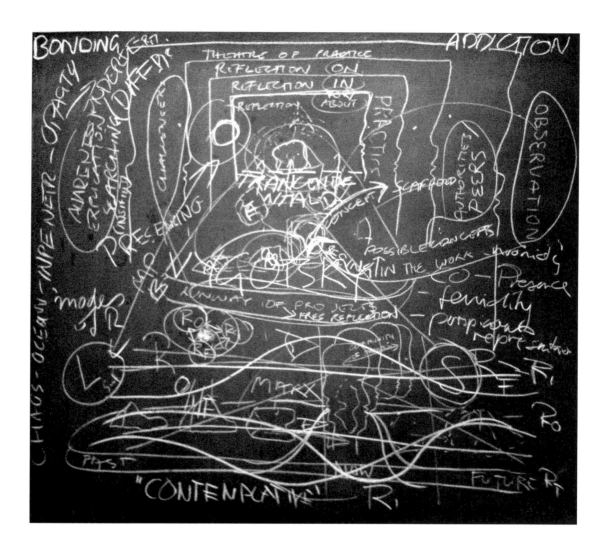

4.8 Drawing made by Richard Blythe and Marcelo Stamm at the Aarhus School of Architecture, November 2011, building upon the key concepts of the reflection model

to again use Leon's model: a theatre of practice that includes those with whom we share a position as well as our challengers: those who to some extent resist, call to account and probe what we do by holding alternative positions (Figure 4.7).

Now I would like to introduce a concept of dynamic reflection, as developed in conversation

with Marcelo Stamm – a conversation captured in the chalkboard drawing shown in Figure 4.8, and included here to illustrate our own process of thinking by drawing, each over the top of the other. Figure 4.8 includes hints of the ideograms that I have presented so far, including 'R-o', 'R-i' and 'R-f', along with other words and marks that point to ideas to be explored in a later paper.

Instead, what I want to propose here is that the reflection is not just between projects, but we can also say that the projects themselves begin to 'talk back' or to reflect back to us from the work, criticisms and confirmations of our challengers, peers and mentors. To illustrate how this happens, I can describe how when a challenger issues a challenge to practice, that challenge sits for some time in the background of the ongoing activity of practice. It forms, if you will, a kind of subconscious *alter ego* for the work-in-progress, the voice on the shoulder, and is to that extent then present when we are also working on the next project. The challenge sensitises us to the issue, as it were, and as a result we might notice something, something jumps out at us, or in a more gentle way emerges, becomes apparent – this 'something' speaks to the challenge from the design act.

Reflection is then also social in what might be understood in Vygotskian terms. The reflection model as described so far can be further placed in a larger theatre of practice. The final move in this ideogram describes how it is also necessary to talk outwards, to explicate what is happening inside this model to an external audience. In research terms, the research of the designer needs to sit in some ways outside of this entire frame to be able to make the observations and to do the searching that is critical in this notion of research. In our blackboard conversation this is the point at which Marcelo Stamm observed:

> Ah, what's going on here with the projects, with the 'back-story', is that while working on a current project there's a reflection in which an earlier instance is reflected, re-membered, in the current project. This is one way of identifying where the reflection is: it is in the surfaces of the family tree of projects.

The past project appears in a slightly altered manner and in fact all the projects are slightly altered through reflection. So what we see is that in the very act of creating a new project practitioners see in past projects the opportunities and possibilities for new projects which are emerging, as it were, from the ghosts of projects past, and that this new gap, new window, or new view was not possible without the act of creating a new project.

In a quite palpable Nietzschean sense, a new history of the family of projects is invented. This transformative reflection is then also about the emergence of a new proposition that exceeds the boundaries of the condition from where it came. I referred to this idea in my own PhD thesis as searching for the 'cracks in the surface of things', through which creative practitioners strive for a glimpse of new possibilities.[23] The reflection is then a dynamic one whereby the past condition itself is not fixed, but remains dynamic, and is altered by the continuing development of each new project: a dynamic reflection model. The research is then grounded in and qualified by (that is gains its quality from) differences and shifts, and by the extent to which new propositions are enabled by this process to exceed the boundaries of their original context. The extent to which the design researcher has been able to 'crack open the surface' of an existing condition and to extend out through that surface a scenario or proposition that exceeds – even if in some incremental way – precedent, is the measure of the success of the research.

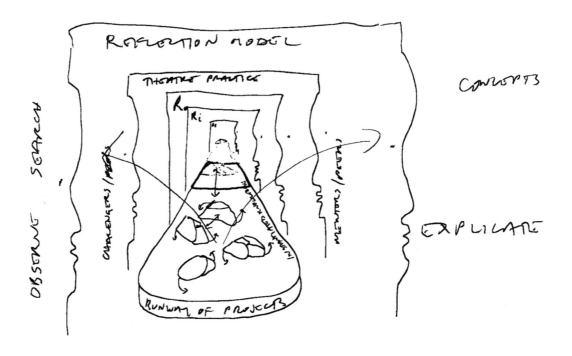

4.9 The dynamic transcendental moment:
Step 5 of the Reflection Model ideogram

LEON VAN SCHAIK (CONCLUSION)

This emphasis of Richard Blythe on shifts and differences brings us back to the original scholarship cone, but with a renewed understanding. It also reveals that in our ideograms we fail to account for the position of the author who is actually constructing the theatre. Our most recent work with practitioners is revealing the ways in which designers adjust their mental space to put themselves in the position to be authors for different projects. These implied authorship positions are represented in this axonometric version of Richard Blythe and Marcelo Stamm's assembled ideogram (Figure 4.10).

The discussion in this chapter has described what we at RMIT have done over the past decades in addressing the belief that design practice contains bodies of knowledge that can be revealed through the medium of design itself. It describes how we have worked – and are working – with practitioner researchers to uncover some of this knowledge. It describes some of what we have discovered and illustrates dynamic aspects of reflection as it has been observed in our research. For those who might want fuller accounts, these are given in past publications, notably the books on *Mastering Architecture* and *By Practice, By Invitation*.[24] Further publications are imminent.

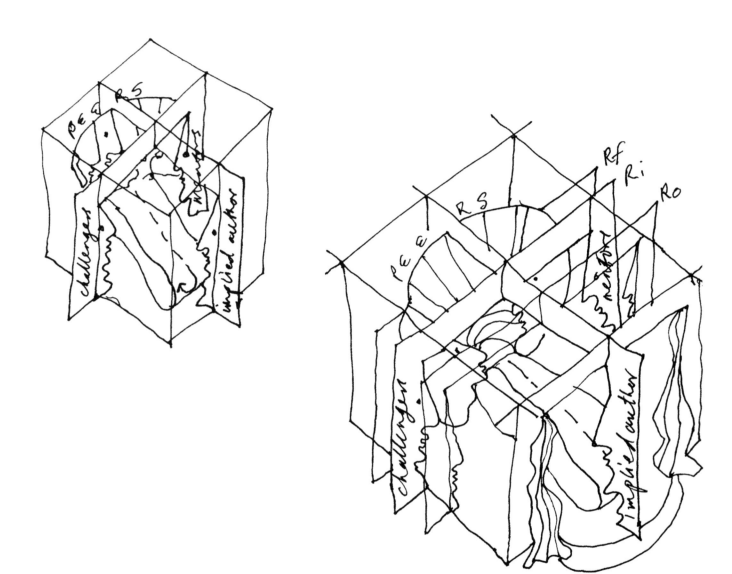

4.10   Here the different kinds of reflection –
'R-i', 'R-o', 'R-f' – are seen as drops on the stage.
Mentors and challengers face onto the stage
from the wings and peers form a panorama at
the rear. Facing into the stage is the profile of
an 'implied author': the characterisation of the
position adopted in order to make a work

Notes

1   Richard Blythe was the primary author of the submission documents for the EU Marie Curie ITN grant, *Architecture, Design and Art Practice Training Research* (ADAPT-r), with input from Johan Verbeke of the Sint-Lucas School of Architecture, who led the submission process, and Claus Peder Pedersen of the Aarhus School of Architecture; Marcelo Stamm provided excellent editorial input.

2   Richard Blythe, 'A Terroir of TERROIR (or, a Brief History of Design-Places)', Unpublished PhD Thesis, Royal Melbourne Institute of Technology, Melbourne, Australia (2008); Graham Crist, 'Sheds for Antarctica: The Environment for Architectural Design and Practice', Unpublished PhD Thesis, RMIT University (2010); Sand Helsel, 'A Search for Common Pleasures: Curating the City', Unpublished PhD Thesis, RMIT University (2009); Martyn Hook, 'The Act of Reflective Practice: The Emergence of Iredale Pedersen Hook Architects', Unpublished PhD Thesis, RMIT University (2008); Paul Minifie, 'Design Domains: Their Relations and Transformations as Revealed Through the Practice of Paul Minifie', Unpublished PhD Thesis, RMIT University (2010); Vivian Mitsogianni, 'White Noise PANORAMA: Process-Based Architectural Design', Unpublished PhD Thesis, RMIT University (2009); Marcelo Stamm, 'Constellating Creativity', GRC Keynote Address, RMIT University (2011); SueAnne Ware, 'Anti-Memorials: Rethinking the Landscape of Memory', Unpublished PhD Thesis, RMIT University (2005); Gretchen Wilkins, 'Manufacturing Urbanism: An Architectural Practice for Unfinished Cities', Unpublished PhD Thesis, RMIT University (2013).

3   Charles Nicholl, 'Death in Florence: Charles Nicholl writes about a 15th-century mystery', *London Review of Books*, vol. 34 no. 4 (2012), pp. 9–10.

4   I lament the lack of successors to Judith R. Blau, *Architects and Firms: A Sociological Perspective on Architectural Practice* (Cambridge, Mass: MIT Press, 1987); Robert Gutman, *Architectural Practice: A Critical Review* (Princeton: Princeton Architectural Press, 1988); Reyner Banham, *The Architecture of the Well-Tempered Environment* (London: Architectural Press, 1969).

5   These were known formerly as GRCs, as in Graduate Research Conferences.

6   This ideogram depicts a shoebox theatre with the work of the practice at the centre (flat cylindrical volume) flanked by side curtains with overarching proscenium and cylinder segment behind. Each element describes key concepts and texts arranged spatially within the shoebox theatre.

7   Howard Gardner, *The Disciplined Mind: What All Students Should Understand* (New York: Prentice Hall, 2000).

8   Leon van Schaik, *Spatial Intelligence: New Futures for Architecture* (Chichester: John Wiley, 2008).

9   Randall Collins, *The Sociology of Philosophies: A Global Theory of Intellectual Change* (Cambridge, Mass: Harvard University Press, 2000), pp. 42, 380, 879.

10   Richard Blythe, 'Topological Errors in Creative Practice Research: Understanding the Reflective Hinge and the Reflective Gap', in Dag Boutsen (ed.), *Good Practices. Best Practices: Highlighting the Compound Idea of Education, Creativity, Research and Practice* (Antwerp: Artesis, 2012).

11   E.L. Boyer, C.E. Glassick, M.T. Huber & G.I. Maeroff, *Scholarship Assessed: Evaluation of the Professoriate* (San Francisco: Jossey-Bass, 1997).

12   This ideogram has been informed by a reading of Otto Friedrich Bollnow, *Human Space* (London: Hyphen Press, 2011), and Bruno Latour, *On the Modern Cult of the Factish Gods* (Durham, NC: Duke University Press, 2009).

13   Leon van Schaik, 'Differentiation In Vital Practice', in Pia Ednie-Brown (ed.), *The Innovation Imperative: Architectures of Vitality – Architectural Design Profile no.221* (January 2013), pp. 106–13.

14   Stamm, 'Constellating Creativity'.

15   This problem is discussed in more detail in Richard Blythe, 'Topological Errors'.

16   Donald Schön, *The Reflective Practitioner: How Professionals Think in Action* (New York/London: Basic Books, 1983).

17   See for example Joyce Scaife, *Supervising the Reflective Practitioner: An Essential Guide* (London/New York: Routledge, 2010).

18   'Project' in this argument is used as a catch-all term to describe the many different forms that architecture can take, from systems of social engagement to urban thinking, and also includes single buildings. In this sense, 'project' should not be understood as a purely formalist notion.

19   Scott Balmforth & Gerard Reinmuth, 'TERROIR as a State of Mind', Unpublished Master of Architecture Thesis, RMIT University (2007).

20   Blythe, 'A Terroir of TERROIR'.

21   Friedrich Nietzsche, *The Gay Science: With a Prelude in Rhymes and an Appendix of Songs* (New York: Random House, 1992/1974).

22   Lev Vygotsky, *Mind in Society: The Development of Higher Psychological Processes* (Cambridge, Mass: Harvard University Press, 1978).

23   Blythe, 'A Terroir of TERROIR'.

24   Leon van Schaik, *Mastering Architecture: Becoming a Creative Innovator in Practice* (Chichester: John Wiley, 2005), Leon van Schaik & Anna Johnson (eds), *Architecture and Design, By Practice, By Invitation: Design Practice Research at RMIT* (Melbourne: RMIT Publishing, 2011).

Plate 1   Antinous at the end of the Long Walk
at Rousham, Oxfordshire (1737–41)

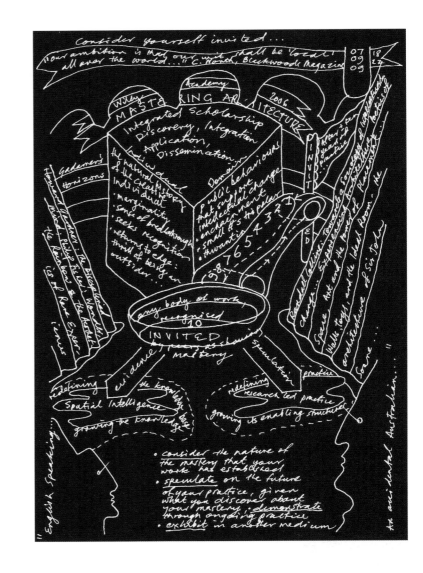

Plate 2 Poster created by Leon van Schaik
in 2009 describing RMIT University's
PhD programme

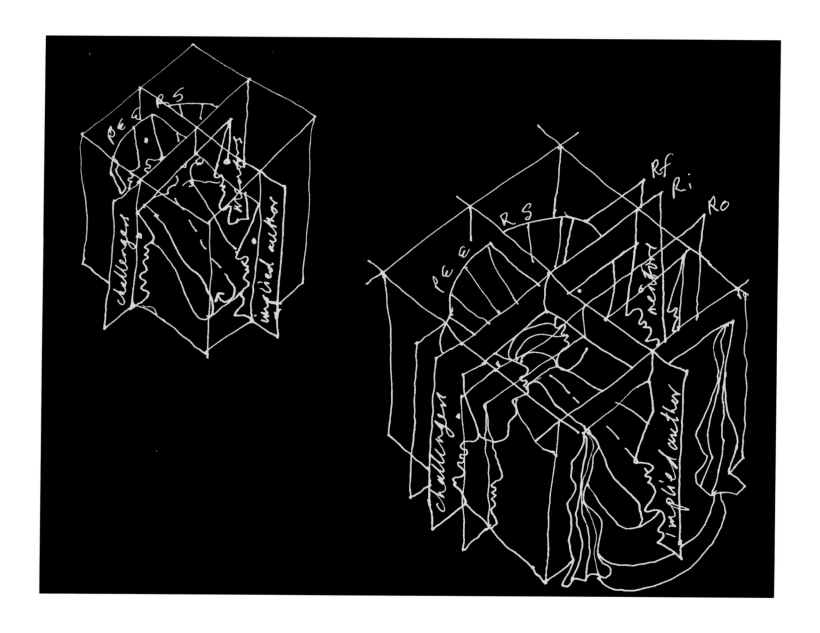

Plate 3   Here the different kinds of reflection – 'R-i', 'R-o', 'R-f' – are seen as drops on the stage. Mentors and challengers face onto the stage from the wings and peers form a panorama at the rear. Facing into the stage is the profile of an 'implied author': the characterisation of the position adopted in order to make a work

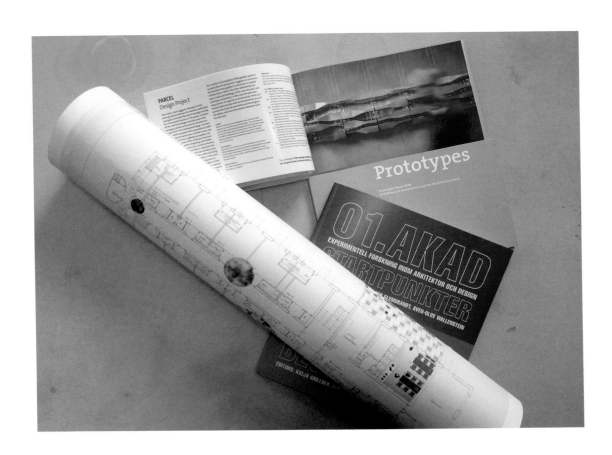

Plate 4   Samples of research by design outputs from the KTH School of Architecture, Stockholm

Plate 5 Cover of the February 2011 issue
of the Swedish journal *Arkitekten* featuring
FATALE and the development of feminist
architecture pedagogy at KTH Stockholm.
Source: Katja Grillner

Plate 6   Speculative design by Monash
Architecture Studio (MAS) for a dispersed
infill housing precinct in Melbourne

Plate 7   Melbourne-Manhattan,
a night view drawn by MAS looking
towards Melbourne's CBD

Plate 8   'Folly' structure by muf architecture/
art at Barking Town Centre, east London (2010)

DESIGN RESEARCH AND CRITICAL TRANSFORMATIONS: SITUATING THOUGHT, PROJECTING ACTION

Katja Grillner

Design is not just a building, an interior, or a preserved landscape; it is a means of acting in and transforming the world.

[Michael Speaks, 2011][1]

If the above statement – as uttered by Michael Speaks, the Dean of the University of Kentucky College of Design at the time, and well known for his advocacy in the early 2000s of a post-critical stance (and for a doing away with critical theory in architecture at large) – is to be embraced, it is interesting to ask what happens if the same argument is put forward for design research.[2] Can research too, be a means of acting in and transforming the world? Well, that seems to very much be the case. In fact in most circles it is exactly what is expected. In order to receive research funding, with few exceptions, whether public or private, strong arguments must be made about the acute relevance of the research project in the light of societal impact and its direct (or at least long-term) applicability. From a more theoretical standpoint, however, the direct link from research to action is neither self-evident, nor is it unproblematic. What, then, is at stake when boundaries are blurred between academy and industry, researcher and designer, or activist?

In the area between pure research, as it were the comfortable 'ivory tower' position, and research as 'product' (direct innovation, product development, buildings, or even urban planning and design inventions), we find a plethora of both critical and much less critical agents and positions. These range from political activists to pragmatic reformers, to curious inventors, to clever advocates for a radical commercialisation of the university world. They all believe, in some way or another, that knowledge development can and should be put to use, and that the direct link between research and actual transformation in the world is important (or, put in another way, profitable). For example, the Swedish goverment agency, Vinnova, which funds research and innovation projects to the tune of around £200 million (Sterling) per year, is now explicitly stating that its top priority is to support research and development projects that are likely to promote and expand Swedish industry, especially in terms of export capacity.[3] Advanced visionary research into systems for sustainable environmental planning and design is thus only seen as interesting if it is backed up by competitive and commercially successful Swedish industrial companies. This construction reflects directly on the agency's governmental mission and as such it has a simple and understandable logic. But at the same time it places the researcher in an ethically tricky situation. For whom does one work, who or what controls the decisions on where the greatest potentials lie for furthering sustainable societal development, and how does this steer the nature of both the resulting knowledge and the developed applications?

Opening this essay with a quotation from Michael Speaks is not an accidental choice. Invited in 2012 as one of four speakers from the Nordic countries to a faculty symposium at Kentucky University on 'Scandinavian Design Research', I found myself immersed in lively, generous, but also at times rather provocative debates about the conditions and possibilities for academic research today, and on the role of the university in the light of radically decreasing public funding and the demand for more creative academic/industrial partnerships.[4] On one hand, Speaks himself does appear, in his role as Dean, along with colleagues, to have generated a vital faculty-led research environment which has several examples of intensive and long-term design studio/community/industry research collaborations, with these catering to a sincere and critical engagement in current post-industrial challenges for local communities there.[5]

On the other hand, in our discussions about the current funding challenges faced by the university sector in the USA, Speaks voiced – not surprisingly given his public calls for architectural education to follow rather than resist capitalist 'logic' – some forthright opinions.[6] He frankly dismissed any critical concerns expressed in the room regarding the ethical risks involved in the commercialisation of academic research, or in the formation of specific partnerships with private investors. I could perhaps understand this position if the only thing that matters is the potential to transform the world, and if the researcher can use his/her own ethical compass (or departmental policy) to judge which kind of business one interferes with. In the River Cities Projects, for example, the Kentucky College of Design had clearly secured some very productive liasons.[7] But if, in addition to transforming the world, one also believes that these transformative processes produce new knowledge and alternative understandings, and that bringing these out is the responsibility of the academic researcher, then the critical conditions controlling these processes and the public acccessability of their outcomes really do matter, and need therefore to be discussed.

This chapter, or at least its framing, is partially provoked by those conversations with Michael Speaks, and by the realisation that further qualifications need to be articulated in order to differentiate the positions, aims and ambitions of different apporaches within the growing field of design research field in architecture, and the engagement with epistemological questions that these positions provoke. With the assistance of Christopher Frayling's now classic differentiation between research 'into', 'through' and 'for' design, I will begin by providing a structured starting point through which to qualify the debate.[8] Following this, and by introducing examples from and around my own practice as researcher and educator, I hope to suggest ways in which I believe it is possible to further a critically tranformative design research practice. The aim is to embrace the necessity of acting in and transforming the world, while saving in the academy always a spot for the 'ivory tower' – however temporary or fragile its construction may be, and however much the researcher and activist must run up and down the ladder to gain alternative viewpoints of the problems at hand.

RESEARCH, SCIENCE, SCHOLARSHIP

> Research is, after all, nothing if we do not in some way change ourselves as well as our buildings. The best architectural research … is therefore that which asks us to consider not only what we understand and undertake by way of architecture and buildings, but also who we think we are and how we want to reside, play and work together.
>
> [Iain Borden, 2008][9]

Frayling's distinctions between research 'into', 'through' and 'for' design is in turn an adaptation of Herbert Read's analysis of fine arts teaching. It begins with the idea of research 'for' art, which can be understood as the realm of the romantic artist genius, for whom nothing matters but the work in itself.

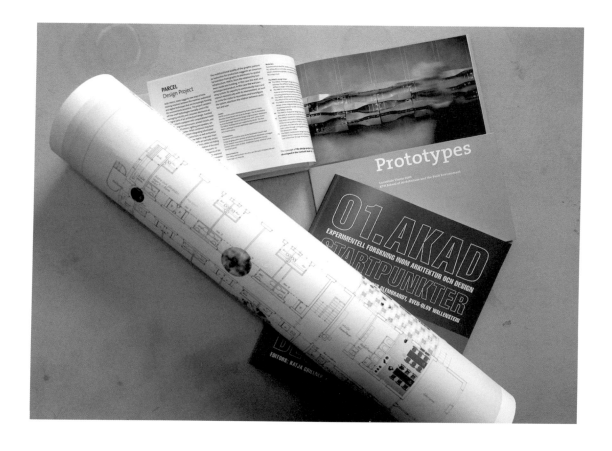

5.1 Samples of research by design outputs from the KTH School of Architecture. Clockwise from left to right: Chinese-Whisper by FATALE, subtle layers of alterations to the design by Swedish architect Ingeborg Waern-Bugge (1899–1991) for a single mothers' housing block; Prototypes for Architectural Design (2008), Licentiate thesis by Jonas Runberger, featuring a book design that formally articulates the complex layers of epistemological reflection inherent to design research when Frayling's categories of 'into', 'through' and 'for' are all in operation; *01.AKAD – Experimental Research in Architecture and Design* (Axl Books, 2005), a publication of works and projects developed from 2003-5 within the framework of AKAD, a collaborative platform for Swedish architectural schools

Frayling cites Pablo Picasso's claim that 'to search means nothing in painting. To find is the thing.'[10] Research 'for' art, or design, or architecture, is thus to be understood as the process of exploration, discovery and fact-finding which makes it possible to produce a particular artwork. This process can both be careful, deep and systematic, as well as spontaneous, associative and serendipitous. But the journey, to use a common metaphor for research process, is as such not really of interest to the artist(s) or designer(s) at work, and there is no systematic analysis or documentation that takes

care of the 'knowledge spill' that is bound to come out along the way.

Frayling spends a lot of time in his analysis in mapping the stereotypical perceptions of the artist, designer and scientist, but in the end points to the fallacies involved and how these feed into present concerns about how we might understand research in relation to artistic practice. Historical examples such as Leonardo da Vinci and John Constable are used to counter the position of Picasso, since they in their respective times contributed directly through artistic methods of observation and documentation

5.2 Pages from Katarina Bonnevier's PhD dissertation on 'Behind Straight Curtains: Towards a Queerfeminist Theory of Architecture' (KTH, 2007), showing textual as well as visual articulations of critical fictions, projecting thought into other grounds, and shifting perspectives on what architecture is and could become

to the development of knowledge about, for example, anatomy, physiology and meterology. Here, then, we are offered some classic examples of research 'through' art. Their objective – or one such objective – is the act of research, and in this sense the artistic methods, ambitions and perceptions provide the means to do so. Some 20 years after Frayling's essay, and looking at the now rather substantial portfolio around the world of design-driven, or practice-led, MPhil or PhD dissertations, we can find a wide range of examples that sit between the 'through' and 'for' positions. I have to confess at this point that I would also position my own and related practices in both categories, not necessarily always being able to distinguish between them. I will come back later to explain how and why this might be the case.

Frayling's other category of research 'into' is perhaps the easiest to comprehend. Here we have a clear outsider's perspective, with the researcher launching an investigation into art, design, architecture – or rather, particular aspects of its practices, its artefacts, or its effects. With recourse to established research methodologies drawn from the humanities, social sciences or natural sciences, a design researcher can get by very well in this arena. If in the other two categories it is assumed that engaged researchers will have access to, or personal experience of, methods which are, if not unique, then at least characteristic of art or design practices, in the category of research 'into' this situations is by no means implied or even deemed necessary. One might argue that it is here that research (with a capital 'R') has by far the longest history within architectural and design research, a history that can trace at least one point of origin back to the late nineteenth century with Heinrich Wölffllin. It is however also very possible to argue the opposite case, in relation to a much longer lineage of development of design-based knowledge as articulated most notably through the history of the architectural treatise.[11]

Of what use, then, are Frayling's distinctions to qualify the opening discussion about the possible mission or responsibility for design research to 'transform the world'. The three categories carry different expectations about the relationship between a design outcome (whether a product, prototype, architectural project, building, urban development scenario, planning document and so on) and the process of knowledge creation. In the case of research 'for', knowledge is seen to develop within the artistic process, but no real effort is made to articulate that gain or to spread it beyond the parties who are directly involved. In the case of research 'through' and research 'into', the act of knowledge development is considered to be explicit, and is thus expected to be clearly articulated during the course of the research process. The research outcome in either of these two categories is generally not identical to a design outcome. In research 'through' design, however, any design outcomes from the research process are usually presented as an integral part of the research outcome, whereas research 'into' generally does not include such a component.

TRANSFORMING THE WORLD? IN WHAT DIRECTION, FOR WHOM, AND TO WHAT PURPOSE?

> I am a passionate advocate for interdisciplinary research, because to truly engage in such work is often a difficult and transformational experience, combining critical engagement with the emergence of new forms of knowledge that are not yet classifiable.
>
> [Jane Rendell, 2004][12]

In interpreting the mission to 'transform the world' quite boldly, we can imagine innovations or interventions that succeed in changing an important aspect of life, or way of living, in the world.

The effects may be local or global in scale, but they need to address a broader community and have a sustained impact to qualify as a real 'transformation'. How and where do such things happen? Clearly in terms of politics, in industry, in community actions, in science and technology and more. For a research project to be able to do this in a direct way (that is which is not simply producing knowledge that in a next step might be put into use by other agents), it clearly needs to become involved on the ground, and perform the research at the same time as it works to transform, by teaming up or collaborating with external partners. It constitutes as such an action research project.[13] For our purposes here a particular interest is to understand whether and how such a project can produce something which can be communicated as a research outcome, and whether it is being performed 'through' design, or is based on an enquiry 'into' design, or indeed both. Technically, following Frayling's distinctions, this is what legitimates it as a genuine research project.

Jane Rendell's essay on 'Architectural Research and Disciplinarity' from 2004 moves beyond Frayling's category of 'through' design by emphasising on one hand the potential for interdisciplinary intersections within complex architectural design inquiry, and on the other hand by showing how this condition places architectural research in a particular position due to its potential to engender 'new forms of knowledge', and thereby to adress a wide range of critical questions for politics and society at large.[14] It is an important qualification. Design research which engages directly in architectural analysis, interpretation, alteration and design does not only hold the capacity to develop knowledge and applications in direct relation to an

5:3 Textual collage production at the Architecture Writing Workshop convened by Hélène Frichot and Katja Grillner at the KTH School of Architecture in May 2012. Working around the table on this occasion were Jane Rendell, Mona Livholts, Stephen Loo, Undine Selbach and Malin Alenius

articulated design problem, but, further, to hold also the potential to structure an investigation which by means of architectural design methods can explore research questions that reach far beyond the scope of its actual design applications.

In an essay co-written with Lars-Henrik Ståhl on 'Practice-based Research in Architecture and Design', I identified the same characteristic as being a typical feature of the studio tradition in architecture schools – that is, the critical framing of design projects through larger societal or philosophical concerns – but also noting that typically this broader methodology appeared to be being lost in the transition from studio design to PhD research.[15] Now ten years later, I would argue that the situation has changed somewhat, as will be discussed below. So far, the discussion in this chapter has not engaged with specific matters or subjects, but has dealt with conceptual definitions and general distinctions. In reality, however, few research projects are as simple to classify as has been implied above. And of course, in the absence of examples, we have no idea of what really could be at stake here. It is time to look more closely what direction, for whom, and to what purpose might potential design research projects transform the world.

FEMINIST ALTERATIONS

> The Altering practices are named after the process they induce, by what they do. They rely on the transformative power of 'altering', on both its positive and critical dynamics. In the syntagm 'altering practices', 'altering' could mean 'undermining', 'subverting' received identities and authoritative rules, norms and tools and working out other shared meanings throughout their transformation ... the Altering practices are about what we want the world to become.
>
> [Doina Petrescu, 2007][16]

In 2007, together with four of my colleagues at the KTH Royal Institute of Technology School of Architecture, I formed the feminist architecture group FATALE.[17] Our ambition was to transform architecture, the discipline, the profession, and its spatial articulations, through a mixture of research, education and practice.

Among other things, the group quickly established new elective courses and a Masters-level design studio which offered feminist design tools and perspectives. 'Altering practices' is both the title of the last design studio course in the fourth year of studies, and stands for a critical reflexive position that is activated from the beginning and runs through the core of our teaching practice. As a notion it has been developed in the publication *Altering Practices*, as described in the quote above by its editor, Doina Petrescu. It is driven by a central question: what do we want the world to become?

The Critical Studies Design Studio, as developed by FATALE, engages in design and research in an integrated way by looking at architectural projects as producers of knowledge and instigators of change.

5.4   Cover of the February 2011 issue of the Swedish journal *Arkitekten* featuring FATALE and the development of feminist architecture pedagogy at KTH. From left to right: Brady Burroughs, Katja Grillner, Katarina Bonnevier and Meike Schalk

5.5   FATALE salon on 'Anthology Works'
at IASPIS, Stockholm, May 2009. A shifting
conversational space through alternative
seating arrangements with pilates balls swept
in red fabric, here playfully experimented with
during the workshop hours

5.6 FATALE salon on 'Shifting Perspectives' at IASPIS, April 2010. Dialogical furniture designed by Meike Schalk

In our own projects we frequently return to questions such as, what knowledge have we gained here, how will this project alter the conditions right here, and who might benefit from this change and who might not? Research, as practiced in our design studio, is pursued both as individual portfolios of design projects and is built up collectively as we test out and develop new critical design methods in a collaborative process. A series of research methodology seminars – support this aspect of the studio, which through selected readings and assignments seeks to clarify individual design and research questions, programmes, methodologies and concepts. Students are required to make a

connection between their work and the effect it may have 'outside' of the academic environment, raising questions about social responsibility through architectural means.

Combining resources between the Masters-level design studio and the elective courses of FATALE, such as various lecture series, and an experimental writing/studio course taught along with international guests, we provide opportunities for a vital exchange amongst participants with various backgrounds, as well as the shaping of critical networks for future work collaborations. Our student projects range from complex buildings, landscape design and urban redevelopment, to small scale design interventions

5.7   The dialogical furniture designed by Meike Schalk has also been used in different FATALE salons and workshops, here at Uppsala University. Participants can select four pieces of plywood to be assembled into a stool (or a small table depending on use). Each piece has a word in red or black selected from a vocabulary generated out of our 'Anthology Works' workshop. For this Uppsala workshop, the participants gathered in groups with their individual pieces of furniture to have coffee and converse around the stories which unfolded from the stools, tables and positions temporarily constructed through this act

and performance pieces, to complex mapping and cataloguing schemes.

As a spatial practice, FATALE has also worked with the arrangement of conversational spaces in the format of what we can call 'performance salons' in a creative sense.

That is, these FATALE events that can be viewed as seminars, as workshops, or as social events which act as gatherings around particular issues, and in which the hosts and guests are involved in co-producing space through arrangement and performance – that is our conversations, clothing, bodies, postures and relational engagements. Three examples of these salons are 'Anthology Works' (2009); 'Shifting Perspectives' (2010), both held at the IASPIS arts foundation in Stockholm; and

'The Incompatible Modalities Salon' (2010) at the Woburn Studios in London, which I will now present in more detail.

It was in relation to the 2010 conference on 'Sexuate Subjects: Politics, Poetics and Ethics', organised by the Bartlett School of Architecture at UCL in London, and in specific relation to the 'Whirlwinds' session, that FATALE invited participants to join 'The Incompatible Modalities Salon'.[18]

Providing some lunch and a space of critical reflection for the conference participants, FATALE shaped a conversational garden around ten 'fluttering follies' each with a different modality of chicks, birds and buildings ('The love nest', 'La Sybille', 'The grotto' and so on). A distinctive soundtrack, projected images and picnic spots articulated each of them. Whatever each participant brought to the scene (in terms of clothing, actions, topics) added to the spatial formation. Performing a guided tour, we articulated the arranged garden through its gendered connotations, and the feminist narratives and figurations it materialised, a momentary realisation of a critical fiction. The format of our salons provides critical potential to transform, through enactment and arrangement, an institutionally and architecturally framed environment in a number of ways. 'The Incompatible Modalities Salon' explored its own specific spatial and social condition, by asking what it meant to be productive of, or what can be argued as, a spatial modality of an essentially incompatible, alternative kind.[19]

The whole event was documented in film and photography. Postcards written during lunch by salon participants remain as a trace of the conversations and imaginations that took place. But, then again, what actually happened there?

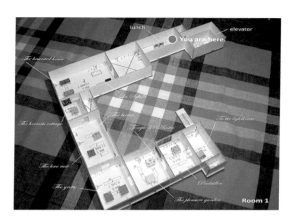

5.8   Model photo and layout presentation of 'The Garden of the Incompatible Modalities Salon', Woburn Studios, London, December 2010

It was an ephemeral event, two hours which passed on the 'Whirlwinds' day. Everyone then returned to further performances, exhibitions, talks and so on in the conference. In what way could this event act as a critical projection, and in what way could this moment be saved, articulated and affect the future? As to its possible effects, one may speak elaborately about collective experience, shared memories, and individual perceptions of different, and in many cases liberating encounters; these were undoubtedly created in our salon, and as such they have a decisive impact. But to determine exactly what is achieved, or to measure its strength, is not necessarily possible, or even desirable. What I would suggest is important is however the continued remediation of the fictional space, the fictional moment, as it appeared, as reality, as if it were a reflection of the world, as a garden where incompatible modalities belong. In her current research for the state-funded research programme that I am coordinating in Sweden, and which is called 'Architecture in Effect', Katarina Bonnevier (along with Therese Kristiansson and Mariana

5.9   In the pleasure garden. Part of the tour of 'The Garden of the Incompatible Modalities Salon'. The tour guide is accompanied by two garden experts – Chantal FATALE (a garden historian) and Pascale FATALE (a folly expert)

Alvès) is continuing along this path of performative experimentation, by arranging historical clubs and salons of particularly queer significance. Offering through such momentary realisations of utopian situations, the intention is to imagine, to quote Bonnevier, 'the day after the revolution … and propose future utopian/reparative/queer/feminist altering realities'.[20]

TAKING CARE OF RESEARCH

Formalized methods are necessary to protect us from imposing what we think we already know … on that which we seek freshly and more fully to understand. But the informal arts of being together that we also have are necessary to protect us against the thoughtlessness that trained technical and theoretical proficiency can lead to.

[Elizabeth Kamarck Minnich, 2005][21]

5.10 In the hermit's cottage. Lunch and time for postcards in 'The Garden of the Incompatible Modalities Salon'

If we look at the FATALE Critical Studies Design Studio, and a performance salon such as 'The Garden of the Incompatible Modalities Salon', in terms of design research, then it is clear that they are dependent on formats of documentation, critical analysis and discussion in order to qualify properly as research 'through' design. They constitute sites for knowledge production, and in the moment of performance this can be articulated, but there remains a surplus of work that needs to be undertaken to draw out the further research potential from these sites and situations. We can see now that this is beginning to happen with research papers that are being developed from studio work by us in our respective roles as teachers and researchers. Brady Burroughs has for example written a research paper, for future publication, about the sites, situations, imaginations and designs produced by FATALE during the autumn term in 2011. In the courses on 'Feminist Design Tools' and 'Dialogical Interventions', she together with Katarina Bonnevier took the students through explorations of humanimal perspectives and positionings with ficto-critical design methods.[22] Furthermore, Meike Schalk and Hélène Frichot are currently both developing articles and presentations, along with their students, from the work undertaken in their respective design studio projects in 2012.[23] And the current studio project on the Rosenlund Park, which will be discussed more below, has already in the process of preparation engendered research material for publication.[24] Together with Katarina Bonnevier, I have also initiated work for an essay performing a critical reconstitution of 'The Garden of the Incompatible Modalities Salon'. The intention is to fix somehow that ephemeral moment of being within the event, and of articulating the presence of another order.

Individual student projects in themselves also carry through a design process from the production of design outcomes to the presentation of research outcomes that reach beyond the specific design proposal, especially at postgraduate level. One example of such a project is Sara Vall's KTH diploma project from 2010.[25]

In her thesis, Vall undertook a careful study of Slussen, a unique, now severely dilapidated, infrastructural node, and as she shows, a complex building which dates from 1935 and sits in the centre of Stockholm. Through her investigations, Vall entered into the controversial debates that have surrounded this building for almost 30 years about what its place should be in the future. She mapped Slussen as it is now used and experienced, as well as Slussen in its matter-of-fact physical manifestation. Few Stockholmers know that this larger piece of concrete infrastructure consists of a great number of rooms and facilities that house a diverse range of programs. These she mapped with great precision and presented in architectural drawings with an almost anatomical character. By presenting, in the form of a catalogue, the sequence of 28 rooms with their diverse characteristics, Vall's project points to the potential of the site to become – as it is already in its current form – a lively meeting-place for the city. With her catalogue at hand, one can ask questions such as: who has the power in planning, what tools are available to us that may influence the development of the city, and what urban consequences can information such as this have? After the completion of her project, Sara Vall and I co-authored an article about her research project and its further implications for urban design and planning practice.[26]

5.11 Diploma work by Sara Vall on '28 Rum (28 Rooms: A Critical Spatial Investigation of Slussen and its Spatial Potential)', KTH School of Architecture (2010). The photograph shows the catalogue of the 28 rooms investigated

Among our most recent Diploma projects (January 2013) both Jenny Andreasson and Anja Linna developed in thir work new innovative approaches to participatory mapping and altering practices of urban and rural spatial interventions.[27]

At this moment in time, I still think that a lot more can be done, and more time and resources should be invested into the documentation, analysis and reflective processing of the performative research practices as developed by FATALE and within the Critial Studies in Architecture programme at KTH. At the same time, we feel that it is absolutely necessary for us to keep up the performative work, and thus to remain in action and continue to articulate spatially and materially the insights that we gain through educational and performative

design practice. It constitutes a complex balancing act for everyone involved, and a challenge that Minnich's quote above captures particularly well.

WEDDING THEORY TO PRACTICE?

Whether 'old' or 'new,' feminism remains an inherently positive approach: it insists not only on the necessity but also on the *possibility* of change. Feminism weds theory to practice and encourages us to rethink the relationship between architecture schools and the larger professional world ... Feminism's attention to practice ... fosters new ways of understanding and experimenting with process.

[Despina Stratigakos, 2012][28]

In her recent essay on 'Why Architects Need Feminism', Despina Stratigakos outlines the very

SAVE AND NURTURE OR ALLOW THINGS TO GROW

VALUE WHAT IS HERE

edible school yards

EPHEMERAL CARE

COMMON AND COLLECTIVE

ACTIVISM FOR SOCIETAL

beautiful!

TAKE CARE OF FENCES AND BORDERS

MAKE USE OF WHAT IS HERE

INSTITUTIONAL CARE

COMMONIN

SELF-BUILDING

ALTERNATIVE ECONOMIES
CARE FOR OWN FOOD PRODUCTION

Un-employed

UNEMPLOYMENT CENTER

ITUTIONAL

STITUTI

5.12   Diploma work by Anja Linna on 'Urban Caring: Finding Creative Strategies for Care-Full Architectural Practices in Norra Sorgenfri, Malmö', KTH School of Architecture (2013). The photograph shows an interactive mapping tool demonstrating the potential of the process to be applied strategically as a 'careful companion' to planning for change on different locations

concrete discriminatory practices which are still prevalent in the professional and educational world of architecture today. As much as FATALE have consciously chosen to make explicit the feminist agenda of our group, rather than just referring

to gender studies more neutrally, Stratigakos emphasises the political imperative implicit in any feminist position. A very basic explanation of the notion of feminism clarifies that it entails two parts: firstly, an understanding that women on a structural

5.13   Diploma work by Jenny Andreasson on 'Magnifying the Rural: Moving through the past, present and future of a social space in Västergötland', KTH School of Architecture (2013). The photograph shows the spatial installation of a mapping and spatial intervention project spanning in scale from European, to regional, to local community network, to village, to community house, questioning therefore the spatial hierarchies between urban and rural

level are disadvantaged in society (albeit in different ways in different contexts); and secondly, the conviction that this situation ought to be changed. The first point is the arena for research on this situation, currently and historically, with the aim to further our understanding on what is the 'matter of concern' (to borrow a critical concept from Bruno Latour).[29] The second point is the political arena, in the sense of what are the means by which the situation at hand can be changed? This too of course needs to be subjected to research enquiry, and different schools of feminism suggest different approaches for

doing so. This way of describing the notion clarifies the necessary link between theory and practice, and Stratigakos writes of the insistence on a 'possibility for change' and 'feminism's attention to practice'. Our experience of setting up the Critical Studies Design Studio and the FATALE salons confirms the particular strength of feminism as a complex body of theories, practices and activisms, all of them offering a way to work in which criticality aligns with concrete design work and performative action.

Recent developments in the theories and methodologies of participatory action research

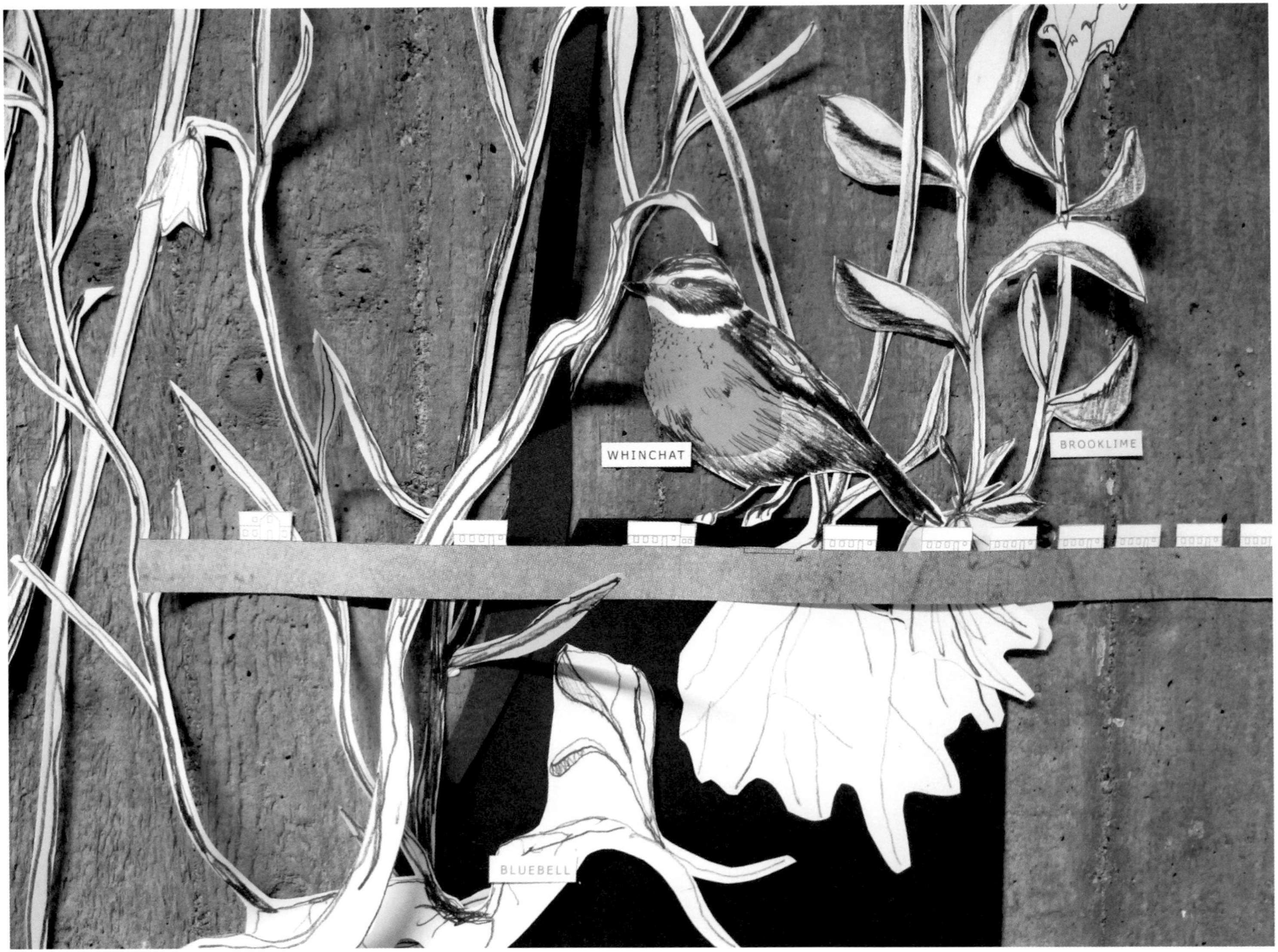
WHINCHAT
BROOKLIME
BLUEBELL

5.14 Diploma work by Jenny Andreasson. Here the photo shows a detailed intervention into the garden of the existing community house, a traditional type of ditch to bring back past ecologies to the present

emphasise the strong relation between feminist research approaches and action research.[30] It is a link that on the other hand is often argued to have long been underdeveloped, or unrecognised, within the dominant discourses of action research. Originating as early as 1946 with the work of social psychologist Kurt Lewin, the field of action research has since been developed to address a broad range of practice contexts in social research from management and organisation studies, to nursing, education, architecture, planning and design.[31] While action research in its broadest sense by definition shares a commitment to transforming existing conditions in real-world settings, a particular strand of participatory action research sets out with an explicit aim towards empowerment and emancipation – that is, in aiming to change political structures and power relations.[32] This then responds directly then to the two intertwined aspects of feminism outlined above, by expanding knowledge *and* taking action. While contemporary theoretical and methodological references are abundant within forms of educational research, it is surprising to note just how little discussed the relation between architectural design research and action research appears to be. There are some interesting examples of writers who outline these relations but as yet not many substantial contributions.[33]

TRANSFORMING KNOWLEDGE: ON-SITE

[H]ow might we, as academic subjects, become open to possibility rather than limits on the possible? What would it mean to view thinking and writing as productive ontological interventions? … How do we actually go about performing new economies … [H]ow can we participate in what is happening on the ground from an academic location? … [S]tarting 'where we are' to engender other worlds.

[J.K. Gibson Graham, 2008][34]

Since 2012, the FATALE design studio has been engaging directly with participatory research, mapping and interventions on a particular site in Stockholm, the Rosenlund Park in Södermalm, the Southern island of the inner city.

The Western part of this park is currently subjected to a planning process that involve proposals for housing development and a new street cutting through the park.[35] This specific situation is highly conflictual, and brings together a number of acute questions concerning urban transformation, gentrication, sustainable development, planning politics and ideologies – and, at the heart of our concern, the absence of situated, local agency and actors. These are, according to the official planning process, completely absent as potential co-producers of knowledge about the existing site, of its history and of its future instantiations. Myself, I am precariously balancing multiple positions in this project as both the lead researcher/design tutor and also an engaged resident in the neighbourhood. This however can be factored into the project as a particular asset rather than a problematic bias. Provided that our engagement with this site partially builds on previous research carried out by myself on performative modes of writing place, using the Rosenlund Park and my residential appropriations of this park as the empirical ground, my own position 'inside' this research context has a history of around five years now.[36] Theoretically this current project draws on feminist critiques of epistemology, in particular Donna Haraway's notion of situated knowledges,

5.15　A hole in the ground in Rosenlund Park, Stockholm, 2012. On what grounds are decisions about radical urban transformation taken? Our current research and studio projects on the park engage in unfolding a complex web of significances that is currently spun around and across its western parts by residents, activists, lobbyists, developers, planners, and politicians

Elizabeth Kamarck-Minnich's attention to philosophical fieldwork, Rosi Braidotti's construction of the nomadic subject, as well as comtemporary applications of these notions through in the work of the feminist economic geographers, J.K Gibson-Graham (the joint *nom de plume* of Julie Graham and Katherine Gibson), in regard to their ideas 'of belonging' and their call for 'diverse economies'.[37]

Together, Gibson-Graham have developed over years a very specific action research practice based on active engagement in local communities where they have – as researchers and representatives of the university sector – constructed themselves as being deeply entangled in concrete transformative processes which have both local and global effects. Carefully mapping the minor economies and local assets essentially overlooked by the capitalist systems of mainstream economics, their methodology aims to empower and activate what lies below the tip of the iceberg. Indeed, the iceberg is a telling figure which they have used to describe just how small a share of the resources for life is counted as 'real economics' from a capitalist viewpoint.[38] In their 2011 essay on 'A Feminist Project of Belonging for the Anthropocene', they argue that they are taking an important step towards an essentially human-centered model for understanding the regional economies in which they are actively engaging through their research.[39] Citing Jane Bennett, they employ the notion of 'vital materialism' to describe the intense engagement with diverse agencies that any future-oriented emancipatory project of 'belonging' must embrace.[40]

Our Rosenlund Park West project therefore aims to test central concepts developed by Gibson-Graham and other action research practices on the current local site context, as a means to develop and specify what situated knowledges implies for an ethics of architectural practice in processes of urban transformation. On a more specific level, the project aims to contribute to the articulation of a critique of current urban planning and development practices, and their discourses, in Stockholm more generally – as well as adding to local empowerment by expanding knowledge about the site and suggesting projective alternative visions for future actions. The project is at the moment in an early but critical phase. A team of Masters-level students are presently working on a participatory mapping project and developing proposals for the site. In parallel, the city council is concluding the first phase of the planning process and is calling for formal stakeholder dialogue. An activist group in which I participate has just now initiated work to assemble arguments and knowledge in preparation for the concretisation of the plan. Once the student design research is concluded, the planning process might well have moved on to another stage, and so the activist group also needs to engage further in public debate. A second phase of theoretical evaluation and conceptual development will therefore have to take place.

TRANSFORMING THE WORLD: ONCE AGAIN

To accomplish this, we are pushed to explore the unfamiliar and often uncomfortable landscape at the edge. It's uneven ground. There we get glimpses of how we might each further transform ourselves as action researchers engaged in transforming the world.

[Patricia Maguire, 2001][41]

Since 2011, I have been engaged as the director for what is termed in Sweden a 'strong research environment' for the development of theories and methodologies for architectural engagement in societal concerns, called 'Architecture in Effect'.[42] This ambitious research programme, funded by the government, engages all of the four Swedish architectural schools: KTH in Stockholm, Chalmers in Gothenburg, Lund and Umea. The research and teaching practices developed within the context of FATALE and within Critical Studies in Architecture, as described above, thus now forms part of a larger context in which political and social issues are specifically foregrounded. In early-February 2013, we arranged an international symposium on 'Rethinking the Social in Architecture' at the Umeå School of Architecture, which featured presentations of over 40 research projects from those in the research environment, as well as invited guests. A 'reader' compendium entitled *The Reader* with long abstracts and associated visual material was published for the occasion.[43] Present in this reader are (and were, at the red round tables in Umeå during three cold winter days) a very wide range of research and design practices spanning from concrete actions of making change – physical, social, mental – in space for community support and creation, through to critical conceptualisations of these practices – theorising, questioning, positioning actions and responsibilities – and also to studies which scrutinise that which is happening anyway today, in local and global contexts. What, then, as one troubling question was posed, is the role of our theoretisations in all this? Do we need a form of critical theory, or philosophy, to make change happen?[44]

With this in mind, we can return to the questions posed at the beginning of this chapter: what is at stake when not only design, but also design research, is engaged in the transformation of the world, and which (as is the case with most projects presented in Umeå) operates from a socially engaged, emancipatory position? If we, in looking at design research here, agree that the implication is for research 'through' and 'into', rather than 'for', it appears necessary always to find, or construct, theoretical or philosophical positions from which one can view, and make sense of, the action that one is performing through the design research process. Exactly how these constructions are articulated, and with recourse to what exact conceptualisations or frameworks, one cannot stipulate. But that they are needed in order to retain criticality and reflexivity is certain. It is in these locations that knowledge takes shape and from where it migrates on to other specific sites, practices, concerns or communities. And it is what secures that action in reality transforms discourse.

ACKNOWLEDGEMENTS

The research for this chapter has been generously funded by KTH School of Architecture and the Swedish Reseach Council, Formas. I wish to thank my dear colleagues and students in FATALE and Critical Studies in Architecture at KTH for great collaborations, discussions, and most importantly the critical design and research work that makes up the key examples cited in this chapter. Thanks also to Michael Speaks and Wallis Miller for the generous invitation to your faculty symposium at Kentucky University, which in many ways provoked the central argument in this chapter. And last to my colleagues in *Architecture in Effect*, a thank you; this chapter forms a contribution to our continued research programme.

Notes

1 Michael Speaks, *River Cities Project*, University of Kentucky College of Design catalogue for exhibition at the 5th International Architecture Biennale, Rotterdam (2011), back cover.

2 In a short essay from 2006 entitled 'After Theory', Michael Speaks summarised his position in relation to the debate on criticality versus post-criticality as it played out in the early 2000s. Speaks himself refutes the term 'post-critical', but maintains a firm rejection of critical theory in its specific relation to architectural design education and practice. He argues that the anti-capitalist resistance towards commercial applications keeps architectural discourse at a distance from significant design practice and architectural action. Michael Speaks, 'After Theory', *Architectural Record*, vol. 193 no. 6 (June 2005), pp.72–5.

3 Vinnova: Sweden's Innovation Agency website, http://www.vinnova.se/en/ (accessed 25 February 2013). The account of the implications of the agency's central mission comes from discussions with a research program director at the agency in December 2012.

4 'Design Research: Four Examples from Scandinavia', Faculty Symposium, 21–2 September 2012, University of Kentucky College of Design, Lexington, Kentucky, USA (symposium hosted by Michael Speaks and Wallis Miller).

5 I am in particular referring here to the set of studio projects on Kentucky's river cities. This project is introduced at http://cargocollective.com/UK-CoD/The-River-Cities-Project-Introduction (accessed 25 February 2013) and is presented in Speaks, *River Cities Project*.

6   Speaks, 'After Theory'.

7   Speaks, *River Cities Project*.

8   Christopher Frayling, 'Research in Art and Design', *Royal College of Art Research Papers*, vol. 1 no. 1 (1993/94), pp. 1–5.

9   Iain Borden, 'The Value of Arts and Humanities Research to Life in the UK', *Architectural Research Quarterly*, vol. 12 no. 3–4 (2008), p. 221.

10   Christopher Frayling, 'Research in Art and Design'.

11   Hanno-Walter Kruft, *A History of Architectural Theory: From Vitruvius to the Present* (Princeton: Architectural Press, 1994).

12   Jane Rendell, 'Architectural Research and Disciplinarity', *Architectural Research Quarterly*, vol. 8 no. 2 (June 2004), p. 146.

13   Connections between action research and design based research is discussed and referenced in some further detail below. Peter Reason & Hilary Bradbury, 'Introduction: Inquiry and Participation in Search of a World Worthy of Human Aspiration', in Peter Reason & Hilary Bradbury (eds), *Handbook of Action Research* (London: Sage, 2006), pp. 1–14.

14   Jane Rendell, 'Architectural Research and Disciplinarity', pp. 146–7.

15   Katja Grillner and Lars-Henrik Ståhl, 'Developing Practice-based Research in Architecture and Design', *Nordic Journal of Architectural Research*, vol. 6 no. 1 (2003), pp. 15–22.

16   Doina Petrescu, 'Altering Practices', in Doina Petrescu (ed.) *Altering Practices: Feminist Politics and Poetics of Space* (London: Routledge, 2007), pp. 3–4.

17   The founding FATALE members were Katarina Bonnevier, Brady Burroughs, Katja Grillner, Meike Schalk, and Lena Villner (†2009). See: Meike Schalk, Brady Burroughs, Katja Grillner & Katarina Bonnevier, 'FATALE Critical Studies in Architecture', *Nordic Journal of Architecture*, vol. 2 no. 1 (2012), pp. 90–96. See also the FATALE website, http://www.FATALE.nu (accessed 25 February 2013).

18   'Sexuate Subjects Irigaray Conference', December 2010, Bartlett School of Architecture, UCL, London, UK. The main organiser of the conference was Peg Rawes, and the session organisers and curators for the 'Whirlwinds' session were Jane Rendell and Ana Araujo.

19   The title 'The Incompatible Modalities Salon' is a reference to Luce Irigaray, as quoted in the text for the 'Whirlwinds' session: '… women diffuse themselves according to modalities scarcely compatible with the framework of the ruling symbolics'. Luce Irigaray, 'The "Mechanics" of Fluids', in Luce Irigary, *This Sex Which Is Not One* (Ithaca: Cornell University Press, 1985), p.106.

20   Katarina Bonnevier, 'Critical Fictions in the Club Scene', in Katja Grillner et al. (eds), *The Reader: Rethinking the Social in Architecture* (Stockholm: Architecture in Effect/KTH, 2013), pp. 64–7. This is a published long abstract of the research project, and is accessible at the Architecture in Effect research programme website, http://media. architectureineffect.se/2013/01/RethinkingTheSocial.pdf (accessed 25 February 2013).

21   Elizabeth Kamarck Minnich, *Transforming Knowledge*, (Philadelphia: Temple University Press, 2005), p. 5.

22   Brady Burroughs, 'Vanity (Fair), Conflicts, Dreams, and Drama, on an Ordinary Day at the Beastlet. On the Possibilities of Critical Pedagogies', in Katja Grillner et al. (eds), *The Reader: Rethinking the Social in Architecture*, pp. 72–5. This is a long abstract of the research paper and forthcoming article, and is accessible at the Architecture in Effect research programme website, http://media.architectureineffect. se/2013/01/RethinkingTheSocial.pdf (accessed 25 February 2013).

23   Meike Schalk et al., 'Participatory Mapping in Bagis', forthcoming chapter in Ola Broms-Wessel & Klas Ruin (eds), *Från loftgångslänga till framtidens gröna sociala boende*, Spridd arkitekter (forthcoming, 2013); Hélène Frichot and students, 'Urban Biopower Stockholm and the Biopolitics of Creative Resistance', paper presented at 'Theory Forum: Urban Blind Spots', November 2012, School of Architecture, University of Sheffield, UK.

24   Katja Grillner, 'At the Western End a Dead-end Park Slot: On "Situated Knowledges and the Science Question" in Urban Planning and Design', in Katja Grillner et al. (eds), *The Reader: Rethinking the Social in Architecture*, pp. 84–7. This is a long abstract of the research paper and forthcoming article, and is accessible at the Architecture in Effect research programme website, http://media.architectureineffect. se/2013/01/RethinkingTheSocial.pdf (accessed 25 February 2013).

25   Sara Vall, '*28 Rum* (28 Rooms – A Critical Spatial Investigation of Slussen and its Spatial Potential)', Diploma Thesis project, KTH School of Architecture, Stockholm, Sweden (2010).

26   Katja Grillner & Sara Vall, 'Samtal om "28 rum": En katalog över nutida Slussens rumsliga potential', in Adam Berglund (ed.), *Röster om Slussen* (Stockholm, 2010).

27   Anja Linna, 'Urban Caring', Diploma Thesis project, KTH School of Architecture (2013); Jenny Andreasson, 'Magnifying the Rural', Diploma Thesis project, KTH School of Architecture (2013).

28   Despina Stratigakos, 'Why Architects Need Feminism', posted 12 September 2012, viewable at the Design Observer website, http://places.designobserver.com/feature/why-architects-need-feminism/35448/ (accessed 25 February 2013).

29   Bruno Latour, 'From Realpolitik to Dingpolitik: An Introduction to Making Things Public', in Bruno Latour & Peter Weibel (eds), *Making Things Public: Atmospheres of Democracy*, catalogue of the show at ZKM (Cambridge, Mass: MIT Press, 2005).

30   Patricia Maguire, 'Uneven Ground: Feminisms and Action Research', in Reason & Bradbury (eds), *Handbook of Action Research*, pp. 60–70.

31   Peter Reason & Hilary Bradbury, 'Introduction: Inquiry and Participation in Search of a World Worthy of Human Aspiration', in ibid., p. 3.

32   Stephen Kemmis, 'Exploring the Relevance of Critical Theory for Action Research: Emancipatory Action Research in the Footsteps of Jürgen Habermas', in ibid., pp. 94–105.

33 See for example Daniel Stokols, 'Transdisciplinary Action Research in Landscape Architecture and Planning: Prospects and Challenges', *Landscape Journal: The Scholarship of Transdisciplinary Action Research: Toward a New Paradigm for the Planning and Design Professions*, vol. 30 no. 1 (2011), pp.1–5. See also Susanna Elfors and Örjan Svane, 'Action Research for Sustainable Housing: Theoretical and Methodological Implications of Striving for Research as a Tool for Change', *The Journal of Transdisciplinary Environmental Studies*, vol. 7 no. 2 (2008).

34 J.K. Gibson-Graham, 'Diverse Economies: Performative Practices For "Other Worlds"', *Progress in Human Geography*, vol. 32 no. 5 (2008), p. 614.

35 On the municipal planning process, see the Stockholm City Council website, http://www.stockholm.se (accessed 25 February 2013). For short publication on the park project, see Katja Grillner, At the Western End a Dead-end Park Slot: On "Situated Knowledges and the Science Question', in Urban Planning and Design', in Katja Grillner et al. (eds), *The Reader: Rethinking the Social in Architecture*, pp. 84–7. This is a long abstract of the research paper and forthcoming article, which is accessible on the Architecture in Effect website, http://media.architectureineffect.se/2013/01/RethinkingTheSocial.pdf (accessed 25 February 2013).

36 Katja Grillner, 'A Performative Mode of Writing Place: Out and About the Rosenlund Park, Stockholm, 2008–2010', in Mona Livholts (ed.), *Emergent Writing Methodologies in Feminist Studies* (London: Routledge, 2011), pp. 133–47.

37 Donna Haraway, 'Situated Knowledges: The Science Question in Feminism and the Privilege of Partial Perspective', *Feminist Studies*, vol. 14 no. 3 (1988), pp. 575–99; Rosi Braidotti, *Nomadic Subjects: Embodiment and Sexual Difference in Contemporary Feminist Theory* (New York: Columbia University Press, 1994); Elizabeth Kamarck Minnich, *Transforming Knowledge*.

38 'The iceberg diagram', as drawn by Ken Byrne, is used by J.K. Gibson-Graham in 'A Diverse Economy: Rethinking Economy and Economic Representation' (2006), as published on the Communities Economies website, http://communityeconomies.org (accessed 25 February 2013).

39 J.K. Gibson-Graham, 'A Feminist Project of Belonging for the Anthropocene', *Gender, Place and Culture: A Journal of Feminist Geography*, vol. 18 no. 1 (2010), pp. 1–21.

40 Jane Bennett, *Vibrant Matter: A Political Ecology of Things* (Durham, NC: Duke University Press, 2010).

41 Patricia Maguire, 'Uneven Ground: Feminisms and Action Research', in Reason & Bradbury (eds), *Handbook of Action Research*, p. 67.

42 Architecture in Effect: Rethinking the Social in Architecture is a 'strong' research environment being funded by the Swedish Research Council, Formas, in the period 2011–16. For further information, please see the Architecture in Effect research programme website, http://www.architectureineffect.se (accessed 25 February 2013).

43 Katja Grillner et al. (eds), *The Reader: Rethinking the Social in Architecture*.

44 This specific concern was voiced in the conference at Umeå University by Hilde Heynen, who said that in relation to some of the projects that were presented, she was not entirely convinced of the necessary relation between theory, philosophy and transformative action.

DESIGN RESEARCH: TRANSLATING THEORY INTO PRACTICE

Shane Murray

Architecture, in general, needs an account of its embodied knowledge and processes in order to substantiate its contribution to the very real and difficult challenges facing cities today. Until this occurs, the discipline risks marginalisation as economists, engineers and official administrators increasingly dominate the formulation of urban growth and development strategies. One important way in which architecture can achieve this account is through the backing of its claims about design research in a comprehensive and systematic manner, and therefore this forms the central issue for this chapter.

WHAT IS DESIGN RESEARCH?

What constitutes design research in architecture is contested territory. The argument moves between those who believe in the possibility of research 'through' undertaking design[1] and those who believe, contrarily, that architectural research can only be conducted by traditional scholarly approaches.[2] There is of course any number of positions existing between these two poles.

This inherent contestation was heightened during the 1980s when, in Australia, a number of independent colleges and technical institutes were incorporated into universities. Design and the creative arts had to work hard to legitimise practice-based modes of inquiry in these traditional research contexts. If the arts led the way, then architecture, which had resided in the university realm for a much longer period, was also subsequently required to legitimise and validate its own practice-based modes of inquiry. This form of research has since become almost institutionalised in Australian universities; however, the discourse continues to focus on problematic questions of what does or what does not constitute design research.

Despite these ongoing discussions, an increasing number of publications have emerged which address the nature of design-based research. The majority of these texts are founded on the ambition of developing a 'designerly' theory of knowledge.[3] There is now considerable support for the concept that designing is a way of knowing that is applied in the wider process of designing, rather than an enquiry directed towards a particular defined outcome.[4] This means that design is future directed and that the more static term, 'knowledge', is rather difficult to apply to what in fact are speculative assertions.[5] Because a form of dynamic knowledge creation is embodied in the process of designing, this form of knowledge can only be contained and communicated through design outcomes, and these outcomes in turn only lead to more design knowledge. However, the practice of design utilises processes that are difficult to discern by an external observer; instead, they are dynamic and are not amenable to tests of repeatability. As a consequence, knowledge generated 'through' the act of design can be difficult to examine other than by the individual designer.

Importantly, most design research processes also involve far more conventional activities that are often described as being research 'for' and 'into'/'about' design. This categorisation of the processes entailed in design research draws heavily on Christopher Frayling[6] – and subsequently Peter Downton[7] – in their tripartite descriptions of the design process. Research 'for' design thus becomes research that enables design to occur. An example of this might be investigations into relevant architectural precedents which act as an aid to consider while designing.

Research 'into' or 'about' design, while very broad as a concept, can be considered through two main approaches. The first of these states what design should be and then sets out to develop methods to achieve it; the second enquires into what takes place when design is undertaken, and then seeks to find methods to improve or refine the observed activity. These aspects of the design research process utilise methods and approaches that are familiar to other fields of inquiry, such as engineering (or other technically based research) or social science (involving detailed qualitative forms of analysis).

In distinction, research 'through' architectural design is not only possible but also fundamentally valuable for the discipline of architecture. However, compared with other practice-based fields of inquiry, the discourse around design research in architecture is still immature. To observers outside the field, architectural design research appears to be unsystematic, dependent on individual whim, and reliant on processes that are largely invisible. As such, it is difficult to see any form of accumulative knowledge base which is being established in the process. Proponents of design research argue that the project outcome – be it an object, building or future proposal – contains embodied knowledge, and thus draws on prior knowledge and that these are visible to those trained in the discipline. However, much of this communication between designers is reliant on tacit understanding and is unable to account for what process was actually undertaken by the individual designer to achieve such an outcome.

Architecture, within the academy at least, is yet to develop a generally accepted research framework in which design research outcomes can stand for new knowledge without considerable accompanying explanation. It is thus very important that that this explanation is as rigorous as possible, and is directed to what actually is taking place in the process of design, in order to demonstrate the validity of the process and to counter the often poor accounts of the design process that currently characterise this discourse. It is also important to remember that design research has relevance in much broader contexts. Rather than the emphasis being placed solely on the productive outcome, speculative design processes can be used to examine the inputs and contextual framework in which design takes place.

Design research in architecture therefore leads to the production of several forms of knowledge with varying degrees of visibility. This places considerable responsibility on the discipline to articulate the processes involved in design research so that important characteristics of design-based inquiries can be addressed. These can be articulated as follows:

1. The 'through' component of design research is hard to examine other than by the designer who is undertaking the design. In this sense, issues and questions emerge through the design process in an iterative rather than linear progression. An important contribution to knowledge about the design process would be an accumulation of accounts of individual designers' research approaches. Architects in industry do not articulate the precise method and structure of the way that their design is carried out.

It is only through critical reflection of a process as it is being done that this design knowledge can be unpacked and made available to others. Indeed, it is through this process that design has a transformative potential.

2. The knowledge revealed in design outcomes is often tacit, easily understood by other designers but often invisible or unclear to those who are external to the discipline. Much of the contemporary discourse surrounding architectural production is directed to theoretical concerns unrelated to what actually takes place in the design process, or when directed to that process it is used to legitimise rather than account for what actually has taken place.

3. The tacit nature of the knowledge that the designing process draws upon, or the cumulative knowledge base of the discipline it is adding to, is often difficult to discern in the design outcome – and again is particularly difficult to discern for those who are outside of the practice of design.

4. The integrative, projective nature of design research has enormous potential to facilitate complex transdisciplinary engagements that are increasingly necessary to solve many of the challenges we face in the world today. In order to contribute to these challenges, design research in architecture needs to offer a much clearer account of what it has to offer.

THE AGEING OF AQUARIUS

Drawing on these principles, 'The Ageing of Aquarius' project was established in 2003 to develop and articulate design-based research, precisely by exploring how to achieve more appropriate housing models for the Australian 'baby boomers' as they entered the retirement period of their lives.[8] As a demographic group that had altered every life stage they had previously entered, and as the most economically powerful cohort in developed society, these baby boomers would be able to shape retirement and retirement dwellings into a completely different form to that which their parents had to accept. The research project analysed the complex range of contextual issues that influences the housing needs of the 'baby boomers' as they approach and experience retirement, and in this way developed a compendium of design exemplars that could address them.

This design research project, which I was involved in leading, therefore incorporated socio-economic and demographic research, and as a result it demonstrated – through the clear application of design research – the physical consequences of this investigation as it relates to the manner in which we occupy our dwellings in Australia. In addition, the research undertook a form of case-study analysis of key architectural exemplars that were then reinterpreted to demonstrate new applications for the embodied design knowledge in each instance. New ways of using dwellings, and diverse and changing household structures, suggested that alternative spatial relationships within new forms of housing – and reconsidered relationships to their exteriors – might better meet the needs of contemporary and future retirement households. One important aspect of this research was the development of methods to communicate the process of interaction between conventional social science research methods and design thinking, as well the articulation of the design knowledge inherent in architecturally designed housing projects.

To demonstrate this level of interaction, we developed a form of relational analysis which we called a 'design matrix'. This design matrix was envisaged as an expanding network in which different forms of research could be introduced into various parts of the network and their inter-relationship graphically mapped. The design matrix was developed from an examination of two adjacent primary research trajectories: key retirement needs, as established from our socio-economic, demographic and contextual research; and our simultaneous research into design compositions that dealt with specific physical dwelling needs and their spatial solutions. Through this design matrix process, the relationship between these two distinct forms of inquiry was revealed. The matrix in this sense acts as an extended and expanding process that links abstract needs to the physical implications of designing new dwellings.

Furthermore, the design matrix process produced a very large network of interrelationships extending for many pages. This leads to an increasingly detailed listing of the possible impact at a physical level of what was originally an abstract concept. The design matrix is extremely detailed. However, the type of interpretive observation which is required to make it is also very familiar to architects. The design matrix makes visible an aspect of the designerly knowing and the application of embodied knowledge which architects tacitly apply each day in their practice.

A conventional response to this design matrix would have been to immediately embark on the design of the dwellings themselves. Instead, the project sought to demonstrate the value of extant but unarticulated architectural knowledge that could respond to these needs. This involved the deep analysis of some 30 case studies in order to reveal design knowledge that would be relevant to the needs established in the earlier research. These exemplar projects were selected on the basis that each demonstrated a number of design elements and relationships which were able to respond to the criteria established in the design matrix. Importantly, the case studies relied on housing models that in many instances were not initially intended as retirement dwellings. This reveals an important aspect of the process whereby architectural knowledge that was intended to address one set of criteria can still be analysed and used for purposes that may not have been initially intended.

The case-study material included both historical and contemporary design, across the globe, and which in the majority of cases were intended for conventional household scenarios. They were family homes sometimes designed for a particular client's needs, or for a non-specified user, and s noted there was no specific intention that they were intended for a retirement-based use. The reasons for their selection were that their spatial design supported the notion of flexible occupation and that this would then facilitate a greater variety of occupation and use. This latter aspect of the research entailed a form of design projection, or designing, which is different to that of simply capturing and communicating the design knowledge that resided in the original architectural case study being analysed.

A good example of this kind of case-study analysis process is the Napier Street housing project in 2002 by Kerstin Thompson Architects of Melbourne.

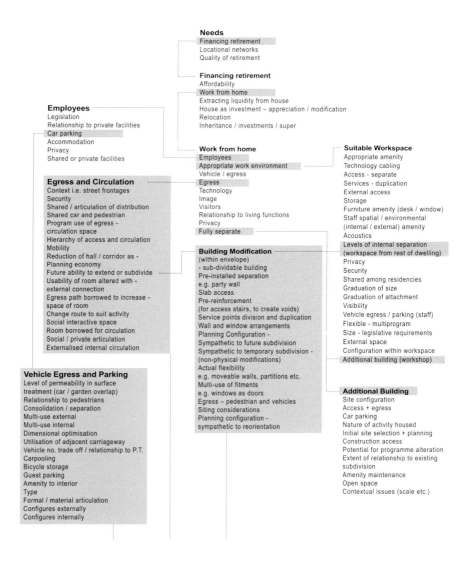

Needs
Financing retirement
Locational networks
Quality of retirement

Financing retirement
Affordability
Work from home
Extracting liquidity from house
House as investment – appreciation / modification
Relocation
Inheritance / investments / super

Employees
Legislation
Relationship to private facilities
Car parking
Accommodation
Privacy
Shared or private facilities

Work from home
Employees
Appropriate work environment
Vehicle / egress
Egress
Technology
Image
Visitors
Relationship to living functions
Privacy
Fully separate

Suitable Workspace
Appropriate amenity
Technology cabling
Access - separate
Services - duplication
External access
Storage
Furniture amenity (desk / window)
Staff spatial / environmental
(internal / external) amenity
Acoustics
Levels of internal separation
(workspace from rest of dwelling)
Privacy
Security
Shared among residencies
Graduation of size
Graduation of attachment
Visibility
Vehicle egress / parking (staff)
Flexible - multiprogram
Size - legislative requirements
External space
Configuration within workspace
Additional building (workshop)

Egress and Circulation
Context i.e. street frontages
Security
Shared / articulation of distribution
Shared car and pedestrian
Program use of egress -
circulation space
Hierarchy of access and circulation
Mobility
Reduction of hall / corridor as -
Planning economy
Future ability to extend or subdivide
Usability of room altered with -
external connection
Egress path borrowed to increase -
space of room
Change route to suit activity
Social interactive space
Room borrowed for circulation
Social / private articulation
Externalised internal circulation

Building Modification
(within envelope)
- sub-dividable building
Pre-installed separation
e.g. party wall
Slab access
Pre-reinforcement
(for access stairs, to create voids)
Service points division and duplication
Wall and window arrangements
Planning Configuration -
Sympathetic to future subdivision
Sympathetic to temporary subdivision -
(non-physical modifications)
Actual flexibility
e.g. moveable walls, partitions etc.
Multi-use of fitments
e.g. windows as doors
Egress – pedestrian and vehicles
Siting considerations
Planning configuration -
sympathetic to reorientation

Vehicle Egress and Parking
Level of permeability in surface
treatment (car / garden overlap)
Relationship to pedestrians
Consolidation / separation
Multi-use external
Multi-use internal
Dimensional optimisation
Utilisation of adjacent carriageway
Vehicle no. trade off / relationship to P.T.
Carpooling
Bicycle storage
Guest parking
Amenity to interior
Type
Formal / material articulation
Configures externally
Configures internally

Additional Building
Site configuration
Access + egress
Car parking
Nature of activity housed
Initial site selection + planning
Construction access
Potential for programme alteration
Extent of relationship to existing
subdivision
Amenity maintenance
Open space
Contextual issues (scale etc.)

6.1   Extract of the design matrix derived from
'The Ageing of Aquarius' research

Half of the development is for owner-occupation and the balance consists of seven terraces for rent that are aimed at professionals moving into the area. What is of interest in our analysis is that, in addition to its obvious architectural qualities, the project contains careful and considered design elements relevant to a range of issues established in our research on the 'baby boomers'. These design elements were, as noted, not initially intended for application to this group. The case study began with a simple architectural explanation of the building type.

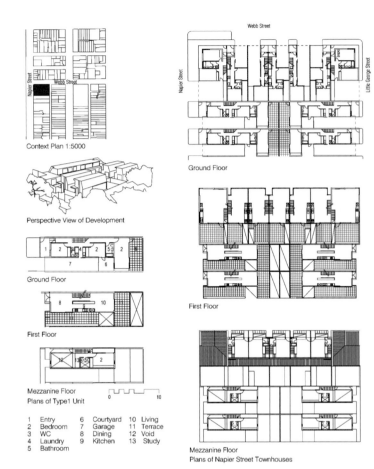

Context Plan 1:5000

Perspective View of Development

Ground Floor

First Floor

Mezzanine Floor
Plans of Type1 Unit

1	Entry	6	Courtyard	10 Living
2	Bedroom	7	Garage	11 Terrace
3	WC	8	Dining	12 Void
4	Laundry	9	Kitchen	13 Study
5	Bathroom			

Ground Floor

First Floor

Mezzanine Floor
Plans of Napier Street Townhouses

6.2   Case study extract of the Napier
        Street housing project by Kerstin
        Thompson Architects (design
        drawings of the project as built)

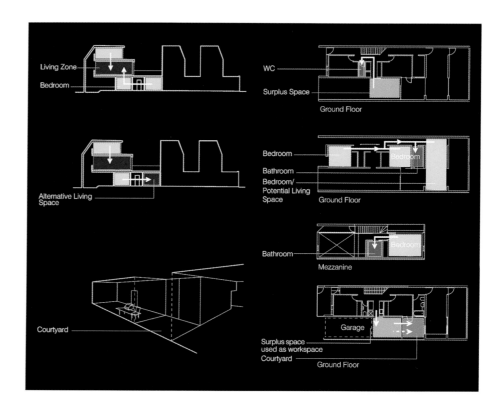

6.3   Front view and bird's eye view of the
        Napier Street housing project

6.4   Case study extract of Napier
        Street housing project

Subsequent analysis established a number of criteria that had also been identified in the earlier design matrix project. These include the treatment of private open space in collective housing, flexibility of use through appropriate spatial planning, opportunities for zoning the interior to accommodate different forms of occupation, and the relationship to external space in achieving this flexibility. Figure 6.4 shows a detail of one element of the analysis which demonstrates how the internal finishes, the provision of a window onto a courtyard, and the proximity to a bathroom permit the garage space to be re-occupied as a workroom or even a bedroom.

By the time we has established this type of information for the 30 selected case studies, the resulting data sheets comprised almost 200 pages of analytical drawings. From the lists which we developed, many solutions began to repeat themselves. Key themes emerged throughout the design matrix and drove the hierarchy of choices of case studies to look at. These themes can be demonstrated through different physical arrangements across several case studies, revealing the very flexible nature of design as a problem-solving technique. An array of possible physical consequences and related design concepts were duly revealed through this process.

The extraction of embodied knowledge as part of the case-study process can never be exhaustive. New aspects of this knowledge are bound to be revealed in subsequent iterations of the analysis. The incorporation of this emerging knowledge into the design of new dwelling models will also not be a direct process. New and unforeseen design knowledge is bound to enter whenever the actual dwellings are designed. However, even articulating this process through a number of modes makes available a much more detailed overview of the design knowledge that might be applied to the design of a particular dwelling. This knowledge can also be presented in the format of simple diagramming, which makes the knowledge communicable beyond the discipline. This aspect of the research demonstrates the integrative potential of design research to forge new and previously unrecognised connection between extant knowledge and new or unforeseen applications. How this knowledge is then utilised by designers is difficult to assess because of the individual nature of each design project. 'The Ageing of Aquarius' project was somewhat fortunate to have an accompanying PhD study in which the relationship between the extracted knowledge from the case-study research was able to be applied in practice, and this process was also fully documented.

BARACCO AND WRIGHT ARCHITECTS

Louise Wright, a practising architect and a director of Baracco and Wright, was deeply involved in 'The Ageing of Aquarius' project, and undertook much of the case-study analysis as well as working on the design matrix for the larger project. Wright was studying for her PhD while working on the Aquarius project, and the analysis of one of the designs from her doctoral research provides an insight into the possible application of the knowledge principles developed. The example shown here consists of a design by Baracco and Wright for a proposed multi-family vacation house. In developing this scheme, Wright was able to draw upon one of the case studies she had previously analysed in the Aquarius project, the Farfor Houses (1968),

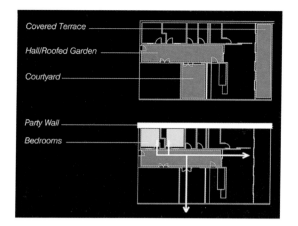

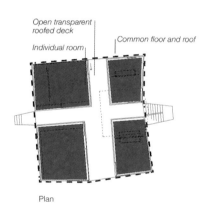

Plan

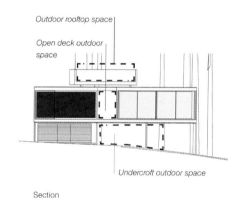

Section

6.5 Case study extract of the Farfor Houses by Romberg & Boyd Architects. Plan diagrams of shared semi-enclosed circulation and internal courtyard, derived from 'The Ageing of Aquarius' research

6.6 Photograph of semi-enclosed circulation space in the Farfor Houses designed by Romberg & Boyd Architects

6.7 Extract from Louise Wright's doctoral thesis as a retrospective design examination of the multi-family house by Baracco & Wright Architects. Plan and sectional diagrams of the semi-enclosed circulation space and vertical connection of common outdoor spaces

as designed by the distinguished Australian architect, Robin Boyd. The Farfor Houses utilise a series of wide, multifunctional corridors and linear courtyard spaces to maximise the potential for layering program onto the corridor spaces. While possibly never explicitly intended in the initial design, this disposition and treatment of circulation spaces provides us with considerable spatial knowledge for reapplication into other contexts. The case-study analysis thereby established a number of scenarios in which this responsive spatial strategy could provide differentiated egress for scenarios that included working from home, where egress would not disturb other occupants, or the ability to utilise the same dwelling by unrelated households, or the opportunities to layer different programs onto the flexible corridor spaces.

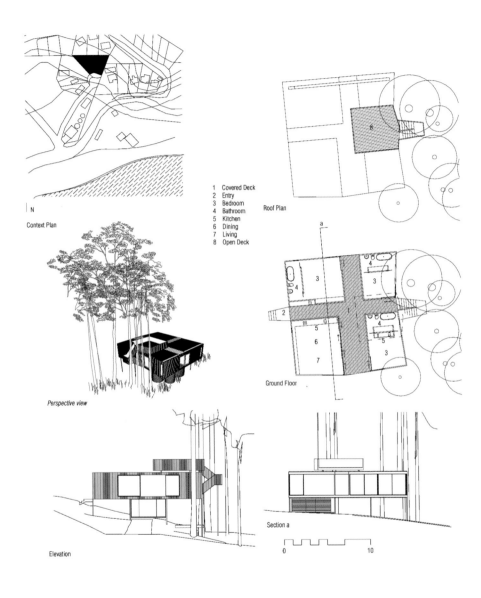

Context Plan

N

1 Covered Deck
2 Entry
3 Bedroom
4 Bathroom
5 Kitchen
6 Dining
7 Living
8 Open Deck

Roof Plan

Ground Floor

Perspective view

Elevation

Section a

0   10

6.8   Design drawings for the multi-family
       house by Baracco & Wright Architects

Baracco and Wright's innovative plan for multi-family dwellings utilised a widened corridor configuration that separates the four contained zones of the house. These private zones can be opened incrementally to the corridor space. This cruciform corridor is sufficiently generous to be utilised for a number of activities other than simple circulation. In one mode, the three separate couples – one with children – are able to occupy the dwelling simultaneously. In this instance, the individual bedrooms are self-contained private zones and the over-scaled corridors become living areas for relaxation, play, and even work. When occupied by one or two families these private spaces can open up to provide a range of permeability between private zones and the flexible corridor space.

In developing this project, Wright was explicit in demonstrating the influence of the Farfor Houses on her own design. Through this process she has demonstrated how designers transform knowledge which they observe in a particular precedent example and apply this within a different context to create new knowledge. Architects do this all the time; however, in most instances, this transformation is not articulated and the majority of architectural discourse seems to be disinterested in explaining these connections. In this particular example the designer, through textual and diagrammatic analysis, validated this kind of connection. Through the unusual opportunity of a PhD candidature, the knower (the designer) carried out the new design in which this knowledge was transformed and articulated. If this process was repeated more frequently by designers, an accumulative knowledge base of the design process would begin to develop.

CONTINUING DISCOURSES: THE MONASH ARCHITECTURE STUDIO (MAS)

The research that was developed through 'The Ageing of Aquarius', as well other research into the articulation of the knowledge embodied in designing, provided the foundations for a new research group at Monash University.[9] In 2008, the Monash Architecture Studio (MAS), was formed concurrently with the new architectural programme at the university.[10] From the outset, MAS has embraced the concept of design research in architecture as a way of engaging with the compelling issues of our time: climate change, resource limitations, rapid population growth, changing household demographics. Its ambition is to demonstrate the contribution that design can make to these significant challenges in the development of our future cities.

MAS undertakes traditional modes of research as well as various forms of design-based spatial inquiries, including projective case studies (following on from 'The Ageing of Aquarius'), commissioned designs and design competitions. Research is interdisciplinary and collaborative, and as such involves government agencies, the development industry, community organisations, the professional design community and academics from Monash University and other institutions. The work of MAS differs from that of a private practice because it is located in a major research university where all activities are required to demonstrate rigorous scholarship. The manner in which design research takes place and the communication of its outcomes are steered by this context. This means that design-based inquiries have to be extensively documented and subjected to detailed analysis.

6.9   Infill housing redevelopment in Melbourne in various stages from 2002, 2006 and 2012 (left to right)

The research undertaken involves considered speculation about the future urban environment and the forces acting upon it: social, political, economic and environmental. Outcomes from this design research may not have immediate commercial applications by industry. Rather, the particular forms of knowledge generated through research by MAS are an attempt to provide a vehicle for subsequent design investigations in architectural practice more generally.

An example of this can be illustrated through 'Greyfield Precincts', an ongoing body of research being developed by MAS which utilises a range of architectural and urban design investigations. The initial study was a collaborative undertaking between three partner institutions offering complementary expertise within the fields of urban economics, social science, architectural design and construction.[11] Funded by the Australian Housing and Urban Research Institute (AHURI), the project was intended to scope the inputs and processes required for a new model of infill housing that could deliver better quality and more effective outcomes for regenerating established and underperforming suburbs. Transitioning these 'middle' regions of our cities into more sustainable urban environments is a particularly difficult challenge and one that the private market has failed to address.

The scoping study was carried out through a formal Investigative Panel process involving government, industry and community experts. It was primarily concerned with the slow take-up of strategic development policies in 'middle' suburbs and the comparatively high levels of ad hoc, informal housing infill which happens in across these contexts, as seen in Figure 6.9.[12]

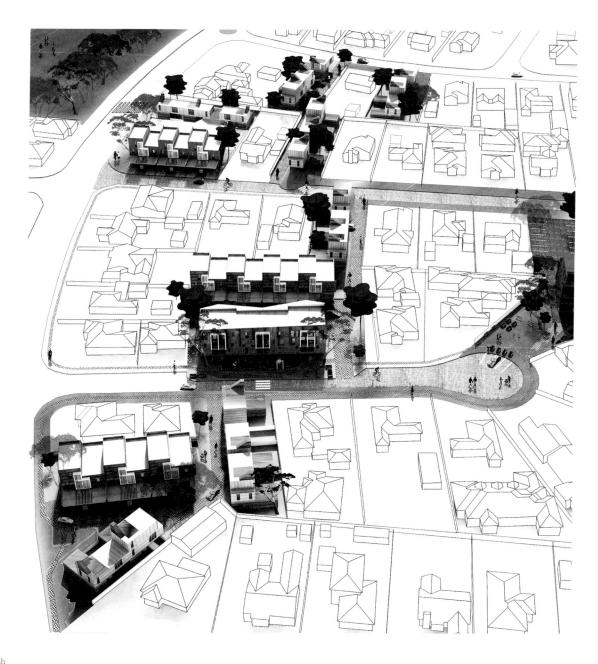

6.10   Speculative design by Monash
Architecture Studio for a dispersed infill
precinct in Melbourne

The research substantiated why small scale, piecemeal infill was a less than optimal outcome in relation to contemporary urban policy for improved spatial, economic, social and environmental outcomes. Concurrent research examined the factors driving these outcomes, including industry practices, regulations, land ownership regimes and so on. A speculative design process was also undertaken to arrive at an alternative redevelopment strategy that might be possible within this highly constrained context, as well as providing a new understanding of these locations.

This research ultimately led to a development model that recognised the difficulty of assembling land for effective redevelopment in these areas, and instead proposed a precinct design approach that operates over a field of non-contiguous allotments (Figure 6.10). The concept of coordinating redevelopment for greater benefit (for example the savings achieved through economies of scale) was not reliant on design research taking place. However projective and spatial engagement with the issues arising from the initial concept revealed several other advantages which were unlikely to have been discovered other than 'through' design.

One example was the re-conceptualisation of settlement patterns and programme distributions in these homogenous suburban contexts. Consolidation through redevelopment of existing allotments typically repeats programmes and services such as car parking and private open space on a plot-by-plot basis. The strategy proposed in the 'Greyfield Precincts' research eliminates these spatial, servicing and programmatic redundancies. The precinct approach distributes such elements over a disaggregated field where, rather than repeating provisions for each allotment, they are strategically allocated. Open space and car parking can be consolidated in key locations through the precinct, thereby freeing up particular sites for higher density and more diverse dwelling typologies. The whole precinct approach therefore presents possibilities for a communal provision of workspaces, childcare and health facilities because there is a larger number of contributory developments to support them. The public infrastructure of the street can be utilised to link the various elements of the development and provide connectivity for precinct-level systems of waste, water and energy distribution. This strategic reconfiguration across a precinct provides a new degree of flexibility for more appropriate housing and urban design solutions that can create high-quality, high-amenity and denser mixed-use environments (Figure 6.11). In turn, these spatial and programmatic variations foster new possibilities for development procedures and governance, including innovative development finance arrangements. The approach also presents a chance to improve efficiencies and increase innovation in construction and delivery, economic viability, the creation of community capital, and environmental systems associated with the model. Finally the single most difficult obstacle to adopting such an approach – that is, the need for the cooperation and coordination of individual allotment owners – is being investigated through the development of 'smart market analytics', whereby the increased capital value of individual allotments, if they join the integrated system of development, can be readily demonstrated.

Speculative design, in this research context, acted as the unifying element that enabled the integration of a broad range of expertise necessary

6.11 Plan of dispersed infill precinct by Monash Architecture Studio. The speculative design model begins to transform the existing suburban morphology through connections in open spaces and a diversity of programmatic distributions

for the formulation and substantiation of an alternative redevelopment approach. Design can hence operate in and engage with projective scenarios in a manner that materialises specificities about an unknown future condition. The medium used to describe these specificities is a spatial one. The creative ability to simultaneously generate and manipulate a virtual, imagined reality provides an environment for other disciplines to directly engage with each other and with the future-directed subject matter. It is the direct engagement that is significant here, and is what makes design-based research so valuable, particularly in terms of problem solving in complex scenarios. Design, quite literally, involves the spatialisation and reconfiguration of different

inputs for the creation of a new entity, which in itself is new kind of knowledge.

URBAN SPECULATION: PROPAGANDA VS. INFORMED DEBATE

While the 'Greyfield Precincts' research was generated by investigating the realities of development delivery in suburban contexts, other examples of projects by MAS show how design research can explore an invented construct, or a seemingly absurd scenario, as a means of uncovering new knowledge about the 'real' urban challenges we face. This type of imaginative investigation offers two advantages: firstly, it exposes potential opportunities that could not

6.12 'Gotham City' as a fictional representation by Monash Architecture Studio to expose alarmist media rhetoric about the State Minister's plan for expanding Melbourne's CBD footprint

be arrived at through normative and often highly constrained research processes; and secondly, it produces a demonstration of a counter-condition which can provoke new thoughts and higher levels of engagement with an extant condition or problem. This mode of working has particular relevance for raising awareness within a public context, where positive changes in behaviour are also necessary components for successful urban transitioning.

'Melbourne-Manhattan: Rhetoric & Response', as carried out by MAS in 2012, was a speculative design exercise instigated by a ministerial announcement which proposed to expand Melbourne's central business district (CBD) through an extensive zoning change.[13] The State Government's intention was to alleviate development pressure on existing residential suburbs by concentrating intensive redevelopment within a new city footprint. The political communiqué described it as a 'bold vision' that reflected strong leadership from a government which was inviting debate about Melbourne's urban future. Beyond a basic map delineating the extent

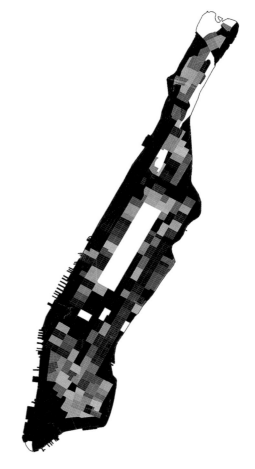

6.13   (Left) The island of Manhattan superimposed onto Metropolitan Melbourne; (Right) Highly variegated distributions of population density in Manhattan

of the proposed new CBD zone, no other visual material accompanied this 'vision' and very little detail was provided about what the plan might achieve. In short, there was actually very little to debate.

Perhaps due to this lack of explanatory content, the ministerial announcement was soon be propagandised in the mainstream media; the rhetoric was alarmist. Under the plan, it was claimed, all development controls would be 'abolished', resulting in 'wall-to-wall skyscrapers' and a Manhattan-style metropolis, five times its present size'.[14] This misrepresentation incited a shallow and reactionary dialogue, largely involving people's supposed like or dislike of towers, and criticising the government's motivations for the zoning change. There was a notable lack of discussion about the future of the city.

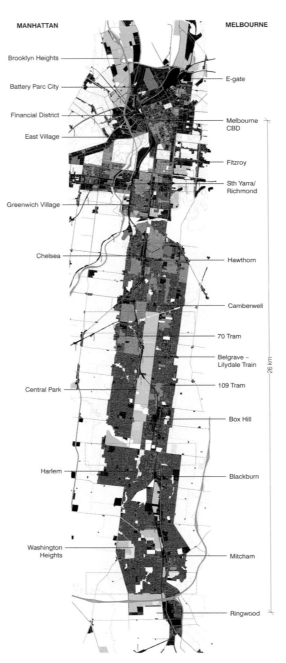

MANHATTAN   MELBOURNE

Brooklyn Heights

Battery Parc City   E-gate

Financial District   Melbourne
                                       CBD
East Village

                                       Fitzroy

                                       Sth Yarra/
                                       Richmond
Greenwich Village

Chelsea   Hawthorn

                                       Camberwell

                                       70 Tram

                                       Belgrave –
                                       Lilydale Train

Central Park   109 Tram

                                       Box Hill

Harlem   Blackburn

Washington
Heights   Mitcham

                                       Ringwood

6.14   Plan transposition of Manhattan onto
Melbourne, adjusted for Melbourne's physical
terrain and context

For MAS, the provocation of creating a Melbourne-Manhattan presented an opportunity to speculate on an alternate urban condition that could challenge conventional thinking around sustainable urban growth, and also test the group's existing body of research. MAS therefore 'unpacked' the rhetoric engendered by the State Minister's containment strategy, and its subsequent reporting, by examining the potential realisation of a Melbourne-Manhattan and what this might mean for the broader metropolitan area were this to come about. The public context of the announcement also pointed to another obvious question: how can design research contribute to a more ingenuous and informed debate about these complex urban issues?

Manhattan's urban fabric is considerably more variegated than that of Melbourne, and despite the usual 'skyscraper' characterisation, contains considerable extents of low- to mid-rise fabric. Preliminary spatial analysis of the two different contexts led to a simple plan transposition of Manhattan's urban morphology onto Melbourne's new CBD footprint (Figures 6.13 and 6.14). The 'dumb' spatial exercise immediately exposed the fallacy of 'wall-to-wall skyscrapers', and in doing so uncovered important relationships between the built form, transport infrastructure, open space amenities, mixes of activities and such like in the two cities. These relationships were then embedded in a dynamic spatial model for a hybrid city that could register the impact of various design decisions in real time. This created a feedback loop between the quantitative measures adopted by the different iterations of the future city and its qualitative reading by the designer.

The research not only yielded projective and unorthodox design outcomes which warranted further consideration, but also illuminated several new concerns regarding Melbourne's current growth strategies. In realising this absurd Frankenstein's monster of a city, the specific consequences of an otherwise uncertain or ill-defined 'vision' were made visible. At the same time, the process also revealed productive and quite feasible possibilities for managing rapid urban growth. For example, three Manhattan Islands would be needed to accommodate Melbourne's expected population in 2056, representing more than 8,000 hectares of redevelopment with an average density of 115 dwellings per hectare accompanied by new employment and amenity provisions modelled on that in New York. The proposed expansion of Melbourne's CBD could only absorb a small proportion of that growth, and hence substantial transformation of existing low-density suburbs would still be required. That being said, the exercise also proved that the expected population in 2056 could be comfortably accommodated within the existing urban boundary if even modest density increases were delivered in predetermined strategic zones.

Melbourne's existing metropolitan strategies for polycentric activity nodes, linear transport corridors and urban fringe expansion were countered by the possibility of a model of contiguous belts of development (the size of Manhattan Island) which delivered 'Manhattan-style' diversity, amenity and intensity (Figure 6.15). The important conceptual shift here was to envision future development as part of an ecosystem that incorporated the existing urban fabric, rather than as discrete new urban zones that replaced it. The zone of redevelopment then becomes a plaited urban belt which contains both new and existing environments; the development approach understands the dependencies between the two environments, and allows for their separate existence and areas of negotiation, as well as areas for a new urban type that result from the adaptations occurring within the ecosystem. Redevelopment permeates the belt at the different scales, speeds and densities necessary for the initial transitioning of that urban ecosystem, as well as its sustained resilience.

In this chapter, I set out to demonstrate how the discourse around architectural design research has been translated into practice, or rather, how design research has contributed to the built environment. I attempted to do this through a discussion of the various kinds of knowledge generated in different project examples and by demonstrating the value of that knowledge applied in different contexts. However, through the compilation of projects and formulation of the discussion, I have also chartered my evolving approach to building up a body of knowledge around the conduct of design research in architecture.

In fact, I began this inquiry 15 years ago with my own doctoral work, focusing on the relationship between architectural design and discourse.[15] I sought to develop both a method that could account for what I did in undertaking design, as well as to demonstrate how my design projects drew on architecture's considerable accumulated design knowledge. This led to an increasing interest in the contributory potential of architectural design knowledge for enhancing built environment outcomes, where so much is delivered without design engagement. I realised that if architecture as

6.15 Melbourne-Manhattan, a night view looking towards Melbourne's CBD. Speculative design by Monash Architecture Studio for potential belts, or ecosystems, of contiguous redevelopment to accommodate Melbourne's projected population growth up to 2056, and fostering a 'Manhattan-style' mixture of uses, amenity, and built-form diversity

a discipline was to make a collective contribution, it would first need to account for what it could contribute, and how.

My evolving approach to constructing a body of knowledge around architectural design research relates less to 'what' kinds of knowledge are generated, and more to 'how' it makes a contribution. 'The Ageing of Aquarius' was the first project founded on a design research process to be funded by the Australian Research Council. As such, the research carried with it an obligation to show how design knowledge could be applied in areas of housing delivery normally devoid of design expertise. In so doing, the project also addressed the necessity for this contributory knowledge to also be available outside of the architectural discipline. Baracco & Wright's design for a multi-family holiday home created the fortuitous opportunity to demonstrate how this same knowledge might be applied to a new design problem, thereby explaining how that existing knowledge could be incorporated and also extended to create new design knowledge.

As the founding Professor of Architecture at Monash University, I again felt a heavy obligation to articulate the contributory role of design research in the establishment of the new architecture programme and its research arm. The remit of MAS is to explore the potential contributions of architecture for the sustainable transitioning of our cities. This has necessarily involved the integration of architectural design research with a complex array of disciplinary inputs, and has extended my understanding of how design research can contribute to enhancing outcomes in the built environment. The Monash Architecture Studio offers an important bridge between academic and professional contexts. The practice environment will always be the site of design innovation, but the institution forges new arenas for this innovation to take place.

Population growth, demographic transformation and climate change are creating enormous challenges to the future viability of our cities. As noted, architecture appears to be becoming marginalised because other groups – economists, engineers, administrators and so on – are increasingly dominating the formation of strategies to address such challenges. The ability of architectural design to provide projective platforms that can integrate a broad range of disciplinary contributions, as well as demonstrate a collective outcome, is currently ignored. In order to become more involved as architects, we will require a more substantial account of what we can contribute.

Notes

1 For example, see: Ranulph Glanville, 'Why Design Research', in Robin Jacques & James A. Powell (eds), *Design, Science, Method: Proceedings of the 1980 Design Research Society conference* (Guildford: Westbury House, 1981); Christopher Frayling, 'Research in Art and Design', *Royal College of Art Research Papers*, vol. 1 no. 1 (1993/94), pp. 1–5; Peter Downton, *Design Research* (Melbourne: RMIT Publishing, 2003).

2 Ken Friedman, 'Theory Construction in Design Research. Criteria, Approaches, and Methods', *Design Studies*, vol. 24 no. 6 (2003), pp. 507–22; several academics have also expressed such views in (unpublished) peer review feedback and assessment of research funding applications.

3 Nigel Cross, 'Designerly Ways of Knowing: Design Discipline versus Design Science', *Design Issues*, vol. 17 no. 3 (Summer 2001), pp. 49–55.

4 For example, see: Ilpo Koskinen, John Zimmerman, Thomas Binder, Johan Redstrom & Stephan Wensveen, *Design Research Through Practice: From the Lab, Field and Showroom* (Waltham, Mass: Morgan Kaufmann, 2011); Simon Grand & Wolfgang Jonas (eds), *Mapping Design Research* (Basel: Birkhauser, 2012).

5 Downton argues that the verb 'knowing' is more appropriate than the noun 'knowledge' in his consideration of the epistemology of design research.

6 Frayling, 'Research in Art and Design'.

7 Downton, *Design Research*.

8 'The Ageing of Aquarius: Designing New Housing Solutions for Australia's Baby Boomers', RMIT University, Melbourne, Australia (2002–3). The investigators were: Shane Murray, Professor M. Berry, Peter Downton, and the industry partner was Mirvac Property Ltd. The project was funded through Australian Research Council Linkage Projects Funding.

9 Shane Murray, 'Architectural Design and Discourse', *Architectural Design Research: Project-based Design Research and Discourse on Design*, vol. 1 no. 1 (2005), pp. 83–102. My thinking around design research was developed with colleagues, including Leon van Schaik and Peter Downton, during my long-time involvement with the Architecture Programme at RMIT University.

10 MAS (Monash Architecture Studio) was co-founded by myself and Diego Ramirez-Lovering. The current research team includes Shane Murray, Diego Ramirez-Lovering, Nigel Bertram, Catherine Murphy, Lee-Anne Khor, Rutger Pasman, Deborah Rowe, Barend Meyer and Tom Morgan.

11 Peter Newton et al, 'Towards a New Development Model for Housing Regeneration in Greyfield Residential Precincts' (Australian Housing and Urban Research Institute, July 2011), viewable at the Australian Housing and Urban Research Institute website, http://www.ahuri.edu.au/publications/p50593/ (accessed 5 January 2013).

12 'Investigative Panels are designed to bring about direct engagement between experts from the research and policy communities, and potentially practitioners from industry and community sectors … The process will draw on the existing evidence base and the experience and expertise of the members of the Investigative Panel … This research vehicle is designed to address

single questions that are of immediate practical relevance to policy development ... researchers are encouraged to devise their own process for running Investigative Panels ... It is important to treat the Investigative Panel as a research method and explain how this process contributes to the generation of new knowledge ... Researchers are encouraged to be innovative in the form that reports take, and in proposing other outputs that may be generated by this process'. This extract is taken from AHURI's research agenda, which is viewable at the Australian Housing and Urban Research Institute website, http://www.ahuri.edu.au/downloads/Research_Agenda/NHRP/2013/AHURI_NHRP_2013_Guidelines_for_applicants.pdf, (accessed 5 January 2013).

13   Matthew Guy, Minister of Planning for the State Government of Victoria in 2012, 'Bold new vision for expanded Melbourne CBD', 17 February 2012, viewable at the State Government of Victoria website, http://www.premier.vic.gov.au/media-centre/media-releases/3179-bold-vision-for-expanded-melbourne-cbd.html (accessed 5 January 2013).

14   Grant McArthur, 'Mega Melbourne plan for skyscrapers in the suburbs', The Herald Sun, 17 February 2012, viewable at The Herald Sun website, http://www.heraldsun.com.au/news/victoria/mega-melbourne-plan-for-skyscrapers/story-fn7x8me2-1226273223639 (accessed 5 January 2013).

15   Shane Murray, 'Architectural Design and Discourse', Unpublished PhD Thesis, RMIT University, Melbourne, Australia (2004). The supervisors were Leon van Schaik at RMIT University and John Macarthur at the University of Queensland, and the thesis was undertaken as part of RMIT's 'invitational stream' of practice-based architectural doctorates.

A WAY WITH WORDS: FEMINISTS WRITING ARCHITECTURAL DESIGN RESEARCH

Jane Rendell

Architecture could be defined as a subject that operates using a number of different disciplinary research methodologies, and four in particular: those of science in the building sciences area; those of the social sciences and the humanities in the study of buildings in terms of culture and society; history and theory; and those of practice-led research in architectural design. To date (and rather bizarrely given that the core activity of architecture is the design of buildings) the most dominant academic modes of research have been science- and humanities-based, and work in both these areas has often been conducted in ways that is rather self-contained and which often follows accepted and long-standing methodologies.[1] This situation has changed recently though, slowly at first, and now rather more rapidly, such that design or practice-led research is coming to be recognised as one of architecture's core research activities – and at the same time, different strands of architectural research are talking to each other and starting to loosen their historic methodological attachments.

In lots of subtle, but important, ways, design research differs from more traditional modes of research, for example, by reversing the order of research methods. Instead of posing research questions and then finding answers, in much design research the process operates through generative modes, producing works at the outset that may then be reflected upon later. And, in terms of context, while a researcher in the humanities might first explore the context or background for a research question in order to find out the current state of knowledge in a specific field, in some cases design researchers will investigate ideas through the production of a work first, and then later consider the larger field to ask who else is researching the same questions, in order to argue how the particular knowledge they have generated is original.

In academic research there has been a shift over the past decade towards supporting multi- and interdisciplinary research. Although the two terms are often used interchangeably, I understand them to mean quite different things. Multidisciplinary research for me describes a way of working where a number of disciplines are present but maintain their own distinct identities and ways of doing things; whereas in interdisciplinary research individuals operate between, across and at the edge of their disciplines and in so doing question the ways in which they usually work. This can occur when one individual's work moves from one discipline to another, and it can also occur when individuals from different disciplines work with one another getting closely engaged in the procedures and ideologies that structure each other's research modes and practice paradigms.

For a subject like architecture, which already involves a number of different disciplinary processes, this support for interdisciplinary research by those that fund and assess research has the possibility of opening up opportunities. However, since such a turn towards the interdisciplinary has been paralleled, in the UK at least, by a call for applied work or research that has impact beyond the sphere of the academy, the situation is not without tensions. Certain definitions of 'application' run counter to the qualities of interdisciplinary research as those in the humanities have understood them historically. In calling for interdisciplinary *and*, or even *as*, applied research, the very particular ways of working that come out of arts and humanities research, which are often critical in intention, may be subsumed in relation to those methods supported by those who have 'industry links'. If we are not careful, this could lead to the marginalisation of those areas that do not immediately and obviously demonstrate economic or corporate benefit.

Of the different modes of architectural research, it is design which appears to offer the most potent set of possibilities in the field of application. Yet architectural design research can have many different purposes. It is certainly possible, and some do argue that architectural design research should be driven by the logic of 'application' and the need to solve problems, to produce artefacts that are functionally useful and can be 'taken to market'. However, it is also the case that architectural design research can raise questions rather than provide answers, and it can make 'problematic' artefacts whose function is to pose critiques of architecture's position and role – cultural, economic, ideological, material, political and social.

Architectural design research that puts forward questions and/or reflects on its own methods can be productive of new knowledge in research terms, but increasingly such knowledge may not be valued if it is not seen to be of direct relevance to the needs of commerce and industry. In the wake of the disastrous outcomes for the economy visited on the majority by the international banking sector, we find the British government – amongst many others – willing to sacrifice the public good. Rather than take measures to redistribute the assets acquired by the financial élite, they have instigated so-called 'austerity' measures, in order to balance the books, in the form of cuts to education for example. In the UK, we have seen public support for teaching in higher

education withdrawn, against fierce opposition, and the future of publicly-funded UK research is becoming increasingly tied to government agendas and to the market. In such a precarious moment we need more than ever to protect interdisciplinary research, for rather than adopt the underlying neoliberal agendas of the architectural profession and construction industry, this kind of work often produces critiques of the capitalist system of building production, acquisition and use.

In exploring questions of method or process that discussions of interdisciplinarity inevitably bring to the fore, Julia Kristeva has argued for the construction of 'a diagonal axis':

> Interdisciplinarity is always a site where expressions of resistance are latent. Many academics are locked within the specificity of their field: that is a fact ... the first obstacle is often linked to individual competence, coupled with a tendency to jealously protect one's own domain. Specialists are often too protective of their own prerogatives, do not actually work with other colleagues, and therefore do not teach their students to construct a diagonal axis in their methodology.[2]

In my view, engaging with this diagonal axis demands that we call into question what we normally take for granted: in other words, that we question our methodologies, the way we do things, and our terminologies, the words we give to the things we do. The construction of 'a diagonal axis' is necessarily a difficult business. Kristeva's phrase 'expressions of resistance' points to the unconscious operations at work in interdisciplinary practice. And the cultural theorist Homi Bhabha also describes the encounter between disciplines in psychoanalytic terms as an 'ambivalent movement between pedagogical and performative address' – thereby suggesting that we are both attracted by and fearful of the interdisciplinary.[3]

It is precisely for this reason that I am a passionate advocate for interdisciplinarity, because such projects are for me critical, ethical and political and also emotional – interdisciplinary work *is* difficult, not only materially and intellectually, but also psychically. In demanding that we exchange what we know for what we do *not* know, and that we give up the safety of competence and specialism, and instead enter a terrain beset with fears of inability, lack of expertise and the dangers of failure, the transformational experience of interdisciplinary work produces a potentially destabilising engagement with existing power structures, allowing the emergence of fragile forms of new and untested experience, knowledge, and understanding. It engenders multiple modes of operation, which explore the boundaries of disciplinary knowledge in order to reveal and expose the workings of power.[4] This is in order to allow for the emergence of marginal and often complex forms of research that are at once questioning of dominant ideological and economic systems and capable of proposing alternatives.

In this chapter I will go on to explore three of these more alternative forms of architectural design research. First, I will consider 'critical spatial practice' as one way of investigating the multiple possibilities of interdisciplinary architectural design research, particularly through the practice of muf architecture/art; second, I will examine, with special reference to the projects of Jennifer Bloomer, a specifically feminist mode of critical spatial practice which places emphasis on subjectivity and which also

emphasises the critical and creative role of writing in architectural design research; third, and finally, I will offer some reflections on my own practice of site-writing, as a form of architectural design research which through acts of configuration aims to produce textual spaces which relate the spatial experiences of writing and reading.[5]

CRITICAL SPATIAL PRACTICE

In 2003 I came up with the term 'critical spatial practice' to describe projects located between art and architecture, and the standpoints theory offered for playing out disciplinary definitions.[6] I developed this concept further in my book, *Art and Architecture: A Place Between*, in which I defined a series of projects located between art and architecture as critical spatial practice since they critiqued both the sites into which they intervened as well as the disciplinary procedures through which they operated. I argued that such projects were situated at a triple crossroads: between theory and practice, between art and architecture, and between public and private, and I was keen to stress three particular qualities that arose from this condition. First, I proposed that the definition of the term 'critical', as taken from Frankfurt School critical theory, be extended to encompass practice – particularly those critical practices that involved self-reflection and the desire for social change, that sought to transform rather than to only describe.[7] Second, and drawing on the work of Michael de Certeau and Henri Lefebvre, I made a distinction between those strategies (for de Certeau) or representations of space (for Lefebvre) that aimed to maintain and reinforce existing social and spatial orders, and those tactics (for de Certeau) and spaces of representation (for Lefebvre) that sought to critique and question them, defining the latter as 'critical spatial practices'.[8] Third, I was most interested in practices which desired to investigate the limits of their particular disciplinary procedures and to explore the interdisciplinary processes at work in between them.

I found Edward Soja's examination of the interrelation of the conceptual categories of space, time and social being to be highly productive.[9] Reading his texts suggested to me that my understanding of critical spatial practice, in terms of the interdisciplinary place between art and architecture, needed to be understood through three distinct aspects: the spatial, the temporal and the social. To explore this further, I would like to focus here on the work of muf architecture/art – as an example of an architectural design practice drawn from my exploration of the social aspect of 'a place between' – in order to examine how the 'work' of architectural design research can be understood less as a set of 'things' or 'objects', and more as a series of exchanges that take place between people through such processes as collaboration.

It is worth starting out by considering an early work, which in many ways began to define muf's approach. In Hanley, in 1998, muf architecture/ art won an open competition set up by Stoke City Council with the Public Art Commissioning Agency.[10] The brief was to make a lifting barrier to prevent illegal traffic entering Hanley town centre, and was part of a larger urban regeneration project. In dialogue with the council planner at an initial stage of the project, the brief was opened out to reveal how 'art can contribute to a safer, more social environment'.[11] The proposal was to make two ceramic benches in close collaboration with Armitage Shanks, the British sanitaryware manufacturers, from a design generated by muf. The Stoke area has a strong tradition of ceramic production, today branching out into sanitary ware, and this was the inspiration for the design of the bench, ceramic patterned with oversized fragments of a blue dinner plate design positioned among white birches and roses. Projected overhead, in close physical proximity to the benches, a video showing portraits of people's faces, was a documentation of the design process and underscored the roles of the benches in tracing the relationships between the various people who produced the work, as well as their position as prompts for future conversations between those who lived and worked around them about the site and its culture of ceramic production: 'We wanted to reveal this as the place where the hands of the person you sit next to on a bus or pass in the street are the hands of the person who shaped the plate from which you eat your dinner.'[12]

As an architectural practice, muf's work has made inspirational contributions to the definition of what architectural design might be over the past 20 years. There was a period in the first decade of the twenty-first century when muf was frequently criticised in mainstream architectural discourse for not actually producing any 'architecture', although I suggest that this was due to the blindness of a discourse unable to recognise architecture as the production of anything but stand-alone object-buildings. Instead, muf develop new approaches to architectural design which I would define as critical spatial practices precisely because the way of working critiques a disciplinary specific architectural design methodology that emphasises object-making.

7.1 Scheme by muf architecture/art for
Barking Town Centre, East London (2010)

7.2   'Folly' structure at Barking Town Centre

7.3 Hypocaust Pavilion at Verulanium, St Albans, Hertfordshire, by muf architecture/art (2004)

Muf's working method highlights the importance of exchange across art and architecture, the participation of users in the design process, and the importance of collaborating with other producers. For muf, the architectural design process is not solely an activity that leads to the making of a product, but is rather the location of the work itself. In their award-winning project for a new town square for Barking in East London, completed in 2010, which contains more formal urban design elements, the scheme also involved a 7 m high folly which invents an imagined and lost history for Barking. This art project, involving the participation of a diverse range of groups – for example, students from the Theatre School, elders from the Afro-Caribbean lunch club and apprentices from the

7.4   Interior of the Hypocaust Pavilion

local bricklayers' college – forms a fourth wall to the square, and was conceived by muf as integral to their architectural design approach.

In an earlier architectural project, muf's work in St Albans, UK, their brief was to protect and enclose a Roman mosaic and hypocaust. Here muf's wish was to juxtapose what was once the Roman city of Verulanium with the contemporary life of the park. This building is a simple structure with a few key elements: a roof whose underside is tilted upwards with a mirrored soffit reflecting the activities of the park and that drains into an ancient Roman well filled with pieces of crockery rejected by the archaeological dig. A glazed strip allows the passers-by to see the mosaic but also layers their reflections onto the view of the mosaic within: 'is this a football game in a Roman city or a mosaic interrupting a football game? Is this building standing in for an attitude, a methodology?'[13]

Muf's methodology is established out of a critique of the brief, and through the ensuing development of a dialogue between clients, artists, architects and various other material fabricators, between those who produce the work and those who use it. In architecture, to position a building as a 'methodology' rather than as the end result of the method or process that makes a building, is a radical proposition. As a form of architectural design research, muf's work therefore emphasises a particular angle to practice, which proposes that the process is the product. Such an approach is perhaps more familiar to those working in the field of fine art, for whom the terms 'social sculpture' and 'relational aesthetics' are commonplace, and where it is not hard to consider the making of relationships or the processes of materialisation to convey aesthetic values. Yet architecture and other built environment disciplines continue to be challenged by the idea that aesthetic values might not only be object-driven but also related to time, process, ethics and subjectivity. Thus muf's work remains important as an example of architectural design research that challenges a linear conception where research as a process leads to design as an object, instead showing how design is a research-led process, while research can also be thought of as a form of design.

FEMINIST CRITICAL SPATIAL PRACTICE

Although muf have never (or at least almost never!) referred to themselves as feminists, their work has had a huge influence on the development of feminist architectural design, enriching an approach which in recent times – certainly from Matrix onwards[14] – has challenged those definitions of architecture carefully guarded by the architectural profession, working collaboratively to critique the single architectural signature and resisting notions of architecture as simply a formal object.[15]

One particularly important aspect of feminist critical spatial practice has been its desire to relate theory (often, but not always feminist) to architectural design, to make connections between built practice and written text.[16] The drawn and written projects of American architect and critic, Jennifer Bloomer, have been highly influential in this respect.[17] Bloomer's work follows Derridean deconstruction, aiming to reveal the insufficiency of logical and rational structures such as spoken language to explain the world, and instead bringing into operation the irrational and subversive elements in written texts: the feminine. Her work demonstrates that the feminine, and perhaps theory, can be a radical element in architectural practice. Drawing parallels between the creation of a building, assumed to be a clean act of control and precision, and the mess of childbirth, Bloomer has questioned the gender of creativity. Through her dirty drawings and her incorporation of parts of the female anatomy – breasts, milk, fluids, blood, hatching, udders – into architecture, Bloomer generates a critique of the sterility of the architectural drawing process. The feminine in her work is to be found in the so-called slippage of words: for example, the term 'big jugs' placed within an architectural context, suggests many things, including large breasts, but she also points to the role of the feminine and female body as a container or empty signifier used to represent patriarchal ideologies.[18]

In Bloomer's writing, text has a materiality and is carefully constructed and spatially structured, operating as a metaphoric site through which imaginative narratives are explored. For Bloomer, different modes of writing express different ways of understanding architecture through the intimate and personal, the subjective as well as the objective, though sensual rather purely visual stimulation. Bloomer's text is her architecture: her textual strategies are used not only to interpret architectural drawings and spaces but also to create new notions of place and creativity, allowing links to be made between architectural design and history, theory and criticism. In this way it is possible to see that Bloomer's work offers an approach to architectural design research which emphasises the key role that writing plays in contributing to understandings of creativity in architecture both as a critical tool, but also as a form of creative production in its own right.

Another important aspect of feminist work in architectural design in the late 1990s, which has also tested architecture's professional and disciplinary boundaries, was demonstrated through the projects of architects who developed an artistic aspect of their practice, such as Maya Lin and Elizabeth Diller.

Diller showed how processes from fine art could inform the development of architectural design through a work, where feminist critiques of women's role as domestic labourers could be used to suggest a different approach to architectural design.[19]

Diller's project involved a complex choreography, where, by performing a series of folding movements similar to origami a number of shirts were ironed into perfectly useless forms. This project can be understood as a parody of the precision of housework and a reworking of the skills of the housewife perhaps for a new function: feminist architectural design! More recently, architectural designers such as Penelope Haralambidou and Yeoryia Manolopoulou have critiqued architectural representational techniques and design processes, and offered instead new approaches to drawing and design, such as 'blossoming' in the case of Haralambidou and 'chance' and 'indeterminacy' for Manolopoulou.[20] While these projects are not explicitly feminist, they do offer new design processes and approaches which resonate with the critiques of representation offered by feminism.

Other architects have worked and continue to do so with or as artists and other spatial practitioners

7.5 Elizabeth Diller and Ricardo Scofidio, 'Bad Press: Dissident Ironing' project (1993-8)

in the public spaces of the city expanding the definition of what constitutes architectural or urban design.[21] Collaborating with those operating through other modes of spatial practice – for example in dance, film, art and writing – has provided architecture and urbanism with new feminist spatial tactics and strategies, whereby the role of audience, user and critic has become increasingly vital to the construction of subjectivity through aesthetic and spatial processes.[22] In working across the boundary between theory and practice, and between architecture and other disciplines, these significant and influential feminist projects of the 1990s informed by a political concern with subjectivity offer critiques of disciplinary boundaries and procedures.[23] Their work suggests new modes of enquiry and action which have moved from providing a gendered critique of architecture and its multiple forms of representation, to the production of work inside and outside the academy and profession where subjects, selves and spaces are understood to be performed and constructed rather than simply represented.

The infusion of the insights of psychoanalysis into architectural theory in recent years has helped to destabilise understandings of the boundaries between the subject of architecture and the researching subject him/herself. Although architecture has been informed for quite some time by psychoanalysis at the level of the theoretical analysis, critique and interpretation of buildings, images and texts, what is new in work in this area is the degree to which understandings of subjectivity and performativity are informing the ways in which subjects are constructed, as well as texts and works. Formerly rather underdeveloped,

especially in comparison to practice-led research in the visual and performing arts, this has helped to increase the level of self-reflection in debates around architectural design. The particular angle that architecture as a spatial discipline offers to this discourse is a materialised and conceptual understanding of the position or situated-ness of the architectural designer or writer herself, and thus the interior as well as exterior relations between criticism and practice in research.[24] Through the theme of 'architecture-writing', I have been keen to bring the discussions on art-writing, which engage closely with debates around criticism and critical practice in the visual and spatial arts, into architecture in order to re-examine the relation between criticism and design practice – such that criticism might be understood as a form of creative production, rather like design, while design itself might be considered as a self-reflective process which can offer critical insights.[25] Reformulating the relation between criticism and design plays an important role in re-conceptualising architectural design research, allowing design to play a role in critical analysis, and criticism to perform creatively.

SITE-WRITING

In my own architectural design research, as a critical spatial practitioner, I have suggested that, with their responsibility to convey an experience of the work to another audience, the critic occupies a discrete position as mediator and that his or her *situatedness* conditions the performance of his/her interpretative role.[26] Site-writing, in taking the location of the critic with respect to his/her object of study or subject matter, as a determining factor in the construction of a critical position, questions the terms of reference that relate the critic to the work positioned 'under' critique. Instead it proposes alternative positions, so functioning as a mode of practice in its own right. This is an active writing, which aims to perform the spatial qualities of an artwork or piece of architecture through textual approaches, reconfiguring the sites between critic and work, essay and reader, as an 'architecture' of criticism.[27] Here site-writing operates as a form of architectural design research exploring how architectural processes of structuring and detailing spaces through can work through textual media, offering new insights into what architecture is and what it might be.

To Miss the Desert was a site-writing written in response to Nathan Coley's *Black Tent* (2003), curated by Gavin Wade.[28] *Black Tent* had developed out of Coley's interest in sanctuaries in general, but particularly the evocative and precise description of the construction of the tabernacle given in the Bible.[29] Wade had read a piece of my writing in which I questioned whether it was possible to 'write architecture', rather than to 'write about architecture', and so he asked me to 'write a tabernacle'. I felt that the text in the Bible had already written the tabernacle, so I decided instead to write *Black Tent*.

Black Tent consisted of a flexible structure, a number of steel-framed panels with black fabric screens stretched across them, and smaller 'windows' inserted into them. *Black Tent* moved to five sites in Portsmouth, reconfiguring itself for each location. My essay echoed aspects of *Black Tent*: each of its five sections was composed around a different spatial boundary condition, such as 'around the edge'. Yet in order to critique Coley's choice of sanctuary as a specifically religious and Judeo-Christian one, my choice of

spatial motif was the secular sanctuary of home.[30] Like the squares, the voice of my text was two-sided, setting up a dynamic between private and public sanctuary. One side of my piece remembered a childhood spent in various nomadic cultures in the Middle East. The other adopted a more professional tone by taking texts from construction specifications that I had written when designing contemporary sanctuaries – a series of community buildings for different so-called minority groups.[31]

A couple of years later, for an exhibition entitled 'Spatial Imagination', I selected 'scenes' from this essay and reconfigured them into a text, three by four, in response to the grid of a window, on which I wrote the word 'purdah' on the glass in black kohl eye liner. This two-part text installation *An Embellishment: Purdah* – one part sited in a book and the other in a building – responded to the window as a boundary condition, performing the interface between inside and outside.[32]

The discipline of performance studies is increasingly becoming a central reference point for feminists writing in architecture, mainly because it is within performance practice – including theatre, but also more specifically in performance writing – that one finds the conceptual depth to the thinking-through of 'performativity'.[33] The autobiographical approach to Peggy Phelan's commentaries on performance art have informed a mode of writing criticism that declares its own performativity and the presence of the body of the critic in the writing as 'marked'.[34] In drawing attention to the conditions of its own making at the level of the signifier, not only the signified, much autobiographical writing is performative. In Della Pollock's highly informative discussion of the key qualities of performance writing,

7.6   Jane Rendell, *An Embellishment: Purdah*
in the 'Spatial Imagination' exhibition at the
domoBaal Gallery, London (2006)

she includes being subjective, as well as evocative, metonymic, nervous, citational and consequential as exceptional aspects of this type of writing.[35] For the art critic Gavin Butt, the attempt by critics and practitioners to 'renew criticism's energies' within fine art occurs specifically through a 'theatrical turn'.[36]

Across the arena of experimental and critical writing, new possibilities are being invented, often performative, which question the distanced objectivity of academic writing styles.[37] This includes artists producing text-based works,[38] writers exploring the poetics of criticism,[39] as well as performance writers,[40] poet-artist practitioners,[41] and philosophers who question subjectivity through alternative visual writing forms.[42] Spatial practitioners can draw inspiration from this intensely creative and theoretically rigorous strand of speculative criticism, yet within it there is also a very particular focus for those engaged in architecture: to enhance writing's spatial qualities and in so doing to explore the 'position' of the writer through the spatial and material qualities of the text. This approach brings writing closer to architectural design processes and so to the heart of architectural design research, showing how writing is not only a way of communicating research findings, but also a tool through which to investigate architectural ideas, and at the same time allowing writing to indicate different spatial, material and conceptual possibilities for ways of knowing and being in architectural design research.

Undoing Architecture was the first piece of writing where I juxtaposed my own voice with those of various critical theorists, and referred to my own life as the subject matter for theoretical reflection.[43] This incorporation of the personal into the critical had different kinds of effect depending on the reader, and so raised many questions for me concerning the ethical responsibility a writer has to those others who become subjects or characters in a narrative form. The essay was inspired by a house where I had lived with a co-inhabitant who invented an unusual mode of DIY, much of which involved the removal of building elements, as well as the use of objects against the purposes for which they were originally designed.

The text was a trialogue constructed out of eleven scenes, in which three voices performed the doing, undoing and overdoing of architecture. My own practice of living or 'overdoing' architecture followed my ambivalence towards the trajectory of a form of DIY set against the grain. This was positioned as a third voice, in fluctuating allegiance, between the 'father' who set out normative procedures for 'doing' architecture, described in terms of the modernist design principles still largely adhered to by the profession, and the 'mother' of feminist critique, Luce Irigaray and Hélène Cixous, whose words of 'undoing' suggested alternative modes of writing and using space which differed from the masculine economy of appropriation and the self-same.

Several years later I produced another triadic text in which I also referred to my personal life as subject matter for architectural criticism. It drew attention to the subject not simply as a research topic for architectural design, but also to the figure of the researcher herself as an embodied subject who brings specific emotions and life experiences to inform her investigations into and through architecture and design. This time the work took the form of a text-based installation positioned

*ARCHITECTONICS – 'A SERIES OF PROCEDURES FOR THE MATERIAL
ORGANISATION AND STRUCTURING OF SPACE.'*

on a public street. With voices drawn from autobiography, psychoanalytic theory and building specifications, *Confessional Construction* explored the confession as a form of story telling which concealed rather than revealed the 'I' of the author.[44] In order to demonstrate how material concerned with an interior can be used to build an exterior covering, the text comprised a main statement – an autobiographical detail – interwoven with more critical reflections from upon what it means to confess. Footnotes consisting of architectural specifications concerning the detailing of walls and openings were located down the side of the page, numbered from bottom to top, to read upwards as one builds a wall.

Although some critics are also beginning to consider the possibilities that the written medium of their work affords, fewer have actively exploited the material possibilities of texts for architectural design research. These possibilities include the patterning of words on a page, the design of a page itself – its edges, boundaries, thresholds, surfaces, or the relation of one page to another. The literary critic Mary Ann Caws's concept of 'architexture' is helpful here in allowing us to take texts – that is, structures which are not buildings – as architecture, a move which is rather more closely guarded against in architecture itself, where the professional view still tends to dominate. As a term that refers to the act of reading rather than writing, for Caws, architexture 'situates the text in the world of other texts', thus drawing attention to the surface and texture of the text, and suggesting rather implicitly (or certainly this is what I draw out of her work) that we might consider the text as a form of material construction or architecture.[45] And if not architecture, then surely we can agree that

each medium has its own architectonics – a series of procedures for the material organisation and structuring of space – and that coming to understand the architectonics of writing offers a new way of imagining architectural design.

Responding to a collection of essays constructing a debate between the seemingly opposite facing disciplines of urbanism and interiors – one looking outwards to the spaces of the city, the other towards the world inside buildings – I will now move on to describe a piece of site-writing configured as a series of *intermezzos* inserted into the book as a built structure. An *intermezzo* is a composition that fits between other musical or dramatic entities, such as acts of a play or movements of a larger musical work. In this context, the *intermezzo* consisted of double-sided 'joints' that were located between the interior territories of the nine essays situated within the larger-scaled 'urban' texture of the book. I took the first line and last line to constitute the exterior edge of each essay, and responding to the content of these texts through association, I positioned quotes from other practitioners and theorists which touched on similar subjects, objects and spaces, back-to-back on pages inserted between the essays.[46] The result was to create a series of interfaces between adjacent 'interiors'.[47]

Opportunities for producing this kind of work, and for developing its critical and creative potential, are now finally possible because of the emerging body of architectural design research exploring the spatial qualities of writing. This can be seen, for example, as a form of materialised philosophy in the work of Hélene Frichot,[48] Stephen Loo, Peg Rawes[49] and Katie Lloyd Thomas; or as poetic practice in the artefacts and texts created by Linda Maria Walker;[50]

architecture and landscape criticism in the essays of Katja Grillner[51] and Sarah Treadwell;[52] and architectural theory in the performative texts of Katarina Bonnevier[53] and Naomi Stead.[54] With the current flourishing of this field, the time is ripe to consider how this kind of research – which takes place through writing as a form of designing – defines a new relation between these two architectural processes.[55] This relation is no longer one of opposition or negation, nor one where writing, as a handmaid, simply documents and comments upon the architectural design research activities of 'her' master. Instead, by confronting the institutional limits of both architectural research and academic writing, feminists offer reconfigurations of architectural design research through new conceptualisations of positionality, subjectivity and textuality. You might say we are finding our way with words.[56]

Notes

1   For a more detailed discussion of architectural design research related to the RAE 2008 research assessment exercise in the UK, see Jane Rendell, 'Architectural Research and Disciplinarity', *Architectural Research Quarterly*, vol. 8 no. 2 (2004), pp. 141–7.

2   Julia Kristeva, 'Institutional Interdisciplinarity in Theory and Practice: An interview', in Alex Coles & Alexia Defert (eds), *The Anxiety of Interdisciplinarity*, De-, Dis-, Ex- (London: Black Dog, 1997), pp. 5–6.

3   Homi K. Bhabha, *The Location of Culture* (London: Routledge, 1994), p. 163. In an interview with W.J.T. Mitchell, the cultural critic Homi Bhabha discusses the operation of two different forms of interdisciplinarity in academic institutions over the past 30–40 years. The first, which he names 'Interdisciplinarity 1', assumes that different disciplines have 'foundational truths', but that by putting 'two foundations in proximity' then a 'wider base' can be created. Bhabha believes that institutions are quite comfortable with Interdisciplinarity 1, but that there is another interdisciplinary mode, which he calls 'Interdisciplinarity 2'. For Bhabha, Interdisciplinarity 2 'is not an attempt to strengthen one foundation by drawing from another; it is a reaction to the fact that we are living at the real border of our own disciplines, where some of the fundamental ideas of our discipline are being profoundly shaken'. In his view, 'questions to do with the

indeterminate, with contingency, with intertextuality, have become central – the issue of ambivalence too.' Bhabha adds: 'It's because Interdisciplinarity 2 is fired with a desire to understand more fully, and more problematically, that its posed at the point of our disciplines' liminality, and that it requires us to articulate a new and collaborative definition of the humanities'. See 'Translator Translated', (interview with cultural theorist Homi Bhabha) by W.J.T. Mitchell, *Artforum*, vol. 33 no. 7 (March 1995), pp. 80–84.

4   In Gary Genosko's excellent book on the psychoanalytic philosopher, Félix Guattari, he describes how for Guattari, the interdisciplinarity (of the 1968 movement) was compromised, in that it relied too much on the disciplines between which it was located, and served to strengthen rather than question their dominance. See Gary Genosko, *Félix Guattari: An Aberrant Introduction* (London: Continuum, 2002), p. 24. In many ways, the problems of the interdisciplinarity of 1968 as recounted by Genosko, in terms of being 'team-based', adopting 'brain-storming' and the 'growing influence of the marketplace', resonate both with the characterisation of multidisciplinarity as I have described it, and with Homi Bhabha's definition of interdisciplinarity 1 as discussed in the endnote above. However, to really interrogate the relation between these distinctions I would need to conduct a much longer piece of research thoroughly embedded in the material conditions of these two historical periods and locations: the late 1960s in France and the mid- to late 1990s in Britain and the USA. The limitations of interdisciplinarity inspire Guattari to argue instead that transdisciplinarity that holds the potential of radical critique, related, in his own philosophy, to 'transversality … explicitly a creature of the middle'. See Genosko, *Félix Guattari*, p. 74. The 'trans-' is capable of transversal actions, which, in cutting across existing territories of knowledge, allows them to be experienced differently, thus providing new positions and perspectives.

5   The focus on writing as a potentially active form of design research has been most vibrant in the areas that work most closely with the critical and interdisciplinary methodologies of fine art practice. See, for example: Katy Macleod & Lyn Holdridge (eds), *Thinking through Art: Reflections on Art as Research* (London/New York: Routledge, 2005); Estelle Barrett & Barbara Bolt (eds), *Practice as Research: Context, Method, Knowledge* (London: IB Tauris, 2007), and Marquard Smith & Michael Ann Holly (eds), *What is Research in the Visual Arts? Obsession, Archive, and Encounter* (New Haven: Clark Art Institute/ Yale University Press, 2008).

6   I first introduced the term 'critical spatial practice' in my article on 'A Place Between Art, Architecture and Critical Theory', *Proceedings to Place and Location* (Tallinn, Estonia: 2003), pp. 221–33 (published in English and Estonian), and later consolidated and developed this as a concept in *Art and Architecture: A Place Between* (London: IB Tauris, 2006). Since that time, the same term has been taken up by individuals such as Judith Rugg in her seminars at the RIBA, London, from around 2008; Eyal Weisman to describe activities as part of the MA: Research Architecture course at Goldsmiths College of Art, London; and most recently by Marcus Miessen to identify the MA: Architecture and Critical Spatial Practice launched in 2011 at the Städelschule, Frankfurt.

7 Critical theory is a phrase that generally refers to the work of a group of theorists and philosophers called the 'Frankfurt School' operating in the early twentieth century. The group included Theodor Adorno, Jurgen Habermas, Max Horkheimer, Herbert Marcuse and Walter Benjamin; and their writings are connected by their interest in the ideas of the philosopher G.W.F. Hegel, the political economist Karl Marx, and the psychoanalyst Sigmund Freud. Taken together, their work could be characterised as a rethinking or development of Marxist ideas in relation to the shifts in society, culture and economy that took place in the early decades of the twentieth century. See Raymond Geuss, *The Idea of Critical Theory: Habermas and the Frankfurt School* (Cambridge: Cambridge University Press, 1981).

8 Henri Lefebvre, *The Production of Space* (Oxford: Basil Blackwell, 1974/91); Michael de Certeau, *The Practice of Everyday Life* (Berkeley: University of California Press, 1980/88).

9 Edward Soja, *Thirdspace: Expanding the Geographical Imagination* (Oxford: Blackwell, 1996); Edward Soja, *Postmodern Geographies: The Reassertion of Space in Social Theory* (London: Verso, 1989).

10 muf architecture/art website, http://www.muf.co.uk/ (accessed 21 August 2012).

11 Katherine Shonfield, *This is What We Do: A MUF Manual* (London: Ellipsis, 2001), p. 92.

12 Ibid.

13 Ibid., p. 151.

14 Matrix, *Making Space: Women and the Man Made Environment* (London: Pluto Press, 1984).

15 There are currently many fascinating versions of a collective feminist critical spatial practice. See for example, the work of FATALE at the KTH Stockholm School of Architecture website, http://researchprojects.kth.se/index.php/kb_7796/io_10197/io.html (accessed 21 August 2012) and further discussion in Chapter 5 of this book, and also the taking place group at Katie Lloyd Thomas, Helen Stratford & Teresa Hoskyns, 'Taking Place', *Scroope*, vol. 14 (2002), pp. 44-8; Doina Petrescu & Teresa Hoskyns, 'Taking Place and Altering it', in Doina Petrescu (ed.), *Altering Practices: Feminist Politics and Poetics of Space* (London: Routledge, 2007), pp. 15-38; and so on. Most recently, there has been the emergence of the Parlour website, http://www.archiparlour.org/, an Australian website debating women, equity and architecture, and also texts such as Lori A. Brown (ed.), *Feminist Practices: Interdisciplinary Approaches to Women in Architecture* (Farnham: Ashgate, 2012).

16 muf, *Architectural Design*, vol. 66 no.7-8 (August 1996), pp. 80-83; Amy Landesberg & Lisa Quatrale, 'See Angel Touch', in Debra Coleman, Elizabeth Danze & Carol Henderson (eds), *Architecture and Feminism* (New York: Princeton Architectural Press, 1996), pp. 60-71.

17 Jennifer Bloomer, 'Big Jugs', in Arthur Kroker & Marilouise Kroker (eds), *The Hysterical Male: New Feminist Theory* (London: Macmillan Education 1991), pp. 13-27; Jennifer Bloomer, *Architecture and the Text: the (S)crypts of Joyce and Piranesi* (New Haven and London: Yale University Press, 1993).

18 This type of feminist work influenced a number of other architectural design projects, which, drawing on theoretical concerns, stimulated new forms of design, from the choosing of site to the articulation of services. In work of Clare Robinson, this is clearly formulated in a project which redefines site as *chora* or female container. For Michelle Kauffman, the gaps between buildings and occupied by women in patriarchy gave rise to a design project based on a lacuna wall. See Claire Robinson, 'Chora Work', 'Dear Jennifer', *ANY*, vol. 4 (January/February 1994), pp. 34-7; Michelle Kaufman 'Liquidation, Amalgamation', 'Dear Jennifer', *ANY*, vol. 4 (January/February 1994), pp. 38-9.

19 Elizabeth Diller, 'Bad Press', in Francesca Hughes (ed.), *The Architect: Reconstructing Her Practice* (Cambridge, Mass: MIT Press, 1996), pp. 74-94.

20 See for example, Penelope Haralambidou, *The Blossoming of Perspective* (London: domoBaal Editions, 2007); Penelope Haralambidou, *Marcel Duchamp and the Architecture of Desire* (Farnham, Surrey: Ashgate, 2013); Yeoryia Manolopoulou, 'Drawing on Chance: Drafting Pier 40', *Journal of Architecture*, vol. 11 no. 3 (2006), pp. 303-14; Yeoryia Manolopoulou, *Architectures of Chance* (Farnham, Surrey: Ashgate, 2013).

21 See for example: Nina Felshin, *But is it Art?: The Spirit of Art as Activism* (Seattle: Bay Press, 1995); Suzanne Lacy (ed.), *Mapping the Terrain: New Genre Public Art* (Seattle: Bay Press, 1995).

22 See the collaborations between Dorita Hannah (performance design and scenographer) and Carol Brown (dancer and choreographer) in, for example, *HER TOPIA: A Dance Architecture Event* (Athens: Duncan Dance Centre of Research in Greece, 2005). See also the Carol Brown Dances website, http://www.carolbrowndances.com/gallery.php (accessed 2 September 2012), and also Dorita Hannah & Olav Harslof (eds), *Performance Design* (Copenhagen: Museum Tusculanum Press, 2008).

23 See the fascinating recent analysis of the place of gender in contemporary architectural theory anthologies from 1993 to 2010 in Karen Burns, 'A Girl's Own Adventure: Gender in the Contemporary Architectural Theory Anthology', *Journal of Architectural Education*, vol. 65 no. 2 (March 2012), pp. 125-34; Karen Burns, 'The Woman/Architect Distinction', in 'Women, Practice, Architecture', special issue of *Architectural Theory Review*, vol. 17 no. 2 (December 2012), pp. 234-44.

24 For a book aimed to address this relationship, see Jane Rendell, Jonathan Hill, Murray Fraser & Mark Dorrian (eds), *Critical Architecture* (London/New York: Routledge, 2007).

25 Jane Rendell, 'Critical Architecture: Between Criticism and Design' and 'Architecture-Writing', in Jane Rendell et al. (eds), *Critical Architecture* (London: Routledge, 2007), pp. 87-91, 150-162; Jane Rendell, 'Architecture-Writing', in 'Critical Architecture', special issue of the *Journal of Architecture*, vol. 10 no. 3 (June 2005), pp. 255-64.

26   For a discussion of the politics of spectatorship, see for example: Umberto Eco, 'The Poetics of the Open Work' (1962) in Claire Bishop (ed.), *Participation: Documents of Contemporary Art* (London/ Cambridge, Mass.: MIT Press/Whitechapel Art Gallery, 2006), pp. 20–40; Claire Bishop, *Installation Art: A Critical History* (London: Tate Publishing, 2005), pp. 13, 131.

27   Jane Rendell, *Site-Writing: The Architecture of Art Criticism* (London: IB Tauris, 2010).

28   Jane Rendell, 'To Miss the Desert', in Gavin Wade (ed.), *Nathan Coley: Black Tent* (Portsmouth: Art in Sacred Spaces, 2003), pp. 34–43.

29   Nathan Coley's fascination with places of religious worship runs through his practice. An early work, *Fourteen Churches of Münster* (2000), comprises a street plan and the view from a helicopter circling fourteen churches in that German city, which, during the Second World War, Allied bomber pilots were issued with an order to target them. *The Lamp of Sacrifice, 161 Places of Worship, Birmingham* (2000) and *The Lamp of Sacrifice, 286 Places of Worship, Edinburgh* (2004) consist of cardboard models of all the places of worship in the towns listed in the *Yellow Pages*, have been argued to express the premise of Coley's work – that architectural forms remain empty contained until socially occupied. See Martin Herbert, 'Nathan Coley, Fruitmarket Gallery Edinburgh', *Art Monthly*, vol. 278 (July–August 2004), pp. 35–7. More recent projects, such as *There Will Be No Miracles Here* (2006) at Mount Stuart, Isle of Bute, question the passivity of architecture especially in current religious conflicts. One part of the exhibition – *Camouflage Mosque, Camouflage Synagogue, Camouflage Church* – comprises three models covered in 'dazzle' camouflage, a technique applied to ships during both World Wars as protection from attack. See Andrea Schlieker, 'Negotiating the Invisible: Nathan Coley at Mount Stuart' at the Nathan Coley Studio website, http://studionathancoley.com/works/camouflage-mosquesynagoguechurch (accessed 2 September 2012).

30   Coley's interest in sanctuaries has been related to their role as places of refuge outside state control. See Nathan Coley, *Urban Sanctuary: A Public Art Work by Nathan Coley* (Glasgow: The Armpit Press, 1997); this book consists of a series of interviews with eight people, including a policeman and a *feng shui* practitioner, in which the artist asked each person what the term sanctuary meant to them and documented their answers.

31   Coley's work has examined the representation of architecture through different kinds of media simultaneously. For example, *Minster* (1998), an installation in the Tate Gallery North in Liverpool, consisted of slide projected images of a non-conformist chapel in Liverpool's Toxteth area, a recorded lecture of a guided tour of York Minster, and an explanatory pamphlet describing the correct procedure for establishing a tabernacle or portable sanctuary. See Nick Barley (ed.), *Leaving Tracks: Artranspennine98, an International Contemporary Visual Art Exhibition Recorded* (London: August Media, 1999), pp. 78–81.

32   See Jane Rendell, *An Embellishment: Purdah* (2006), in *Spatial Imagination*, an exhibition at domoBaal contemporary art gallery, London. This had an associated catalogue essay, and an essay by the author on 'An Embellishment', in Peg Rawes & Jane Rendell (eds), *Spatial Imagination* (London: The Bartlett School of Architecture, UCL, 2005), pp. 34–5. See also the Spatial Imagination website, www.spatialimagination.org.uk (accessed 8 July 2008).

33   Here I should note the work of practitioners and writers such as P.A. Skantze, Emily Orley and Ella Finer at the University of Roehampton, and Susan Melrose at the University of Middlesex.

34   Peggy Phelan, *Unmarked: Politics of Performance* (London: Routledge, 1993); Peggy Phelan, 'To Suffer a Sea Change', *The Georgia Review*, vol. 45 no. 3 (Fall 1991), pp. 507–25.

35   Della Pollock, 'Performing Writing', in Peggy Phelan & Jill Lane (eds), *The Ends of Performance* (New York: New York University Press, 1998), pp. 73–103.

36   Gavin Butt (ed.), *After Criticism: New Responses to Art and Performance* (Oxford: Blackwell Publishing, 2005).

37   See for example: Maria Fusco (ed.), 'The Dream that Kicks: Transdisciplinary Practice in Action', special issue of *a-n* (*Artists' Newsletter*) (London, 2006), and *The Happy Hypocrite*, a journal edited by Fusco.

38   Brigid McLeer, 'From "A…" to "B…": A Jealousy', in Peg Rawes and Jane Rendell (eds), *Spatial Imagination* (London: The Bartlett School of Architecture, UCL, 2005), pp. 2223, and more recent work such as Brigid McLeer, *Horizontal Ontologies: One + One (The Reading)* and *Vexations* (2012).

39   For alternative strategies of critical writing by poets and others, see for example: Juliana Spahr, Mark Wallace, Kristen Prevallet & Pam Rehm (eds) *A Poetics of Criticism* (Buffalo, New York: Leave Books, 1994).

40   Iain Biggs, *Between Carterhaugh and Tamsheil Rig: A Borderline Episode* (Bristol: Wild Conversation Press, 2004); Mike Pearson, *In comes I: Performance, Memory and Landscape* (Exeter: University of Exeter Press, 2007); Mike Pearson, *Site-Specific Performance*, (Basingstoke: Palgrave, 2010).

41   See for example: Carolyn Bergvall, *Éclat* (pdf edition, ububooks, 2004), viewable at the Ubu Books website, http://www.ubu.com/ubu/bergvall_eclat.html (accessed 8 July 2008); Carolyn Bergvall, *Fig* (Cambridge: Salt Publishing, 2005); Redell Olsen, *Book of the Fur* (Cambridge: Rem Press, 2000); Kristen Krieder, 'Toward a Material Poetics: Sign, Subject and Site', Unpublished PhD Thesis, University of London, UK, (2008).

42   See, for example: Sue Golding (Johnny de Philo) *Games of Truth: A Blood Poetics in Seven Part Harmony (This is Me Speaking to You)*, Inaugural Lecture delivered at the University of Greenwich, 27 March 2003; Yves Lomax, *Writing the Image: An Adventure with Art and Theory* (London: IB Tauris, 2000); Yves Lomax, *Sounding the Event: Escapades in Dialogue and Matters of Art, Nature and Time* (London: IB Tauris, 2005).

43   Jane Rendell, 'Doing it, (Un)Doing it, (Over)Doing it Yourself: Rhetorics of Architectural Abuse', in Jonathan Hill (ed.), *Occupying Architecture* (London: Routledge, 1998), pp. 229–46; Jane Rendell, '(Un)doing it Yourself: Rhetorics of Architectural Abuse', *The Journal of Architecture*, vol. 4 no. 1 (1999), pp. 101–10; Jane Rendell, *Site-Writing*.

44   This piece of work was originally installed as Jane Rendell, *Confessional Constructions* (2002) *LLAW*, curated by Brigid McLeer at the BookArtBookShop, London. It was then performed as part of a poetry reading at The Foundry, London, in 2003 and published as part of some longer essays: Jane Rendell, 'Between Two: Theory and Practice', in Jonathan Hill (ed.), 'Opposites Overlap', special issue of *The Journal of Architecture*, vol. 8 no. 2 (2003), pp. 221–37; Jane Rendell, 'Architectural History as Critical Practice', Elisabeth Tostrup & Christian Hermansen (eds) *Context: (Theorising) History in Architecture* (Oslo: Oslo School of Architecture, 2003), pp. 17–29; Jane Rendell, 'From Architectural History to Spatial Writing', in Elvan Altan Ergut, Dana Arnold & Belgin Turan Ozkaya (eds) *Rethinking Architectural Historiography* (London: Routledge, 2006), pp. 135–50. I also described my own performance of 'Travelling the Distance/ Encountering the Other', in David Blamey (ed.) *Here, There, Elsewhere: Dialogues on Location and Mobility* (London, Open Editions, 2002), pp. 43–54, as part of *taking place*, University of North London, November 2001, as a 'confessional construction'. A script of this performance was also published as part of Jane Rendell, 'How to Take Place (but only for so long)', in Petrescu (ed.) *Altering Practices*, pp. 69–87.

45   Mary Ann Caws, *A Metapoetics of the Passage: Architextures in Surrealism and After* (Hanover, New Hampshire/London: University Press of New England, 1981), p. xiv.

46   Psychoanalyst Christopher Bollas has noted that Freud's clearest account of his method outlined in 'Two Encyclopaedia Articles: A. Psycho-Analysis', suggests that psychoanalysis takes place if two functions are linked – the analysand's free associations and the psychoanalyst's evenly suspended attentiveness. See for example: Christopher Bollas, 'Freudian Intersubjectivity: Commentary on Paper by Julie Gerhardt and Annie Sweetnam', *Psychoanalytic Dialogues*, vol. 11 (2001), pp. 93–105; Christopher Bollas, *Free Association* (Duxford, Cambridge: Icon Books Ltd., 2002), pp. 4–7; Sigmund Freud, 'Two Encyclopedia Articles: (A) Psycho-Analysis' (1923) in *The Standard Edition of the Complete Psychological Works of Sigmund Freud, Volume 18 (1920–1922): Beyond the Pleasure Principle, Group Psychology and Other Works* (London: The Hogarth Press, 1955), pp. 235–54; Sigmund Freud, 'On Beginning the Treatment (Further Recommendations on the Technique of Psycho-Analysis I)' (1913), in *The Standard Edition of the Complete Psychological Works of Sigmund Freud, Volume 12 (1911–1913): The Case of Schreber, Papers on Technique and Other Works* (London: The Hogarth Press, 1958), pp. 121–44.

47   Jane Rendell, 'Intermezzo', in Rochus Hinkel (ed.), *Urban Interior: Informal Explorations, Interventions and Occupations* (Baunach, Germany: Spurbuchverlag, 2011).

48   Hélène Frichot, 'Following Hélène Cixous's Steps Towards a Writing Architecture', in 'Writing Architecture', special issue of *Architecture Theory Review*, vol. 15 no. 3 (2010), pp. 312–23; Hélène Frichot, 'I Would Prefer Not To: How Bartleby's Formula Troubles Collective Design Practices', in conference convened by Harriet Edquist & Laurene Vaughan on 'Geoplaced Knowledges', 9 July 2010, Design Research Institute, RMIT University, Melbourne.

49   See for example: Peg Rawes, 'Plenums: Re-thinking Matter, Geometry and Subjectivity', in Katie Lloyd Thomas (ed.), *Material Matters: Architecture and Material Practice* (London: Routledge, 2006), pp. 55–66.

50   Linda Marie Walker, 'Of Restless Goings-On, and Actual Dyings', *Angelaki*, vol. 11 no. 1 (April 2006), pp. 117–26; Linda Marie Walker, 'My Friends the Birds', in Barbara Bolt, Felicity Colman, Graham Jones & Ashley Woodward (eds), *Sensorium: Aesthetics, Art, Life* (Newcastle: Cambridge Scholars Publishing, 2007); Linda Marie Walker,' So On, And' in 'Entr'acte: Interval', *Architecture Theory Review*, vol. 16 no. 2 (2011), pp. 157–76; Linda Marie Walker, 'Writing, A Little Machine', *Architecture Theory Review*, vol. 17 no. 1 (2012), pp. 40–51.

51   AKAD: The Academy of for Practice-based Research in Architecture and Design website, http://www.akad.se/progwri.htm (accessed 21 August 2012); Katja Grillner, 'Writing and Landscape – Setting Scenes for Critical Reflection', in Jonathan Hill (ed.), 'Opposites Overlap', special issue of *The Journal of Architecture*, vol. 8 no. 2 (2003), pp. 239–49; Katja Grillner, 'Ramble, Linger and Gaze: Dialogues from the Landscape Garden', Unpublished PhD Thesis (2000), KTH Stockholm, Sweden.

52   Sarah Treadwell, 'Pink and White Descriptions', in Naomi Stead & Lee Stickell (eds), 'Writing Architecture', special issue of *Architecture Theory Review*, vol. 15 no. 3 (2010), pp. 266–80.

53   Katerina Bonnevier, *Behind Straight Curtains: Towards a Queer Feminist Theory of Architecture* (Stockholm: Axl Books, 2007).

54   Naomi Stead (ed.), *Semi-Detached: Writing, Representation and Criticism in Architecture* (Melbourne: Uro Media, 2012); Naomi Stead, 'Writing the City, or, The Story of a Sydney Walk', in *NORA – Nordic Journal of Feminist and Gender Research*, vol. 18 no. 4 (December 2010), pp. 226–45; Naomi Stead, 'If on a Winter's Day a Tourist: Writing the Experience of Stockholm', *Architectural Theory Review*, vol. 14 no. 2 (August 2009), pp. 108–18; Naomi Stead, Katrina Schlunke & Trina Day, 'Sydney Letters,' in *Mapping Sydney: Experimental Cartography and the Imagined City* (Sydney: Local Consumption Publications, 2009), unpaginated exhibition catalogue.

55   The issue of the timeliness of this strand of feminist interdisciplinary writing has been addressed directly by the feminist sociologist, Mona Livholts, who with sensitivity and humour draws on performative techniques to describe the sexism of academia. See for example: Mona Livholts, 'The Snow Angel and Other Imprints: An Untimely Academic Novella', *International Review of Qualitative Research*, vol. 3 no. 1 (2010), pp. 103–24; Mona Livholts, 'The Professor's Chair: an Untimely Academic Novella', *Life-Writing*, vol. 7 no. 2 (2010), pp. 155–68; Mona Livholts (ed.), *Emergent Writing Methodologies in Feminist Studies* (London: Routledge, 2012).

56   'A way with words', rather than 'away with the fairies': I use 'finding' to evoke the ongoing present tense, as an indirect gesture of thanks to Hélène Cixous and her magnificent essay on 'Coming to Writing', which has served as a source of inspiration for many of the writers that I reference here, including myself: See Hélène Cixous, 'Coming to Writing' (1977), in Hélène Cixous, *'Coming to Writing' and Other Essays*, as edited by Deborah Jenson (Cambridge, Mass: Harvard University Press, 1991). Cixous writes on page 4 of that essay: 'Writing is good: it's what never ends'.

Plate 9   Overview of the PhD exhibition on
'displacement' by Arnaud Hendrickx from the
Sint-Lucas School of Architecture, held in an
old industrial building in Brussels cleaned up
for the purpose

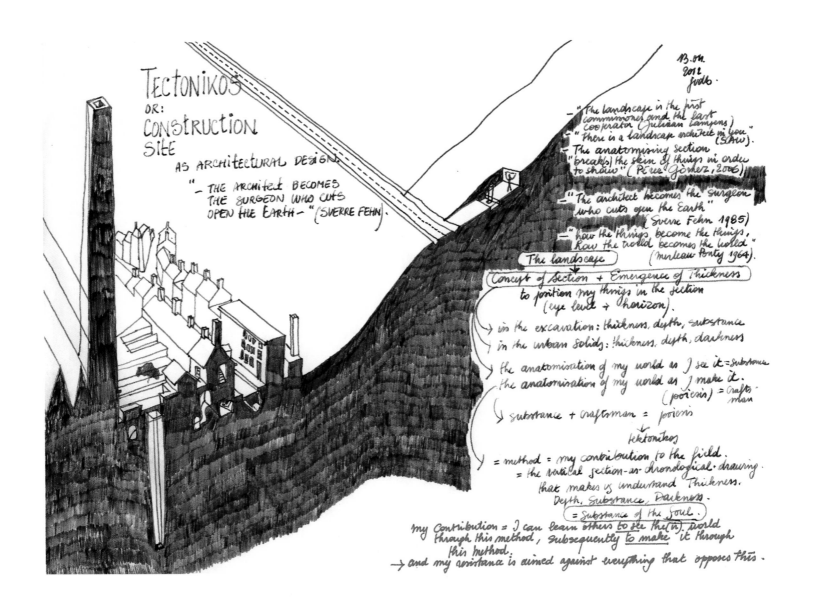

Plate 10 Imaginary section drawn by Johan Van Den Berghe through his grandmother's house in an old Belgian industrial town to help organise his thoughts and projects for his design doctorate at the Sint-Lucas School

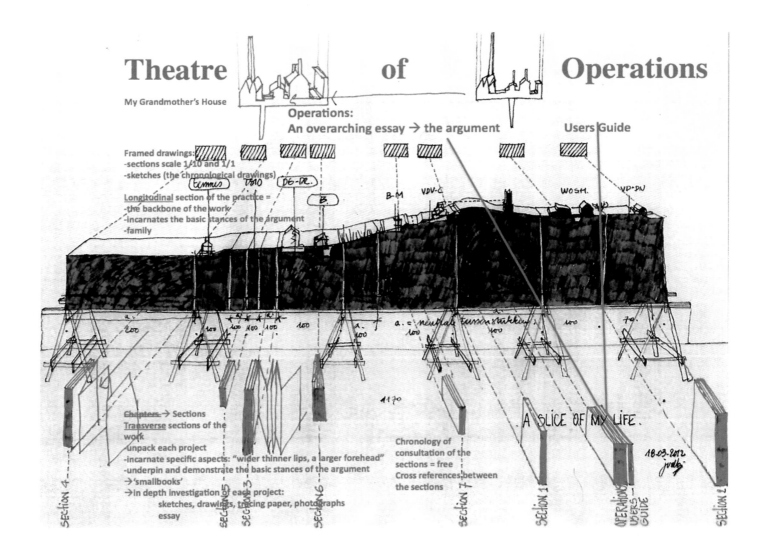

Theatre of Operations

My Grandmother's House

Operations:
An overarching essay → the argument   Users Guide

Framed drawings:
-sections scale 1/10 and 1/1
-sketches (the chronological drawings)

<u>Longitudinal</u> section of the practice =
-the backbone of the work
-incarnates the basic stances of the argument
-family

tammus   T910   DG-DR.   B   B-M   VDV-C   WOSH.   VD-DN

<u>Chapters</u> → Sections
<u>Transverse</u> sections of the work
-unpack each project
-incarnate specific aspects: "wider thinner lips, a larger forehead"
-underpin and demonstrate the basic stances of the argument
→ 'smallbooks'
→ in depth investigation of each project:
    sketches, drawings, tracing paper, photographs
    essay

Chronology of consultation of the sections = free Cross references between the sections

A SLICE OF MY LIFE.

1170   18-03-2012 jvdbj

SECTION 4   SECTION 5   SECTION 3   SECTION 6   SECTION 7   SECTION 1   OPERATIONS USERS GUIDE   SECTION 2

a. = neutrale tussenstukken

Plate 11   Sketch design for the final
exhibition of PhD research work by
Johan Van Den Berghe

Plate 12   Large sectional model for the final
exhibition by Johan Van Den Berghe, bringing
together scaled models of real and imaginary
design projects in an attempt to synthesise the
main conclusions of his PhD research

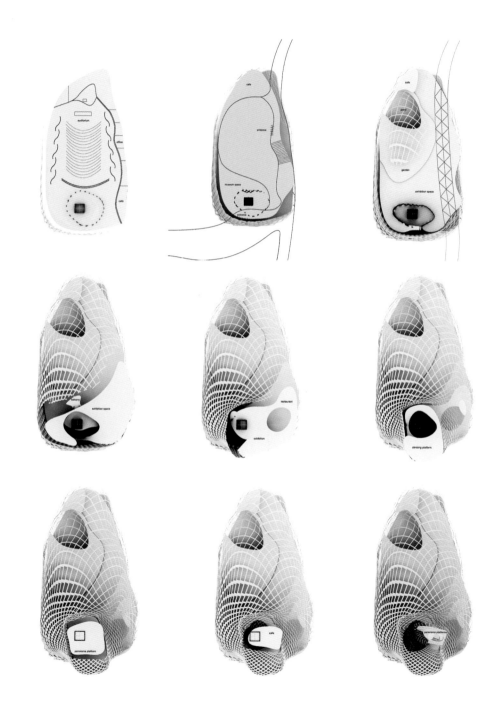

Plate 13   Horizontal sections showing the vertical circulation core interlacing with exhibition spaces, gardens, auditorium and viewing platforms for the historical museum project in Amsterdam by studiokav

Plate 14   Amsterdam historical museum by
            studiokav at night reflected in the
            water of the harbour

Plate 15   Looking at space differently:
the interior of the Pantheon in Rome
photographed by Richard Coyne on an iPhone
using the '360' app by Occipital

Plate 16 'Moving Targets' workshop run by the University of Edinburgh to prototype a system for interfacing social media with streamed media content

THIS IS RESEARCH BY DESIGN

Johan Verbeke

This chapter discusses recent trends in research by design in the field of architecture and, as such, it attempts to introduce the present challenges and weaknesses of the method. Findings from recent developments and positions in artistic research will be analysed in order to introduce key components of research by design. Furthermore, a scheme is introduced that assists in discussing the different ways that design (as an activity) can be relevant when undertaking a research project. A clear definition of research by design is proposed in the hope of improving both transparency and clarity in current discourse. The aforementioned developments in artistic research provide confirmation for the proposed definition. A few examples will also be given in the later stage of the chapter.

Then, reflecting upon the recent developments in research by design, the chapter concludes with some thoughts on the importance of designing as a vehicle to develop understanding and knowledge, as well as of how to keep an open and liberal attitude toward the form and content of design research while simultaneously maintaining high academic standards.

INTRODUCTION

Ever since the joint declaration of the European Ministers of Education convened in Bologna on 19 June 1999, university education in Europe has been evolving toward a strict Bachelors/Masters/PhD structure.[1] The idea is to establish a transparent structure in which every Bachelors degree requires three years of full-time study, a Masters degree requires two additional years, and a PhD a further three. This organisational plan forces schools of architecture (as well as those of art, design and cognate disciplines) to increasingly focus on research endeavours and establish appropriate doctoral degrees. Moreover, recent accreditation procedures, such as in Sweden, Denmark and other European countries, now require schools to clearly report on their research structures and outputs. The consequence of these changes is that architectural schools have begun to explore how the core of the field (that is, designing and artistic activity, and its related activities) can become the basis of, or vehicle for, research. This chapter therefore aims to establish a clear and sharp definition of the term 'research by design'. It is proposed as that kind of research in which the process of designing, as well as experience gained from practice, plays a crucial role in research – not only as inputs to be observed, but, more importantly, as the actual methods and outcomes of the research itself.

A growing number of conferences on research by design and artistic research in general have been organised during the last decade, and many proceedings from these conferences have been one of the tangible results. These conferences include: 'The Unthinkable Doctorate' in Brussels, Belgium (2005);[2] 'Design Enquiries' in Stockholm, Sweden (2007); 'Research into Practice Conference' in London, UK (2008);[3] 'Changes of Paradigms in the Basic Understanding of Architectural Research' in Copenhagen, Denmark (2008);[4] 'Communicating (by) Design' in Brussels (2009);[5] 'The Place of Research/The Research of Place' in Washington, DC, USA (2010); 'Knowing by Designing' in Brussels (2013), and many others. In addition, the European Association for Architectural Education (EAAE);[6] the European League of Institutes of the Arts (ELIA),[7] as well as a number of professional bodies – for example the Royal Institute of British Architects (RIBA)[8] and the Architects Council of Europe (ACE)[9] – are all paying increasing attention to architectural research and its developments, especially that which is grounded on practicing and designing architecture.

Also, after a major effort by an international group of experts, *The Routledge Companion to Research in the Arts* (2010) has been published and includes many interesting experiences and relevant positions for those engaged in artistic research.[10] Likewise, the *Journal for Artistic Research* was established in 2011.[11] Research has clearly become a hot topic: buzzwords like 'research-based education', 'knowledge society' and 'knowledge processes', for instance, have put research endeavours high onto the agenda of politicians and academic policy makers. This is especially the case in architecture and the arts, where a lot of specific PhD degrees have only recently been created.

An example is the situation in Flanders in Belgium, where I am based. After signing the Bologna Declaration, the Flemish Minister of Education began a process to reform the university education system, and the Flemish parliament duly adopted a new Higher Education Act in April 2003. The degree structure, based on the three main Bologna 'cycles', constitutes the core of this legislation, and the structure was introduced for all degree programmes in the 2004–5 academic year. A variety of new doctorates in the arts, music, product design, and architecture (including by design) were created. For all these disciplines, therefore, research is becoming ever more important. And as a consequence, more explicit reporting on research outcomes is required, since it now has a growing impact on governmental financing of Flemish universities.

It is also important to note that teaching staff in the fields of the arts, music, product design, and architecture largely consist of leading practitioners; hence, schools are bringing top-level professional expertise directly into their curricula. These adventurous practices are some of the important foundations of their educational systems. Faced with a period of change in which the development of research has become a crucial concern, most schools in Flanders found they had to address many important questions. What is the context for these educational changes? How should they then develop appropriate methods of research? What indeed is research by or through design? How can it lead to a research project that will eventually lead to a viable PhD award? And what should be the requirements for undertaking research by design?

Within this frame of reference, it seems logical to begin to examine these questions in relation to the highly-developed design competences that are available in almost all the schools of architecture across Europe. On average, half the curriculum for a Bachelors or Masters degree is comprised of practical and design work; this is also in line with European requirements for achieving a balance between theoretical and practical courses (Table 8.1). Thus, it seems logical to try to find ways to extend this kind of balance into new PhD programmes as well, and to acknowledge how designing and making can not only play a crucial role in the intellectual work of the researcher but also contribute to the creation of knowledge.

From the above analysis, it is evident that there was strong pressure from politicians and academic

	CURRICULUM	
	Theoretical components	Practice-based / design components
PhD	?	?
Masters	50%	50%
Bachelors	50%	50%

Table 8.1 Balance of the architectural curriculum for Bachelors and Masters Courses in typical European schools of architecture, posing the question of what proportion to apply to PhDs in a design-orientated school[12]

policy makers following the 1999 Bologna agreement – both in Belgium and other European countries – to increase the research endeavours of universities, and so as to ensure that research activity in Europe would not be eclipsed by that in the USA, Asia, Australasia and elsewhere. This then triggered the organisation of a good many research conferences, and induced research policy documents from European associations in subjects such as architecture. In the following section it will be shown that the understanding of what knowledge is has been shifting over time, with the more recent positions being most helpful for the field.

KNOWLEDGE FORMATION

Following the lines set out in the Frascati Manual, research and experimental development is defined as creative work undertaken systematically to increase the stock of knowledge – including knowledge about humanity, culture and society – and to use of this stock of knowledge to devise new applications.[13] Although this definition has been discussed exhaustively, the focus on a contribution to knowledge is generally accepted and crucial to this discourse. As one example, the RAE 2008 assessment of UK university research applied the following definition:

'Research' … is to be understood as original investigation undertaken in order to gain knowledge and understanding. It includes work of direct relevance to the needs of commerce, industry, and to the public and voluntary sectors; scholarship; the invention and generation of ideas, images, performances, artefacts including design, where these lead to new or substantially improved insights; and the use of existing knowledge in experimental development to produce new or substantially improved materials, devices, products and processes, including design and construction.[14]

This kind of acknowledgement is generally understood as an important step forward for the fields of architecture and the arts, and is seen as an open categorisation that includes architectural projects and artworks as research outputs. As Fraser has pointed out in regard to the UK's RAE 2008 exercise, design research outputs tended to be rated highly by those on the architecture and built environment panel.[15]

How then does this affect the pursuit of design research? The principal criterion for awarding the degree of Doctor of Philosophy is whether a project represents an original and significant contribution to knowledge. This, however, raises the question of what is understood to be knowledge. The following overview describes a wide range of positions toward knowledge in order to show that it is much more than the traditional understanding of explicit written-down knowledge.[16] The important point is that, in reality, far more kinds of knowledge are needed than just the explicit one.

Already in the 1950s and 60s Michael Polanyi started arguing that there was more than factual and explicit knowledge.[17] In his famous book on *The Reflective Practitioner*, Donald Schön introduced the importance of reflective thinking in the development of understanding and knowledge in creative disciplines.[18] His insights and ideas have been quoted widely, especially within architecture, where they are regarded as one of the primary ways of developing knowledge. However, reflection-in-action has also become a key process in all disciplines where doing and making are essential. What is less known is that Schön's underlying intention was to make an argument against the positivist position, and thereby to stimulate focus on the importance of other types of knowledge. In this sense, he was already aware of the aforementioned developments in research and science, and he wanted to balance those with a focus on other ways of understanding – stressing always the importance of *other* types of knowledge.

Gibbons and colleagues introduced the important distinction between 'Mode 1' and 'Mode 2' knowledge.[19] In their view, 'Mode 1' knowledge is defined as:

> The complex of ideas, methods, values and norms that has grown up to control the diffusion of the Newtonian model of science to more and more fields of enquiry and ensure its compliance with what is considered sound scientific practice.

On the contrary, 'Mode 2' is:

> Knowledge production carried out in the context of application and marked by its transdisciplinarity, heterogeneity, organizational hierarchy and transience; social accountability and reflexivity ... It results from the parallel expansion of knowledge producers and users in society.

'Mode 1' knowledge therefore includes the scientific knowledge developed in university laboratories, concepts drawn from architectural theory and so on, whereas 'Mode 2' knowledge is the kind that is transferred by architects from practice into the design studio. These definitions were later used by Halina Dunin-Woyseth to stress the importance of multidisciplinary research in the field of architecture.[20]

Furthermore, based on a distinction raised by Gerard De Zeeuw, Ranulph Glanville has introduced the concepts of 'knowledge of' and 'knowledge for':

> What designers need is knowledge for changing the world, not knowledge of what it is. Scientists want knowledge of what it is. They want to tell us how things are. Designers want to change it. Design is not interested in describing what it is, but changing what is.[21]

All of this must be considered within the general context of human learning. Human learning and (social) constructivist thinking are strongly based on experiences, perceptions, and interactions between people.[22] It is then argued that, as a result, these groups of people develop a mutual inter-subjective understanding.[23] The problem hence with academia today is that it undervalues the diversity in knowledge, as has been clearly formulated by Glanville:

> One of the problems for design and research is that research and the academy has become very specialized; science as a word used to mean knowledge ... It has come to mean a particular type of knowledge formed in a particular way, reflecting a particular world view.

This overly particular interpretation is one of the major problems that the 'creative' and 'making' disciplines currently face as they attempt to incorporate several types of knowledge.

In this context, it is also worth mentioning the difference between 'nomothetic' and 'idiographic' sciences as introduced by Wilhelm Windelbrand.[24] Nomothetic sciences are those that search for general laws (or at least generalised knowledge), as is the case in most of the natural sciences. Windelbrand remarks that even a humanistic discipline like history might have a similar aim, so no intrinsic differences exist between disciplines. However, he maintains as a fact that, in the study of history (or art or architecture, it is tempting to add), general laws are not normally of interest, for example for tracing historical development. Rather the focus is on single events, single periods, and single personalities; here the idiographic disciplines are those which study their subjects in terms of their specificity. For example, Stefan Östersjö's doctoral thesis at Lund University in Sweden, titled 'Shut up 'n' Play' (2008) introduced the concepts of 'thinking-in-action', 'thinking-through-practice', 'thinking-through-performing', and 'thinking-through-hearing'.[25] This PhD nicely describes the critical moments in developing

insight during practice/play; hence, it acts as an exemplar of research where the 'doing' plays a crucial role.

Donald Schön's ideas were, later on, further developed by Nonaka and Takeuchi when they highlighted the different sub-processes of knowledge: combination, internalisation, socialisation, and externalisation.[26] It is the interaction between these sub-processes that brings a field forward. Vital in their arguments is the interaction between explicit and implicit knowledge, something which is especially relevant to the fields of architecture, art and design since they incorporate mainly implicit knowledge (this being transferred in a design studio setting).

The key point that Glanville has made is that there is no such thing as research that is not designed.[27] Research itself is design. It is not just setting up something and doing it – it has to be modified, changed and fiddled with until it works; then the results are looked at and learned from, which changes things, and the process is begun again. His conclusion is therefore that it is ridiculous to try to make design subject to the rules of research, when research itself is only possible because of design.

Hence, in this way, designing has the power to facilitate the generation of knowledge, as indicated by J. Christopher Jones:

> In any creative process, what some of us call the intuition (of the imagination) must have priority. Reason (and science) must be used to support, not to destroy, this essential confidence and vision. Otherwise, the intuition, or creativeness, which does not perform to order, will 'fly out of the window'.[28]

From the above observations, it is clear that the scientific understanding of what is knowledge has been changing over time and has been seriously broadened as a consequence. For the discipline of architecture, it is important to find ways to value the insights and outcomes developed during design activities. In a similar way, creating and making are the core processes of the arts in general.

To wrap up this part of the discussion, the field of architecture incorporates a good deal of tacit knowledge, which is crucial but often very difficult to communicate precisely. This is the challenge for the development of research in the domain: on one hand, researchers need to exploit the possibilities and the competences that have, for centuries, been developed in the field (designing and making); on the other hand, this competence needs to be further developed in order to find ways that allow peers to understand and discuss the knowledge being created. Given that similar debates are taking place in various artistic subjects, the following section describes recent developments and the main positions taken.

WHAT IS HAPPENING IN THE ARTS?

As is well known, architecture and the arts were strongly linked in the past. Therefore, it is worth exploring the recent developments in those kinds of arts in order to reflect back onto the field of architecture. In 2006, Jan Kaila published a fascinating document called *The Artist's Knowledge*.[29] In his introduction, the problem of the relation to knowledge and the interaction between theory and practice was nicely formulated:

> The postgraduate program aimed at producing new knowledge based upon the artist's own artwork, rather than searching for straightforward models from the world of the sciences … In this manner it was hoped that a dialogical relationship could be maintained between artistic research, art audiences and art-related institutions and that the troubling isolation often incurred within academic research could be solved … The so far most unresolved question of the methodology of artistic research and the doctoral studies program is related to theory. How can the artist devise theory from his/her practice, theory which can be linked in part to the almost non-existent tradition of artistic research, which can dispute legitimacy in an investigative manner, but not necessarily resemble traditional academic research methodology.

A similar position comes from Jan Baetens when discussing the relation of literary theory to reading and writing:

> Why do we need literary theory? Because literary theory can enhance the quality of literary practice. If literary theory matters, then practice (of reading as well as of writing) really matters … I have also identified the basic problem of modern literary theory, namely the fact that theory is no longer aimed at producing better practice (of reading as well as of writing), but as something else (and that something else can be extremely diverse, such as theory for theory's sake, for instance). However, linking theory and practice should be the basis of any serious academic education and research … More in general it should be observed that a fruitful relationship between theory and practice seems to work better if initiated by practitioners, not by theoreticians.[30]

Henk Borgdorff has been one of the driving forces in developing artistic research throughout Europe; and he states:

Characteristic of artistic research is that art practice (the works of art, the artistic actions, the creative processes) is not just the motivating factor and the subject matter of research, but that this artistic practice – the practice of creating and performing in the atelier or studio – is central to the research process itself. Methodologically speaking, the creative process forms the pathway (or part of it) through which new insights, understanding and products come into being.

In part, then, the outcomes of artistic research are artworks, installations, performances and other artistic practices, and this is another quality that differentiates it from humanities or social science research – where art practice may be the object of research, but not the outcome. This means that art practice is paramount as the subject matter, the method, the context and the outcome of artistic research. That is what is meant by expressions like 'practice-based' or 'studio-based' research. This points to an important distinction between art practice in itself and artistic research. Artistic research seeks in and through the production of art to contribute not just to the artistic universe, but to what we 'know' and 'understand'.[31]

And Borgdorff continues in his same essay in *The Routledge Companion to Research in the Arts*:

As a rule, an original contribution in artistic research will result in an original work of art, as the relevance of the artistic outcome is one test of the adequacy of the research. The reverse is not true, however; an original artwork is not necessary an outcome of research in the emphatic sense.

The requirement that a research study should set out with well-defined questions, topics or problems is often at odds with the actual course of events in artistic research. Formulating a question implies delimiting the space in which a possible answer may be found. Yet research (and not only artistic research) often resembles an uncertain quest in which the questions or topics only materialize during the journey, and may often change as well. Besides not knowing exactly what one does not know, one also does not know how to delimit the space where potential answers are located. As a rule, artistic research is not hypothesis-led, but discovery-led … whereby the artist undertakes a search on the basis of intuition, guesses and hunches, and possibly stumbles across some unexpected issues or surprising questions on the way.

In another essay in the same book, Helga Nowotny, who chairs the European Research Council, confirms the purpose of endeavours in the arts:

Research is the curiosity-driven production of new knowledge. It is the process oriented toward the realm of possibilities that is to be explored, manipulated, controlled, given shape and form, and transformed. Research is inherently beset by uncertainties, since the results or outcomes are by definition unknown. But this inherent uncertainty proves to be equally seductive: it promises new discoveries, the opening of new pathways, and new ways of problem-solving and coming up with novel ways of 'doing things,' designing and transforming them. To put research (back) into the arts, to (again) make visible and explicit the function of research in the arts and in the act of 'creating knowledge' is a truly ambitious undertaking, because it takes up a vision and a project that originated in the Renaissance. After centuries of separation, it promises to close a loop.

But the techno-sciences, important as they are, are not alone in leading these explorations and pursuits. Artists have quickly realized the artistic challenges offered by hybrid forms and the vast domain of crossing the natural with the artificial. Most significantly, they extend their creativity beyond the range covered by the techno-sciences. True to the humanistic spirit of the Renaissance, they bring the human back into this world that continues to be transformed by the techno-sciences and their societal impact. It is this humanistic impulse that should continue to invigorate research in the arts. It has the potential to bring forth a new Renaissance.[32]

As noted earlier, the *Journal for Artistic Research* has recently been established for the field of the arts. Moreover, networks like SHARE (Step-change for Higher Arts Research and Education),[33] EPARM (European Platform for Artistic Research in Music),[34] and ADAPT-r (Architecture, Design and Art Practice Training – research),[35] and other initiatives indicate that artistic research has become a priority for the leading European art schools, almost all of which are now busy developing artistic research.

What becomes obvious from these kinds of quotes is the central place given to exploration and curiosity-driven activities. Artistic research is not so much hypothesis-driven, but is built on experiences and explorations. It uses the production of art, and of making and performing, as the key paths to develop insight, understanding, and knowledge. Transferring these developments to the field of architecture, it seems logical to use designing as the main knowledge process for developing research. Complementary to research in history and theory, building physics and sociology, and also research connecting to other disciplines, the act of research by design – if developed appropriately – has the potential to bring another dimension to architectural research. Furthermore, it is clear that in the arts, the main processes in research are the core activities of the field – that is, the making of art, the playing of music, the designing of objects and such like. It should be the same in architecture, so let us now ask what is happening in our field.

BACK TO ARCHITECTURE

As prepared by the Research Committee of the European Association for Architectural Education, the following text formed part of the Research Charter approved by the EAAE's General Assembly in September 2012:

In architecture, design is the essential feature. Any kind of inquiry in which design is a substantial constituent of the research process is referred to as research by design … In research by design, the architectural design process forms a pathway through which new insights, knowledge, practices or products come into being. It generates critical inquiry through design work. Therefore research results are obtained by, and consistent with experience in practice

Architectural research meets the general criteria of originality, significance, and rigour. It produces forms of output and discourse proper to disciplinary practice, to make it discussable, communicable and useful to peers and others. It is validated through panels of experts who collectively cover the range of disciplinary competencies addressed by the work.[36]

Later in the research charter, it adds:

The following characteristics could help to guide architectural research to a high level of quality and open up new horizons:
- the research is meaningful and relevant for practice, for the discipline, and for society; it explores limits and expands them;
- it contributes to design practice, to the exploration of spatial understanding and/or the creative design process;
- it contributes to knowledge through intellectual work that is characteristic of architecture and design practice;

- the results are consistent with experience in practice;
- the research endeavors to make its processes and foundations as clear and explicit as possible;
- method, context, process and results are communicated and submitted to regular peer review; they refer to the work of peers;
- the research explores emotional, intuitive and/or artistic aspects of the domain, it engages architectural competences and experience in practice;
- it creates and exploits transdisciplinary connections.

From this EAAE document, therefore, a few points emerge which are important for propelling research by design in a positive manner. Firstly, in terms of research by design, the act of designing is the key process to develop understanding and knowledge. Secondly, peer reviewing is essential to maintain quality (as indeed it is for all other disciplines). Thirdly, research by design needs to be openly connected to practice and studio work. And finally, we should be careful not to impose a strict list of qualitative aspects, as a sort of checklist, but rather keep things open for interpretation by practitioners, reviewers and research assessment panels. Perhaps above all, the EAAE Research Charter repeatedly stresses the importance of the link to practice for research to thrive.

What is common between research by design and scientific research is that their assessment is based on inter-subjective standards which are shared within the specific field; it is precisely this plane of reference that is established through the discourse of peers. And peer review has long since established itself within the field of architecture through the evaluation of design competitions, award juries, etc. The intention of research in all disciplines is to expand the horizon and to enrich the world. High-level research shifts boundaries by discovering new areas and understandings. Careful investigations, explorations, and broadening experiences reveal new aspects of architecture and practice. And the quality of research output is best judged by those in the field itself, including those who practice architecture outside of academia. This principle is not affected by the fact that channels other than traditional academic journals are used.

Unlike other research that is chiefly analytical and seeks to understand current realities, architecture and design try to project into the future, and thus to change things. Research outputs should also follow the media which are most appropriate for the field: maps, drawings, sketches, models and so on. Results have to be related to the practice of designing and making in a meaningful way; this kind of practice, as well as design studio work, are the essential aspects for research by design. A good example of the exploitation of the potential of non-textual communication was the final PhD exhibition by Arnaud Hendrickx, who works at Sint-Lucas School of Architecture and recently got a RMIT degree (see Figures 8.1–8.4). The doctoral research by Hendrickx explored the idea of 'Substantiating Displacement' through a range of design work and installations. In this manner, his final exhibition in the spaces of an old factory created a specific experience aimed to make the audience understand and feel the tangible aspects of displacement.

A SCHEME TO DISCUSS THE ROLE OF DESIGNING AND PRACTICE IN RESEARCH PROCESSES

Based on the work of Gerard De Zeeuw, I developed an investigatory scheme into general research processes that was published in my 2002 essay

8.1 Overview of the PhD exhibition on 'displacement' by Arnaud Hendrickx in an old industrial building in Brussels cleaned up for the purpose

on the nature of architectural research.[37] For the purposes of this present chapter, it is sufficient just to show the diagram in Figure 8.2, and give an explanation of the terms involved:

Input refers to what in relation to the research activity will be known as 'local statements' at the start-up. These may include answers/reports from people who have been interviewed (by the researcher, or by others as reported in the literature, e.g., in interviews, earlier research) about their experiences concerning some tool or some form of support, as well as external observations on people working as architects. The input may also compromise some of the starting ideas and thoughts of the researchers who are interested in the design process. It also includes literature review and what is known at the start of the project.

8.2 Scale models and drawings as part of the
doctoral explorations by Arnaud Hendrickx

8.3 Part of the exhibition showing the reuse of 'found' spaces and materials

Operations refers to anything that is (proposed to be) done to change the input. Operations include getting more input (new interviews, new experiments, new experiences), subdividing and thus combining part of the input, replacing some of the input by improved versions of the input.

Output/Knowing refers to anything which results when the application of an end rule to the process of operating (the applying operations) on the input comes to a stop.

Output may include general statements, but also actual 'design rooms', of which it can be said that they implement the stated conditions, or else 'teaching tools' which ensure that students achieve certain pre-specified results.

Deliverables refers to all tangible manifestations of the outputs. Examples include computer programs, design rooms, design tools and databases, papers and/or exhibitions.

8.4 Uncanny spatial installations created
by Hendrickx as part of his PhD
defence presentation

What is perhaps most important for an understanding of research by design is the question of in which phase of the research process should the design and/or practice work take place? Three different possible situations can be distinguished:

1. Designing and/or practice takes place in the early *input* phase: this is the case when, for example, a designer founds his or her research on earlier designs and experiences. In such instances, drawings, and possibly actual buildings, play a crucial role in the research of or observations on design and/or practice. This is what is sometimes referred to as research 'on' architecture.

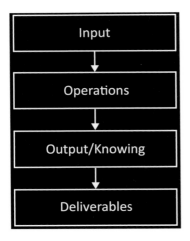

2. Designing and/or practice takes place in the final phase of making the *deliverables*, with it then being part of the illustration of the outcomes from the research process. Hence the research outcomes are incorporated into architectural projects and/or artworks. These projects are thus used as 'illustrations' of theoretical concepts.

3. Designing and/or practice forms the key component of the entire research *operations*. This can happen while realising new design projects, or when work from practice becomes one of the main ways of generating understanding within the research. Hence, designing, making, studio work, practice, and/or artwork are the generators of insight, understanding, and knowledge: they are part of the intellectual work and complementary processes of reflection and knowledge creation.

It is important to note that this kind of distinction is seldom applied exclusively. In a number of research projects, there is a mixture of methods and processes: a combination of the three types formulated above. Yet it is the third category, when the design and/or practice drives the whole research project throughout its entirety, which seems to offer the most fertile condition for research by design.

It is worth explaining why. Traditionally, research tries to take a distant view, as it does in architectural history and theory. In research by design, however, it is the researcher who is also the designer, and who develops knowledge through their design activities. This process thus differs from normal practice in that it also includes explicit knowledge formation that is openly communicated and peer-reviewed.

And this is why it is so important that the term 'research by design' should only really be used for the type of research described under item 3) above, or for that research in which the activities listed in that item are primary and essential. This definition of research by design is proposed here in the hope of improving transparency and clarity in current discourse, so that everyone knows what is being proposed by the term.

As described earlier, designing can be recognised as the core of a type of research process within the field of architecture. This is identical to what is happening in the arts, where the artist-researcher continually produces art or plays music – that is, they utilise the acts of making and doing – as the central process in the generation of understanding and/or knowledge. So, the key issue for developing architectural research is to incorporate practice and design studio work into it. Instead of simply research 'on' architecture, researchers should try to establish research 'in the medium' of architecture:[38] this means to investigate architecture through architecture and not through history, theory, social science or environmental science (although, of course, those types of work are also valuable research).

The basic rationale behind all this is that it is important to value the qualities of designing, and hence to avoid intermediaries when undertaking research. It is the designer themselves who needs to exploit their design competence to obtain understanding and knowledge. In such cases, the designer looks back at finished work and gives an overview, and extracts key aspects of his or her understanding, and explores these aspects through further design work, as well as through connections

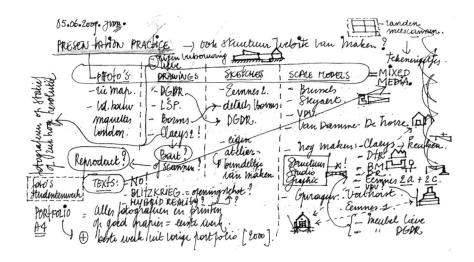

8.6 Initial ideas trying to structure the PhD research progress presentation by Johan Van Den Berghe

to the work of other practitioners. It means that their research work is regularly peer-reviewed. The designer must also project into the future, mentioning key aspects that will be useful for the field. Research results and outcomes are presented through drawings and text in an exhibition and a written exegesis.

This way of working in research by design has been developed, for instance, at RMIT University in Melbourne for many years and has been described in detail by Leon Van Schaik and others.[39] The RMIT approach has lately been extended to Europe, workings with myself and colleagues at the Sint-Lucas School of Architecture in Ghent and Brussels, and as a model it functions as a key example for any serious developments in research by design. As Van Schaik has pointed out, it is the reflection on, and contemplation of, the processes of designing and making which impact on the results of the research in a fundamental way, and as a result give it its unique quality.

SOME RECENT EXAMPLES OF RESEARCH BY DESIGN

The following three cases are given as very different examples of possible ways to undertake research in connection to practice, design, and creative practice work. While these doctorates can be said to be representative of the principles of research by design, they are also extremely distinct in their subject and approach. The first is another, like Arnaud Hendrickx, whose recently completed thesis was mentioned earlier. It also could not have been realised without the crucial contribution of designing and making/performing.

This PhD project was by Johan Van Den Berghe, a member of staff at Sint-Lucas, and it began in, and then went back to, his own award-winning architectural practice. Under the title of 'Theatre of Operations, or: Construction Site as Architectural Design', Van Den Berghe's research was conducted as a series of observations made about past and present design actions. As such, his research could be seen as participant observation that builds on design work

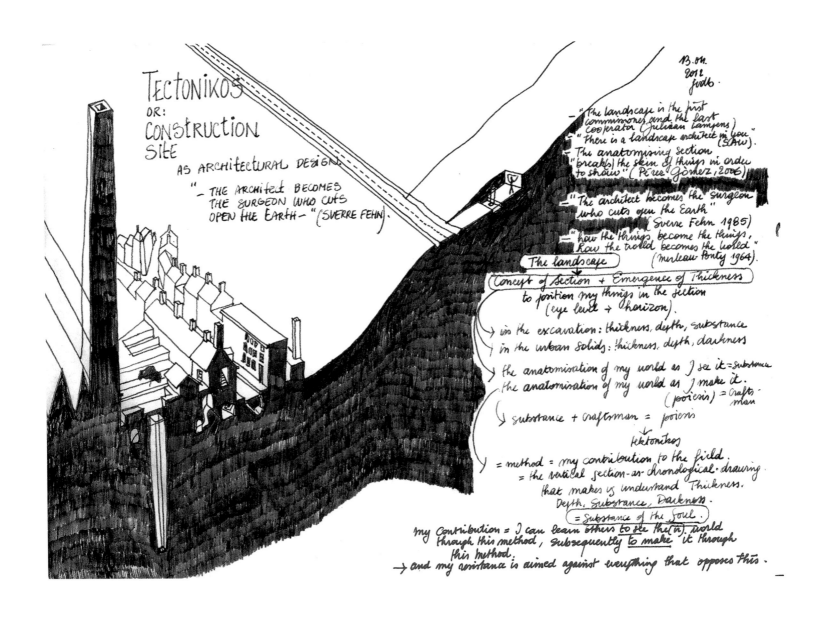

8.7 Imaginary section drawn by Johan Van Den Berghe through his grandmother's house in an old Belgian industrial town to help organise his thoughts and projects

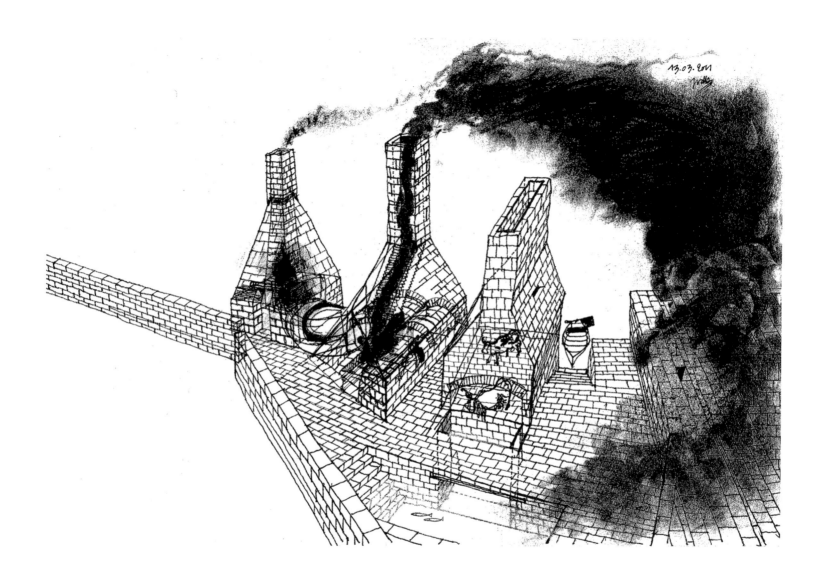

8.8 Exploring the own mental space
of the design researcher through
drawings of past buildings

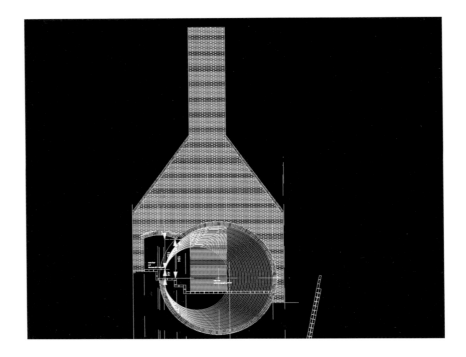

8.9 Detailed constructional drawing for a brick chimney illustrating the impact of materialisation on the 'dream' of the designer

which is an integral part of the doctoral research. Some of the architectural projects in his thesis are described as if they were a crime scene investigation (that is, the projects of his practice as if they were 'victims'). Other projects are treated more like the reconstruction of far older crimes from the past which need to be recreated (such as 'My Grandmother's House'). Still other projects are offered as 'new crimes' which are still in the process of being committed.

Through investigations of his own work and the work of other architects, through intensive reading, by making new designs as the core of his PhD, by self-validation, peer-reviewed presentations and discussions, and writing his text, Van Den Berghe worked his way through the research process.

The contribution to the field is manifold, yet all elements hide under his basic assumption – that is, that it is wrong when the creative process in architecture is considered all too automatically as a unidirectional one that begins with the poetic image of the designer and is then subsequently substantiated on the construction site. Van Den Berghe's research reveals that this assumed unidirectionality is a false assumption, and that the process of creation, including its built substantiation, is much more negotiated and two-directional. He also argues, through a careful analysis of his work and that of his architectural peers, that the poetic image is more often triggered by construction practice. In other words, the 'dream' is triggered by the 'substance'.

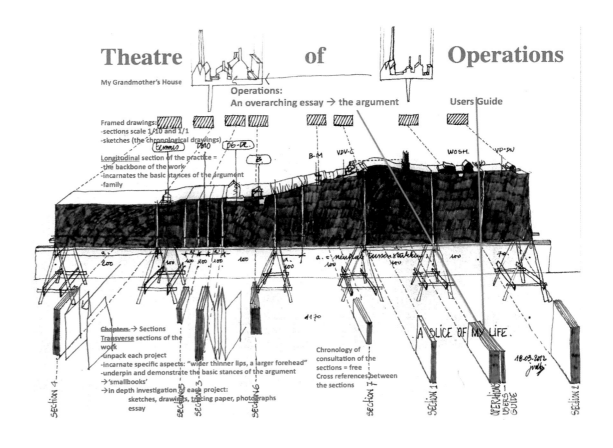

8.10 Sketch design for the final exhibition of PhD research work by Johan Van Der Berghe

Following the framework set out by Leon van Schaik, Van Den Berghe also explored his own mental space by moving from an implicit to an explicit awareness of its potential in the creative process. He discovered in his work, and in the work of others, a series of concepts and made them explicit: these included the emergence of thickness, the concept of section, depth as the first dimension, the meaning of eye level in the perspective, the passing of time, the Greek notion of *tektonikos*, the chronological drawing, x-ray images, and ideas of chronology and substance as found on the drawing table. Together, these investigations were used by Van Den Berghe to support the main argument, and to make it work for his (future) architectural practice; these too are parts of his contribution to the field. They co-exist as a specific moment in a specific place, merging the moment of *to dream* with the place of *to make* into energetic momentum: this is the acute moment of creation when the designing architect is able to place themselves at the strategic intersection of time and space, and thus create new forms. Van Den Berghe calls this moment of acuity the 'State of Emergency'.

8.11 Large sectional model for the final exhibition, bringing together scaled models of real and imaginary design projects in an attempt to synthesise the main conclusions of his PhD research

The other two doctorates that I wish to refer here are taken from music schools elsewhere. One is the aforementioned PhD by Stefan Östersjö, titled 'Shut up 'n' play! Negotiating the Musical Work', which was delivered at the Malmö Academies of Performing Arts at Lund University, Sweden in 2008. The research incorporates the interaction between Stefan Östersjö and several composers. It is through this process of interaction, the playing and performing, that a deeper understanding is able to be developed. As noted, this PhD discusses useful concepts as 'thinking-through-playing' and 'thinking-through-performing': thus the collaborations with the composers are described in great detail to explain the critical moments

in the development of joint understanding and knowledge.

The PhD research of Carl Van Eyndhoven (who works at the Lemmensinstituut in Leuven) reconstructs the *carillon* music (both in terms of repertoire and performance practice) which existed in the southern Netherlands in the seventeenth century. *Carillons* were instruments made up of rows of bells set within a church tower or municipal building. Since there are no primary musical sources with *carillon* music dating from this period, he had to use the so-called *versteekboeken*, collections of arrangements that were placed onto the large drums of the automatic playing systems of the *carillons*. By playing these arrangements himself on a *carillon* – originally, they had only been meant to be played automatically – Van Eyndhoven acquired new knowledge about the way that *carillonneurs* had played music in the seventeenth century. Through this 'research by playing', as performance pieces, he succeeded in reconstructing a historical musical vocabulary which had been lost. Hence in all these examples, the PhD research work serves to report, monitor, connect, and reflect from and upon experience and practice. Practicing and designing are the core processes for developing new understanding and knowledge.

CONCLUSION

It should be clear from the above that artistic research and research by design are developing in a wide manner at this very moment. Research endeavours like these have become crucial for all schools of architecture (and those in the arts). The idea behind this momentum for new PhD research programmes is to build upon the already strong competences of the field in terms of designing, making, and developing projects, as well as to find ways to value knowledge and experience derived from practice.

Research by design is hence high-level research in which these core competences of the field in designing and making – including that also of leading architectural practices – are the main pathways to establish new understanding and knowledge. It creates cutting-edge exploration and progress, both in practice and in studio work. It results in the development of spatial understanding and human ecology which daily impacts upon behaviour and living conditions. It is not about analytical thinking in the narrow sense, but rather about exploration – that is, searching, searching, and searching again to find new insights and aspects of architecture. It is about extending horizons, changing borders, stimulating curiosity and exploration. It is about imaging, visualising and projecting alternative worldviews, as well as developing spatial understanding and making possible future worlds – and thus also contributing to the understanding of underlying processes of the present.

In order to increase clarity in current communications on the subject, this chapter has introduced a scheme with which to structure our discussions of research activities. It also proposes that the term 'research by design' be used only for the kind of research where design activities (including activities undertaken in 'real world' practice) are the central means to develop understanding and knowledge. In establishing research by design as a new development, it is important to continue to explore and develop other directions and research lines.[40] Researchers should learn from these in order to improve the outcomes and research outputs. This continual process of exploration will help to develop the knowledge base for the discipline in all its strength, variety, and plurality. Above all it implies an open and liberal attitude toward the form and content of research by design, while at the same time maintaining high academic standards of the research content. In order to achieve this highest level of quality, it is important to organise peer review on a regular basis, communicating externally and connecting to knowledge and experience drawn from practice. Within the broader debate on what research is, the experience and the perspective of the designer should be valued.

ACKNOWLEDGEMENTS

The author wants to thank Johan Van Den Berghe, Arnaud Hendrickx, Stefan Östersjö and Carl Van Eyndhoven for providing input and material about their PhD projects. He is also thankful to Halina Dunin-Woyseth for her valuable feedback on a first draft. This chapter is a majorly reworked version of my previous paper on 'Recent Trends in Research by Design(ing)', as published in 2012 in the *Proceedings of the 3rd Symposium of Architectural Research 2011: Research & Praxis* by the School of Architecture, University of Oulu, Finland.

Notes

1   The European Students Union, *Bologna with Student Eyes 2009* (Leuven: ESU, April 2009), viewable at http://www.ond.vlaanderen.be/hogeronderwijs/bologna/documents/MDC/BOLOGNA_DECLARATION1.pdf (accessed 5 February 2013).

2   Marc Belderbos & Johan Verbeke (eds), *The Unthinkable Doctorate*. Proceedings of the International Conference (Ghent/Brussels: Sint-Lucas School of Architecture, April 2005).

3. Selected papers are published online in Working Papers in *Art and Design*, vol. 5, viewable on the University of Hertfordshire website, http://sitem.herts.ac.uk/artdes_research/papers/wpades/vol5/index.html (accessed 25 February 2013).

4   Anne Katrine Getting & Ebbe Harder, *Changes of Paradigms in the Basic Understanding of Architectural Research* (Copenhagen: School of Architecture, The Royal Danish Academy of Fine Arts/EAAE/ARCC, 2008).

5   Adam Jakimowicz & Johan Verbeke (eds), *Communicating (by) Design. Proceedings of the 2009 international conference at the Sint-Lucas School of Architecture* (Ghent/Brussels: Sint-Lucas School of Architecture, 2009).

6   European Association for Architectural Education website, http://www.eaae.be (accessed 25 February 2013).

7   The European League of Institutes of the Arts website, www.elia-artschools.org (accessed 25 February 2013).

8   Royal Institute of British Architects website, http://www.architecture.com (accessed 25 February 2013).

9   Architects Council of Europe website, www.ace-cae.eu (accessed 25 February 2013).

10   Michael Biggs & Henrik Karlsson (eds), *The Routledge Companion to Research in the Arts* (Abingdon, Oxon: Routledge, 2010).

11   Journal for Artistic Research website, http://www.jar-online.net/ (accessed 5 August 2012).

12   Johan Verbeke, 'Research by Design is up and running', *AE Architecture and Education Journal*, vol.5 (2011), pp. 111–19; viewable at the *AE: Revista Lusofona Arquitectura e Educacao* website, http://revistas.ulusofona.pt/index.php/revlae/article/view/2682 (accessed 5 January 2013).

13   Organisation for Economic Cooperation and Development, *The Measurement of Scientific and Technological Activities: Frascati Manual – Proposed Standard Practice for Surveys on Research and Experimental Development* (Paris: OECD Publishing, 2002).

14   Higher Education Funding Council for England, *Research Assessment Exercise 2008: Guidance on Submissions – RAE 03.2005* (Bristol: HEFCE, June 2005), p. 32.

15   The feedback report written by the H.30: Architecture and the Built Environment sub-panel in RAE 2008 is viewable in the Main Panel H folder on the HEFCE RAE 2008 website, http://www.rae.ac.uk/pubs/2009/ov/ (accessed on 28 March 2013). For confirmation of the relative success of design research in that UK assessment exercise, see Murray Fraser's contribution to 'Evaluating the Evaluation of Research', *Architectural Research Quarterly*, vol. 14 no. 1 (March 2010), pp. 6–10.

16   Johan Verbeke & Ranulph Glanville, 'Knowledge Creation and Research in Design and Architecture', in Faris Ameziane (ed.), *EURAU 04: European Symposium on Research in Architecture and Urban Design, Marseille 2004 – Considering the Implementation of Doctoral Theses in Architecture*. (Marseille: Ecole Nationale Superieure d'Architecture de Marseille, 2006).

17   Michael Polanyi, *Personal Knowledge: Towards a Post-critical Philosophy* (Chicago: University of Chicago Press, 1958); Michael Polanyi, *The Tacit Dimension* (London: Routledge, 1966).

18   Donald Schön, *The Reflective Practitioner: How Professions Think in Action* (New York/London: Basic Books, 1983).

19   Michael Gibbons, Camille Limoges, Helga Nowotny, Simon Schwartzman, Peter Scott & Martin Trow, *The New Production of Knowledge* (London: Sage, 1994).

20   Halina Dunin-Woyseth, 'Some Notes on Mode 1 and Mode 2: Adversaries or Dialogue Partners?', in Biggs and Karlsson (eds), *The Routledge Companion to Research in the Arts*, pp. 64–81.

21   Ranulph Glanville, 'Design prepositions', in Belderbos and Verbeke (eds) *The Unthinkable Doctorate*, pp. 115–26.

22   Ernst von Glasersfeld, 'Aspects of Constructivism. Vico, Berkeley, Piaget', in *Key Works in Radical Constructivism* (Rotterdam: Sense, 2007), pp. 91–9. This essay was originally published in Italian in 1992, and is viewable at the Ernst von Glaserfeld website, http://www.vonglasersfeld.com/139.2 (accessed 5 August 2012).

23   Alex Gillespie & Flora Cornish, 'Intersubjectivity: Towards a dialogical analysis', *Journal for the Theory of Social Behaviour*, vol. 40 (2010), pp. 19–46.

24   Wilhelm Windelbrand, 'Geschichte und Naturwissenschaft' (1894), in *Präludien: Aufsätze und Reden zur Philosophie und ihrer Gechichte* (Mohr, Germany: Tübingen, 1915).

25   Stefan Östersjö, 'Shut up 'n' play! Negotiating the Musical Work', Unpublished PhD Thesis, Lund-Malmö Academies of Performing Arts, Lund University, Sweden (2008).

26   Ikujiro Nonaka & Hirotaka Takeuchi, *The Knowledge Creating Company: How Japanese Companies Create the Dynamics of Innovation* (Oxford: Oxford University Press, 1995).

27   Ranulph Glanville, 'Researching design and designing research', *Design Issues,* vol. 15 no. 2 (Summer 1999), pp. 80–91.

28   John Christopher Jones, 'A Theory of Designing' (2000), viewable at the softopia: my public writing place website, www.softopia.demon.co.uk/2.2/theory_of_designing.html (accessed 25 January 2013).

29   Jan Kaila, *The Artist's Knowledge: Research at the Finnish Academy of Fine Arts* (Helsinki: The Finnish Academy of Fine Arts, 2006), p. 9.

30   Jan Baetens, 'Allemaal terug naar de klas: Over het nut van retoriek voor literatuur', *Rekto Verso*, no. 52 (2012), pp. 71–3 (original in Dutch, translation by the author).

31   Henk Borgdorff, 'The Production of Knowledge in Artistic Research', in Biggs & Karlsson (eds), *The Routledge Companion to Research in the Arts*, pp. 44–63.

32   Helga Nowotny, 'Foreword', in Biggs and Karlsson (eds), *The Routledge Companion to Research in the Arts*, pp. xvii–xxvi.

33   Share network website, http://www.sharenetwork.eu/ (accessed 25 January 2013).

34   Association Europeene des Conservatoires website, http://www.aecinfo.org/Content.aspx?id=2279 (accessed 25 January 2013).

35   ADAPT-r Marie Curie Initial Training Network website, http://www.adapt-r.org (accessed 28 March 2013).

36   European Association for Architectural Education, 'EAAE Charter on Architectural Research', viewable at the EAAE website, http://www.eaae.be/research.php (accessed 5 January 2013).

37   Johan Verbeke, 'Gerard de Zeeuw and Architectural Research', *System Research and Behavioral Science*, vol. 19 no. 2 (March–April 2002), pp. 159–66.

38   Leon van Schaik & Anna Johnson (eds), *Architecture and Design, By Practice, By Invitation: Design Practice Research at RMIT* (Melbourne: RMIT Publishing, 2011).

39   Ibid.

40   Søren Kjørup, 'Pleading for Plurality: Artistic and Other Kinds of Research', in Biggs and Karlsson (eds) *The Routledge Companion to Research in the Arts*, pp. 24–43.

SPACE IS NOT A THING

Leslie Kavanaugh

Of course, research in architecture takes many forms, from the most necessary technological innovations to the most abstract thinking. My research in architecture came out of a perception over time that architecture was periodically changing styles, but not really fundamentally questioning the nature of architecture itself. We as architects create space, but what is space actually?

This question – what is space? – would lead me many places. Many times I would come up against the predominant and absolute space/time paradigm. Many times I would be forced to confront ideas of architecture as instrumentality, as software manipulations, as commodity, as 'gaming'. I went further. Fortunately, within the history of human thought, I found several ideas that I could hold onto, ideas wherein I thought, 'Yes, this is always what I have felt about space'. Here I will share with you a few conclusions of my years of research, hoping that these ideas will inspire others to think more fundamentally about architecture. Subsequently, in thinking through this research, I will explain one design project from my architectural practice, studiokav (www.studiokav.com), which is for a historical museum in Amsterdam harbour, in order to give an indication of how I as an architect have used this research to inform design practice. Next, I will briefly mention two other architectural practices in Amsterdam that are also thinking about space as an inter-relation, albeit in differing manners. In short, I will discuss space/time as relation, as perception and as existence itself. My conclusion will be that fundamentally space and time are relations, not things.

Funnily enough, I have a tendency to think that I know what space is. I am an architect. I deal with space all the time, so I think I know what space is. Yet historically various concepts of space have arisen and for a time have become paradigmatic. Since the end of the seventeenth century, in the period of 'modernism', the concept of absolute space and time, especially as postulated by Newton, has become hegemonic. Indeed, even now, it is difficult to think outside of this absolute box. In this conception, space and time are a fixed envelope, and objects are positioned within this neutral background. Obviously, this conception is a reduction of the ephemeral nature of phenomenon; however, this static conception allowed for the mathematical manipulation and statistical predictability of nature which brought forth many technological innovations. Yet contemporary with Newton and the birth of modern science was the philosopher and mathematician, Gottfried Wilhelm Leibniz. He proposed a conception of space and time as a relation.[1] Both Leibniz and Newton, separately but concurrently, developed differential calculus for indeed every paradigm has its own descriptive geometry. The Leibnizian relational space/time has the characteristic of being infinite – both infinitely large and infinitely divisible – in a continuous and dynamically changing phenomenal fold or pleat of matter. At the time of Leibniz and Newton, the mathematical difficulty of describing such a continuously dynamically changing universe was almost impossible. Only now can this complexity begin to be mathematically described, providing inspiration to architects, and a challenge to think space and time differently.

Now, what does this have to do with architecture? As an architect, along with many other architects, I tend to be attached to our buildings as objects.

Even with the 'de-materialised' modelling software, the temptation to see our form-giving as something separate and unrelated to its environment is seductive. Indeed, the manner in which space is traditionally represented in architecture betrays that fact that architects are still deeply embedded in Newtonian absolute space/time, in 'object-thinking'. In contrast, I would suggest that the Leibnizian notion of relational space/time provides a fundamentally and potentially fruitful way of thinking about architectural space. In this way, I think not of objects, rather the 'between'; the 'in-common', in which the world is not a static container, but rather merely and only the relation between things, perpetually and continually becoming one thing after another. In relational space/time, all things are related, and indeed are defined by their relation. All things having position and situation only are temporally definable by their relationship to a world defined as a collection of individuals in mutual relation. With Leibniz, I get a perfectly interconnected world with all things in relation.

As a result of this possible paradigm shift to a relational notion, I can no longer speak of 'being' in space and time; rather of 'becoming' in space/time. The implications of this shift are only beginning to be thought. And indeed, the next move would be to investigate what is the precise nature of the 'relation' that is space/time, spontaneously interfacing and continuously changing. Leibniz suggested that the relation was one of 'perception'; yet a full working out of this notion was not accomplished in his lifetime. As a result, the working through of a relational space/time paradigm would need to make an account of the nature of this 'relation'. For this account, I turned to twentieth-century

phenomenology – to Brentano, Husserl, Heidegger, Mach, Levinas, Merleau-Ponty, Bachelard, Bergson and Whitehead.

Phenomenology gives us two important conceptions: 'intentionality' and 'intersubjectivity'. For the founder of phenomenology, Franz Brentano, precisely this question about relationality was the original impetus for his philosophical investigations: what is the relation between my soul/mind and the world? Brentano sought a third way between the physical 'out there', and the psychic 'in here', in my mind. For Brentano, the physical and psychic were not radically different, rather two sides of the same coin as it were. Any object 'out there' in the world is known to us only by first directing our attention toward it, then perceiving it in some way with one or all of our five senses, and then getting a hold of it in our mind through some kind of representation of the object. Therefore, any consciousness of an object is always a consciousness *of* a specific object. This intrinsic connection links 'that which is thought' (*noema*) with the conscious thought or intellection (*noesis*) – to think, to purpose, to intend (*noeo*) with the mind (*nous*), the thinking/perceiving/sensing part of our soul. Brentano uses in his work of 1874, *Psychologie von empirischen Standpunkt*,[2] the term '*Die intentionale Inexistenz*'. This term becomes the foundational conception of phenomenological 'intentionality'.

As such, the *will to know* becomes critical; the world of sensible phenomena 'appears' to us, and our act of intention, our 'attending-to' the world, makes available objects of experience to our mind. The account of the relation between the psychical and the physical, termed by Brentano as 'intentionality', is partly derived from the Scholastic term *intentio*,

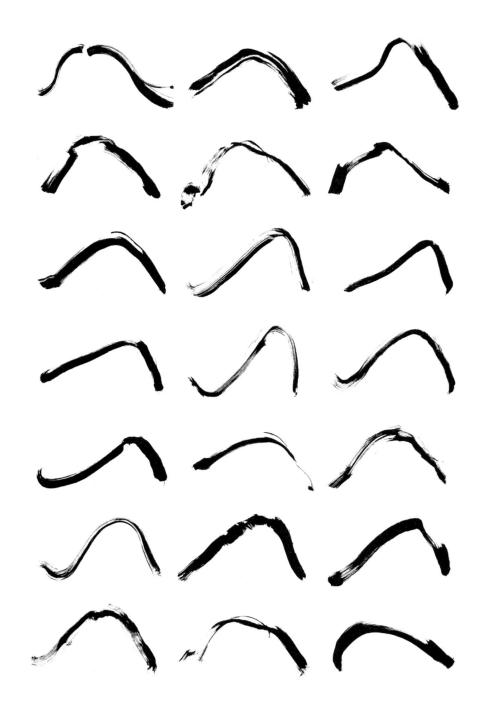

9.1   Chinese ink painting studying the
      curvature of the arch

which means 'directed toward'. An emphasis is put on the 'act' for Brentano, for intention is also dynamic and changing – an enactment of the individual will. Through the *consciousness of* phenomena, each individual has access to spatial and temporal determinations. Consequently, space and time do not need to be determined as a whole, for 'we do nonetheless, possess the presentation of something spatially [and temporally] determinate in general, and also a manifold of determinations of relative spatial [and temporal] differences'.[3] Although Brentano feels that Leibniz had the 'correct insight', the paradox remains as to how an individual *intuition of* the relational spatial outer sense and the temporal inner sense could be made to 'correspond' to some unity of perception of the world. The phenomenal world is a continuum, and yet how can the 'immanent' be said to be a unity as well? As a consequence, Brentano would then be left with the unfinished project of the inter-relatedness of individual consciousnesses.

Nevertheless, Leibniz gives a clue to solving this inter-relatedness problem in his idea of the monadic point of view. Inter-relatedness is assured because each individual perceives the world from his or her own point of view. A complete knowledge of the whole is only given to the architect of the whole – in Leibniz's terms, God. Yet collectively each individual point of view contributes to the whole network of relations, and as such constructs a world of relations. The world is quite simply then the summation of individual perceptions. Even though each individual is capable of perceiving only a small portion of the world, each individual is nonetheless *per se* inter-related with the whole through a system of relations in space and time.

Furthermore, the notion of the interconnectedness of space and time for the French phenomenologist philosopher, Maurice Merleau-Ponty, becomes that which *enables connection*.[4] Just as Brentano, Merleau-Ponty did not see the psychological and the physical as two radically separate terrains.[5] In his chief work, *The Phenomenology of Perception*, Merleau-Ponty develops an important account of perception that is not merely that of the sensible or visible. Perception is not merely looking at the world, or reflecting upon the world as is the case in modern philosophy; rather, perception is the phenomenological relation of intertwining with the world. Notably, Merleau-Ponty states: 'We are not in Space/Time; rather we are of Space/Time.' This position, in contradistinction to modernist thought, harkens back to Aristotle's *Physics*. Aristotle, at the beginning of Western philosophy, had determined that the nature of being was intrinsically tied to situation. Each being is singular and occupies a singular space/time. I am not merely some body that is in space and time, located in some kind of container with respect to some ideal objective viewpoint; on the contrary, I am part and parcel of this world, of this space and time, the very stuff of the world. In *The Visible and the Invisible*, Merleau-Ponty in his turn, would call this singularity of being, 'situational being'. To quote Merleau-Ponty (with the author's emphasis in bold):

I am not in space and time, nor do I conceive space and time; **I belong to them**, my body combines with them and includes them. The scope of this inclusion is the measure of that of my existence; but in any case it can never be all-embracing. **The space and time which I inhabit are always in their different ways indeterminate horizons which contain**

9.2   Wax and clay form studies

other points of view. The synthesis of both time and space is a task that always has to be performed afresh.[6]

In addition, with the standpoint of time as the horizon of Being, Martin Heidegger made an attempt in the twentieth century to account for the fact that as individuals we have our own existential experience, yet belong to the same world. I am 'in' the world, he said, and fundamentally interconnected with the things in it. I am always in relation *with* things in the world, and that relation is fundamentally spatial, characterised by an 'inconspicuous familiarity'[7] and a 'belongingness' (*Gehörigkeit*) and 'insideness' (*Inwendigkeit*).[8] I dwell in space. Or as Heidegger states, 'dwelling is the essence of Being-in-the-World'.[9] Dwelling is an immediate and ever-present commonplace. We all dwell. To say that 'we dwell' is already to say that we dwell *someplace* – that is, localised in space and time. Most importantly, then, Heidegger points out that 'dwelling' has a primordial and essential significance because this relation is how I am in the world fundamentally connected to the things in it. I am in relation with others; I dwell *with* them.

The last topic which I have been researching has been the very status of space and time itself, that is to say the ontology of space/time. In the publication, *Chronotopologies: Hybrid Spatialities and Multiple Temporalities*, the problem was to think about time in its relation to space from multiple viewpoints and scholarly disciplines.[10] My personal research has investigated time from an historical/epochal perspective. To this end, I looked to the philosophers/historians/sociologists Harootunian, Bloch, Foucault, Poulantzas, Koselleck and Gurvitch. In conceptions of absolute space and time, temporality was a static

position, a kind of freeze-frame, with respect to space, so that I could only speak of the position of an object at a certain time. With relative notions of space and time, on the other hand, I could only speak of the 'before' or 'after' with relation to some other body in a state of constant flux. Relativity is a variant, in fact, of Newtonian physics, with the speed of light serving as a constant referent. Yet the question remained: what would space and time *be* if taken not as separate ontological categories, but thought together as one true relation? With this question in hand, research was done on what I came to call 'chrono-topologies'. As such, the task was to problematise history as a spatio-temporal field, comprised of 'layers of time'.

Time, then, could be thought of not just as a simple linear chronological scheme of past, present and future. Consequently, I would have a temporal model of an infinite flow of individual times coexisting on a plane of immanence, thereby privileging the local/individual whilst acknowledging the connectiveness of the whole space/time structure. Space and time, then, are not a background upon which, or behind which, events occur and borders are drawn; rather, space and time are a relationship. I have a tendency to forget that I speak of a specific locality only at a moment in time. Space, too, has its own time.

With historical events, an account must be made to make a common story, yet without reducing history to the history of a few powerful figures, reducing the complexity of history to a totality. Rather, history is a sort of social framework encompassing a multiplicity of temporalities, each having its own rhythm, qualities, speed, migration and duration. As such, any account of historical time must take into consideration that events *per se* occur in a situatedness of plural positions in space/time,

9.3   The promenade and the bridge/arch pass through the historical museum building and continue on to the Overhoeks Tower and EYE Film Museum

in a multi-layered richness of temporal continuity. Without the time of the natural sciences providing a measuring stick, and without a linear conception of history, another theory must be actualised in order to not only tie together synchronic events, but also provide a substratum that accounts for succession and duration. A difficult task indeed, for historicity must provide an account for both the intersubjectivity of various historical persons, and the interconnection of events in space.

CONCEPT

The project for an historical museum in Amsterdam gives an opportunity to ask the question about

'What is history?' Indeed, how do I think time as history? An epochal notion of history is situated within the thought of the history of the earth itself as well as the 'small-scale' history of an individual lifetime. As such, the project becomes a kind of temporal and spatial node in a relational field. And soon the building can be seen as a nexus of interconnectedness reaching out into the infinity of space and time. As a nexus, then, a very particular and dense spatio-temporality occurs on the site of the project. The key task would be to express some kind of collective time known as a shared history, as well as individual experience. Subsequently, the research into the philosophy of space and time enables the conceptual thought of multiple times co-existing within an infinite flow of space. As such, even the present – a present defined as the lifetime of an architecture – is a rich and multi-layered phenomenon. Without an attempt to reduce the variety of spatio-temporal experience, attempts at a false unification which would automatically only speak of the hegemonic, an historical time would seek to preserve the complexity and multiplicity of collective experience. These experiences conceptually can be said to converge and diverge upon the specific site of the historical museum.

Nevertheless, time as history must also be heterogeneous in the sense that the nexus explodes into a notion of futuricity. As Harry Harootunian provocatively states: 'All history is made in the present.' Therefore, the architecture becomes the site for not only for a building, but a productive or generative, open-ended conception of time and space.

DESCRIPTIONS OF THE PROJECT

Of course the move from the abstract to the material is often a matter of standing on the edge of the abyss. This is architecture, the materialisation of an idea. In the following project, a proposal for an historical museum on the shores of the old harbour of Amsterdam, several ideas come to the fore: interconnectedness, historical time versus individual time and situatedness in space/time. How does the architecture reflect or express these notions? Or more importantly, does thinking about space and time in a more fundamental and originary way help to create a more 'commodus' architecture, as Vitruvius would say?

This project proposal for an historical museum on the old harbour of Amsterdam attempts to speak to conclusions of more than two decades of research into space and time. However, such abstract notions can never be literally realised; rather, they are a guiding attitude for the determination of architectural practice. Philosophical thought cannot be translated literally into architectural form. Indeed the form cannot 'represent' the idea, rather it 'expresses' the idea. Undoubtedly, the effluent and temporal nature of all architectural interventions call for a measure of humility. Yet embracing the temporal and often temporary nature of the spaces that I create can also be seen as a brave historical moment in time. One could almost read the history of a city, for example, based upon what kind of buildings populate the urban fabric: Glasgow is an industrial late nineteenth century-city; Naples is a layering of thousands of years of diverse occupying cultures; and the centre of Amsterdam reflects its prosperity in the sixteenth and seventeenth centuries. The harbour specifically was critical for the maritime success and colonial expansion of the republic of the Netherlands. Life was always oriented towards this harbour, with its frenetic activity and fiscal import. In the 1830s, the railroad and the central station were built, joining Amsterdam with the sea at Haarlem and Ijmuiden. After centuries, the harbour was estranged from old system of canals which allowed smaller barges to ferry goods from the sea-faring ships to the weighing stations and the rows of warehouses in the core of Amsterdam. The subsequent shipping activities were moved extrinsically to the centre, and even in the late twentieth century, were moved effectively outside of the city altogether. This estrangement of Amsterdam from its origins and merchant roots not only caused urban impoverishment, but left the

9.4 Plan of Amsterdam harbour showing the proposed bridge/arch, historical museum and promenade

city without a true reason for existing at the mouth of the Amstel River. In the most recent decade, the city planning office has developed policy plans in order to encourage redevelopment of the area into a cultural centre, with links to the already existing important network of museums, concert halls and famous neighbourhoods.

Indeed, a city can be read as a palimpsest with traces, scars and buried layers of historical interventions. As architects, we merely make our gesture, our intervention, into the manuscript of the city to be scraped away, built upon, or obscured by future generations. In the Amsterdam of this present era, the explicit desire is to speak not only of this particular space/time, but also allude to various traces and layers that have existed historically. Compliant with the municipal planning office, the historical museum project contributes to the cultural zoning for the area around the former harbour, both on the South side and what is now called Amsterdam North. Already several important initiatives have begun to populate the area: the Bimhuis and IJ Music Building, further out is the NDSM docks, the new man-made island of IJburg

9.5 Aerial view showing the promenade unfolding along the waterfront and joining together the historical centre of the city with other cultural institutions on the North side

(which is mostly housing), the articulation of the edge with high-end office and apartment buildings, a new passenger terminal for large cruise ships, the renovation of the former Shell headquarters (Overhoeks Tower), and the strengthening the connections by ferry across from the Central Station and traffic behind the station, plugging into the public transportation network, Sixhaven yachting harbour, NEMO Science Museum, municipal library, newly renovated Amsterdam Maritime Museum and most recently the opening of the new film museum, called the EYE. Yet conspicuously lacking is a coherent connection between these elements, a promenade to give the water back to the pedestrian and allow for civic venues such as SAIL Amsterdam to have a jewel from which to celebrate the historical maritime ships. In addition, Amsterdam in turning away from the harbour has also deprived itself of an entrance gate, an announcement of civic pride, a place marker. The municipality holds hope for the future location for the Olympics. Of course, nature and recreation, the encouragement of creative industries, and let us not forget shopping, provide a stable anchoring for the activities in the harbour area. Therefore, this proposal for the harbour of Amsterdam attempts to take these considerations on board, not only in order to relate itself to the particular space/time that is Amsterdam, but also to make a positive contribution to the spatial qualities of this important area in the twenty-first century.

This proposal for an historical museum in the old harbour of Amsterdam addresses these issues by providing a physical connection between the two shores of the harbour as well as a landmark attraction for the people and visitors of the city. Embedded into the design of the building, bridge and promenade is the influence of relations in space/time. The bridge/arch begins on the South shores of the IJ harbour with bifurcating legs arising from the music centre of Aan 't IJ/Bimhuis and from the path along the water that leads from the central railway station to the new passenger terminal for cruise ships. The intention is to have a sloping elevator system to bring visitors to the apex of the arch, where the path gently slopes down to the North side of the harbour. At the apex of the arch, the triangular section of the arch broadens out into a parabolic asymmetrically converging viewing platform for opportunity to see the entire harbour, the outlying city, the passing ships and the coming and going of much activity around the harbour. Proceeding along the archway, the bridge spans the entire harbour, connecting into the historical museum building, skirting along the water and becoming the promenade that interconnects the North side of the Amsterdam harbour. The bridge/arch here follows a groove carved into the side of the building, providing respite to enjoy the view, a close connection with the water and the opportunity to enter the historical museum whilst catching a glimpse of the activities inside. Leaving the Sixhaven site of the historical museum, the interconnection continues by arching up over the sea channel going into Northern Holland and the North–South metro line, landing at the platform where the ferries dock for the central railroad station, connecting to an area in development for creative industries where the former Shell headquarters in Amsterdam were located, wrapping around the Overhoeks Tower, to land upon the shores of the IJ harbour behind the newly opened EYE Film

Museum. As such the bridge/arch connects in a dramatic and spatially exciting way the two shores of the Amsterdam Harbour and interconnects with various cultural institutions, buildings, events and visitor experiences.

The historical museum itself sits in a location at the end of a small island peninsula and docks for yachts and pleasure crafts. Tucked away from the busy shipping channel, the yachting harbour lies at the intersection of various transportation networks of shipping, rail, metro, auto, public transportation, pedestrians and not to forget the all-pervasive Amsterdam cyclists. The historical museum provides an important edge along the waterfront. The museum is entered at a level which is two storeys up from the water. A visitor can enter along the peninsula of the yachting harbour, or from the waterside continuous promenade of the bridge/arch that ties the Southern side of the harbour with the Northern. At this level, the building involutes along the elevation in order to receive the bridge/arch. This seamless walkway is covered by the building itself overhanging, and at two points it offers entrance into the museum, and into the café and museum shop. This place becomes an important public viewing platform for the harbour of Amsterdam without having to enter the museum proper. On the floor below the entrance is an exhibition space, intentionally kept open so as to allow maximum flexibility for curators. In the level which is in fact under the water level, an auditorium as well as archive space is situated. With its own independent access, the performance space can become multi-functional, providing an auditorium for various group functions, not just for the museum itself.

9.6   A viewing platform at the apex
of the arch, over the IJ, creates a
visual relation with the city

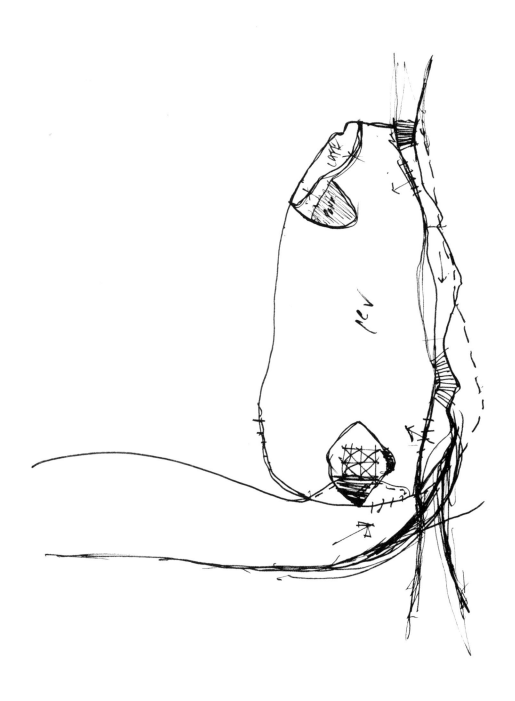

9.7 Preliminary sketch showing the pathway
carving out a channel on the waterside of the
historical museum

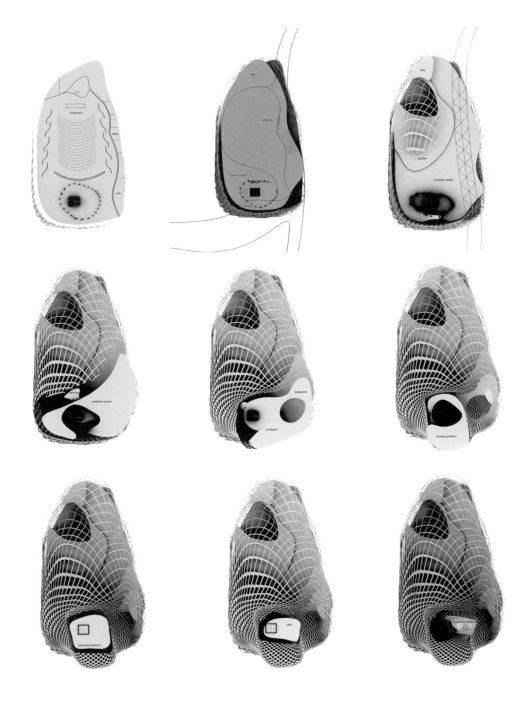

9.8 Horizontal sections showing the vertical circulation core interlacing with exhibition spaces, gardens, auditorium and viewing platforms

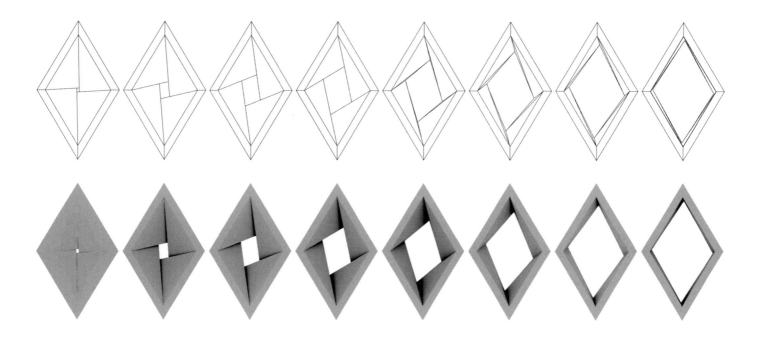

9.9 'Diamond' component for the façade with a variable diaphragm to respond to changing light conditions

Importantly, at the fourth level, the building opens up to the sky in a public garden including a small pond, an outdoor café, lounging and walking areas. Above the garden, the tower of the museum continues, but at various points balconies, bridges, walkways and viewing platforms penetrate the outer skin of the building to make connections with the rest of the building and visually to the harbour of Amsterdam itself. The core tower is also biomorphic and contains the elevators/stairs/toilets/mechanical rooms, having ramps and bridges flying off to connect with exterior skin tower. The core tower is clad with a different 'diamond' component, and at a certain point near the top of the building bursts through the outer building tower which is clad with a heliotropic 'diamond' component. Finally, at the summit of the tower, a 'bird's nest' viewing platform offers the entire panorama of the city to the visitor. As such the historical museum is tied into the harbour as a whole, both spatially and visually.

METHODOLOGY

This project was designed with the most advanced software technologies currently available, alongside the most ancient, time-proven means: a pencil on a piece of paper, a paintbrush filled with Chinese ink, moulding wax and clay, words and gestures. Initially, after the years of research thinking through the nature of space and time, the philosophical position must filter down into the cellular level,

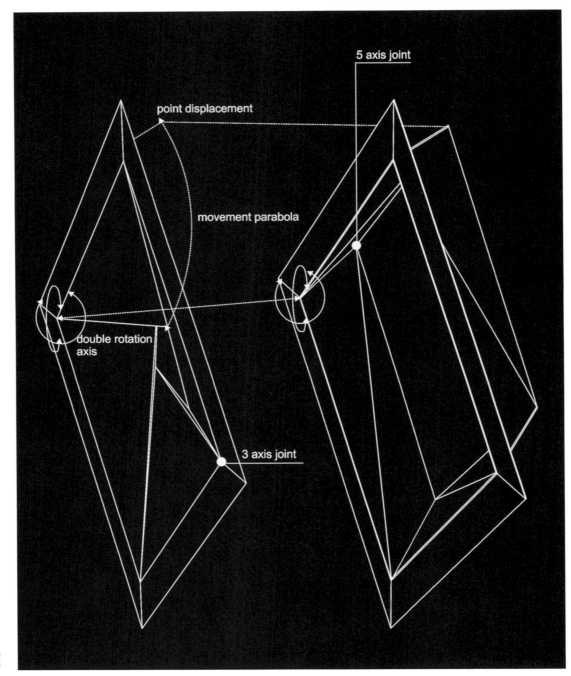

5 axis joint

point displacement

movement parabola

double rotation
axis

3 axis joint

9.10   Detail of the 'diamond' component to be
       plugged into the mesh

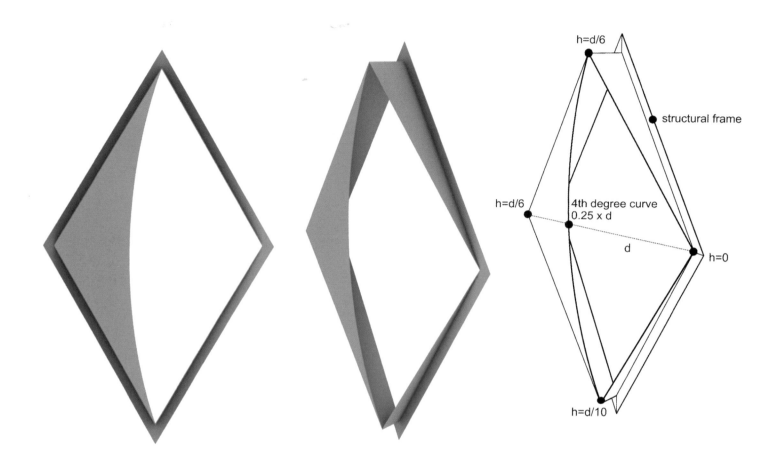

h=d/6

structural frame

h=d/6

4th degree curve
0.25 x d

d

h=0

h=d/10

9.11   Fixed 'diamond' component for use on
the circulation core

so to speak, so that it becomes not just 'thought' but a 'thinking through'. At the point when I could finally understand on an intellectual and analytical level that space and time was not a thing, rather a relation, the main work was yet to be done. This work was the perception of the relation itself. The nature of the relation was grasped through intuitive understanding, a higher faculty of thought than analysis in that the whole is understood in its entirety. This intuitive understanding of the space/time relation then becomes the origin of the creative act.

Given this understanding, architecture is then made from a 'jumping out' of this originary idea.

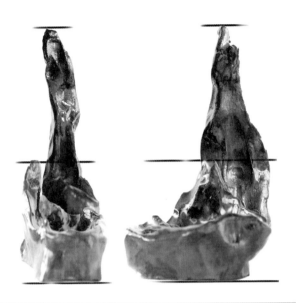

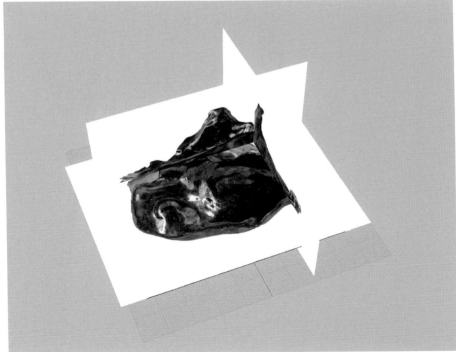

9.12   Rationalising the form study models into
        a parametric mesh

Not an easy thing to do. From the origin comes the creation. The initial studies of this building where simple ink paintings to come to a pure gesture of the bridge/arch, as well as small clay and molding wax models to explore the form of the building. In these studies, most importantly, it was paramount not to 'think'. At the originary moment of creation, the analytic faculty of the mind is obstructive. Instead, I encourage and in fact desperately need to 'not think'. This process is known by the ancient Greeks as '*poesis*', or 'making', which is to say a kind of knowing that comes from getting your hands dirty. 'Not thinking' at this stage in the creative process is in fact quite difficult, but critical. Only after the form emerges from the origin can the rationalisation/ mathematisation process begin.

At this stage of the design process for the historical museum, the project team (including myself as chief architect along with Simona Puglisi, Cristina Ampatzidou, Silvia Roxana Palfi and Gustavo Nascimento) went to work with the tools of Rhino, Photoshop, Bender, V-Ray as well as various state-of-the-art software plug-ins such as Grasshopper. In order to be able to model the building from the form studies, a strategy needed to be developed as to how to best implement softwares that were intended for parametric design. A surface as opposed to a pointed grid is a much easier element to use for parametric design. Nevertheless, the project was 'reverse engineered', starting not from the parameters required to generate form with the methodology of parametric design, but from the old-fashioned modelling techniques. The team began to work with Rhino – a software that works with 'nurbs', and the parametric design was done in Grasshopper – a plug-in for Rhino. However, a surface approach has limitations, and so could not be used for

modelling such a complex geometry. Consequently, the building was modelled as a mesh, which is more flexible and allowed the generation of the required biomorphic geometry.

Yet this mesh approach had limitations as well, giving problems with the initial mesh definition from which the final building had to be sculpted. Several iterations were needed in order to achieve the correct mesh subdivision so that the team could rationalise the shape for the parametric component application. Ultimately the mesh points were used as an input for the surfaces so that the application of two different diamond-shaped components could be applied to the skin. The modelling was then accomplished not by scanning in the original form studies, but by another kind of 'sculpting' in Blender software, as 'pushing and pulling' in order to actually model the building geometry. The basic mesh was first created and then shaped until the desired shape was reached. The first attempt at a model did not have a sufficient amount of mesh subdivisions, which in the process of deformation did not allow the mesh to stretch in order to achieve all the intricacies of the design. Consequently another mesh was created with more subdivisions to provide the articulation of the curvatures. Still, in the end, the complexity of the original form studies was simplified in order to achieve a continuous mesh. The largest challenge was to achieve a shape that could be properly rationalised in order to apply a parametric component on it, while at the same time preserving all the original features of the form studies. Ultimately, as with any true architectural project, the poetry of the original idea needs to be maintained and to shine out in the finished building in spite of multiple iterations, compromises,

9.13 A study of the horizontal sections
connecting the inner circulation
core with the outer mesh

collaborations and the very process itself. In this regard, years of research and experience help to hold on to the idea as it is materialised into architecture.

'Space is not a thing': this is the conclusion of my philosophical investigations, and yet how is it that I can advance this proposition when I have made 'space', I have made architecture? The concept of the building sought to think of history as a multi-layered, spatio-temporally continuous and ever-changing event. The architecture is but a nexus in a relation

9.14   Digital studies of mesh on the
building form

9.15   The Amsterdam historical museum at
night reflected in the water of the harbour

of inter-connectedness and situatedness in space/
time. How does the design reflect or express these
notions? Or more importantly, does thinking about
space and time in a more fundamental and originary
way help to think of architecture itself in a more
originary way?

CONTEXTUALISATION

Briefly, I wish to mention two other architecture
practices that deal with architecture as but a nexus in
a relation of inter-connectedness and situatedness
in space/time, albeit using differing methodological
approaches. One practice in Amsterdam also

advocates a 'process-oriented approach', and that is UN Studio.[11] As Caroline Bos, one of the partners with Ben van Berkel, explains:

> ... movement is the program and the program is moving. Spaces that are dedicated to specific uses are defined more in relation to time than to topography. The time-based topological organization requires a vast input of information ... a knot of flows.[12]

In considering time as methodologically important as space as such, UN Studio breaks with classical mechanics, acknowledging that the phenomenal world is really not as simple as the traditional classical models of physics and mathematics modelled them. Using new software derived from the airplane industry, gaming and animation software, the design methodology reiterates possible solutions to complex problems, effects and flows.

In an attempt to generate time or process-based architecture, non-trivial solutions rely upon the use of parameters. Parameters are, in effect, controlled variables. In order to generate structurally stable systems with these mathematical models, the most important thing is the *relation* of the parameters to other phenomenal variables. Here the relation is emphasised. However, the most important thing is the choice of the parameters themselves in a modelling application – quite simply, the more variables the more complex the nonlinearities become. Subsequently, the relations between the parameters will generate multiple simultaneous solutions.

Parametric design mirrors the contemporary pluralistic world view in that it considers any intervention as a complex system of a great many variables and interacting relations. In a system of inter-relatedness, an architect still chooses which parameters to consider important, which relations are dominant, and which moment in time to express. As such, an architect makes a 'subjective' judgment, albeit while trying to acknowledge that this judgment can never function independently of other forces. In the end, even though only one possible solution is chosen – as one 'attainable' solution (affordable + sustainable) – architecture is 'not the object itself, but the sets of relationships between the component parts [which] are articulated and defined'.[13] With the design research and methodology of UN Studio, architecture seems to emanate from space/time relations.

Another way to consider architecture as a nexus in a relation of inter-connectedness and situatedness in space/time, is within the context of the ecological or sustainability debate. In this way, any specific architectural intervention would always be seen in a wider whole world, both impacting and being impacted by a global ecology and economy. Inter-relatedness is quite simply the acknowledgement of our mutual interdependence on this earth. What one individual undertakes – either constructively or destructively – impacts upon the whole. Another architectural practice in Amsterdam, Thomas Rau Architects, takes this ideology as a foundational concept for design.[14] Far more significantly than merely designing ecologically responsible buildings, Rau looks at architecture from the micro-material scale as well as from the perspective of global economies and equitable societies. Most importantly, Rau began a collaboration that is modelled also on a productive humane working paradigm called the oneplanetarchitecture Institute.[15] Through the oneplanetarchitecture Institute, Rau approaches design as a social phenomenon in a holistic approach. Of course, as an architect, Rau also creates beautiful spaces – this hardly seems exclusionary – for beauty is also 'humanistic'. Nevertheless, Rau emphasises methodology rather than product, seeing architecture as situated in a specific place, yet intrinsically connected with the whole.

Finally, what could 'space is not a thing, rather a relation' mean for architecture? Here I would quote Prigogine:

> Whatever our professional preoccupations may be, we cannot escape the feeling that we live in an age of transition, an age that demands constructive modification of our environment. We must find and explore new resources, must understand our environment better, and must achieve a less destructive coexistence with nature.[16]

In the end, space and time are the ground from which all human experience is determined. An intuitive understanding of the space/time relation then becomes the origin of the creative act. Architecture begins as a node within this relational field, but then projects or 'expresses' itself into a productive or generative act. The architect merely steps into a moment in time in order to create situatedness, in order to create a relation.

Notes

1 For a fuller account, see: Leslie Kavanaugh, *The Architectonic of Philosophy: Plato, Aristotle, Leibniz* (Amsterdam: Amsterdam University Press, 2007).

2 Franz Brentano, *Psychology from an Empirical Standpoint* (London: Routledge, 1995).

3 Franz Brentano, *Philosophical Investigations on Space, Time, and the Continuum* (London: Routledge, 1988), p. 169. This citation comes from Leibniz's Letter to Volder, *Die philosophischen Schriften von Leibniz, von Gottfried Wilheml Liebniz; hrsg. von C.I. Gerhardt* (Berlin: Weidmann, 1875-1890), GPII, p. 221.

4 Maurice Merleau-Ponty, *Phenomenology of Perception* (London: Routledge, 1994), pp. 243–4.

5 Ibid., p. 10.

6 Ibid., p. 140.

7 Martin Heidegger, *Being and Time* (New York: Wiley-Blackwell, 1962), p. 137.

8 Ibid., p. 134.

9 Martin Heidegger, 'Letter on Humanism', in David Farrell Krell (ed.), *Martin Heidegger: Basic Writings* (New York: Harper Collins, 1977), p. 236.

10 Leslie Kavanaugh, 'The Time of History/The History of Time', in Leslie Kavanaugh (ed.), *Chronotopologies: Hybrid Spatialities and Multiple Temporalities* (Amsterdam: Rodopi, 2010), pp. 91–124.

11 UN Studio website, http://www.unstudio.com (accessed 21 March 2013).

12 Caroline Bos, 'Techniques and Effects', in Kari Jormakka, *Absolute Motion*, DATUTOP no.22 (Tampere: University of Technology, School of Architecture, 2002), p. 115.

13 Ibid., p. 112.

14 Rau Architects website, http://www.rau.eu (accessed 21 March 2013).

15 oneplanetarchitecture Institute website, http://www.opai.eu (accessed 21 March 2013).

16 Grégoire Nicolis & Ilya Prigogine, *Exploring Complexity* (New York: W.H. Freeman, 1989), p. 1.

EVEN MORE THAN ARCHITECTURE

Richard Coyne

In this chapter I argue that architecture draws inevitably from disciplines outside its immediate orbit. This impulse to borrow from elsewhere supports healthy and vital architectural research – especially design research, which is further aided by the growing use of online media. Drawing on ideas from hermeneutics I conclude that exposure to the 'otherness' of disciplines that may be regarded as 'alien' disrupts knowledge structures and keeps architectural research relevant and engaging.

Architecture is a robust discipline.[1] The mass media publicises celebrity architects, high-profile competitions, prizes, important iconic and economy-boosting flagship building projects, as well as high-profile cost overruns and architectural controversies. The demand for places in architecture schools is perennially high. Most urban dwellers in developed countries exercise an informed interest in buildings, and recognise that the procurement and design of buildings require coordinated effort by specialists with many years of training.

To what extent does architecture's authority reside in the concept of a disciplinary core? During his foray into the world of architects in the 1980s, the philosopher Jacques Derrida tried to identify what could be the core, or foundation, of architecture.[2] His purpose was to show that architecture could never be the truly radical or deconstructive discipline advocated by his newly found architectural compatriots. He identified four key concepts to which architects lay claim and on which architecture seems to depend. The first was the concept of home and related ideas about dwelling and hearth. Second was the nostalgia within modern architecture for a centre, an origin, a set of primary principles, an ordering, including belief in the sacred origins of architecture (for example in the primitive hut or the place of architecture in the symbolic union between the microcosm and the macrocosm). Third, he noted how architecture is wedded to ideas of social betterment and the service of humankind (for example social improvement through better housing). And fourth, the pursuit of beauty, harmony and completeness – what Derrida called 'the fine arts'. From Derrida's point of view, as a philosopher of radical hermeneutics, architecture cannot escape its dependence on these foundations, even though they are shaky. Such is the tactic of post-structuralism to identify dilemmas, contradictions and paradoxes where others seek certainties.

It was Bernard Tschumi who brokered the interaction between Derrida and architecture, or at least with the architectural formalist, Peter Eisenman. Tschumi reports that on their meeting, Derrida inquired of Tschumi why architects should be interested in his work since 'deconstruction is anti-form, anti-hierarchy, anti-structure – the opposite of all that architecture stands for'.[3] 'Precisely for this reason', was Tschumi's reply. The flirtation between architecture and philosophy was here predicated on differences rather than similarities.

Whether or not Derrida was right in his identification of the supposed core of architecture, in fact architecture's conservatism proves to offer no disservice to its practice. Not least this conservatism provides the requisite target for onslaughts and challenges from radical continental philosophy. Architecture is a strong adversary and worthy target of critique from all quarters. Buildings and cities tend to stay around whatever people say about them, or about architects.

For 'conservative', think also of conservation and preservation. The favourable reception of architecture has time on its side. In European cities at least, architecture lays out its history before us, and the positive reception of architecture in general is abetted in no small part by the growth in global tourism, competition between nations and cities for business, and a desire to create living environments attractive to a productive work force. The past sells cities.

As a further indicator of architecture's esteem, consider the proliferation of architectural commentary, analysis, and images generated by amateurs and professionals on the Internet. Architecture's security as a high-profile asset in the public imagination is indicated by the popularity of 'architecture' as a search tag in crowd-sourced image repositories such as Flickr and Pinterest. Here architecture is in the elevated company of 'weddings', 'health' and 'travel' in the popular imagination.

I think that architecture's wide appeal is one of the reasons it can afford to be reckless and permissive in its boundaries – secure because buildings are solid, grounded and conspicuous. However we define architecture, there really is no need to exclude other disciplines from its orbit, or to be reluctant to encroach into the territory of others. This has been my own working hypothesis about architecture while at times overseeing its position in the multidisciplinary context of a large university. Professional accreditation provides a further boost to this esteem. Any group of qualified architects or associates inherits architecture's institutional legitimacy.

As suggested by Derrida's reference to the grounding of architecture in the fine arts, architecture is indebted to the classical tradition.

The classicists, descendants of Vitruvius, add historical legitimacy to the conceit that, after all, architects are polymaths with a grasp of all the arts and sciences, a boast sustained into modernity. It is no wonder therefore that architecture departments in colleges and universities, as well as those innovative practices to whom they are often connected do not restrict themselves to buildings, landscapes, urban environments and construction, but have played host to activities and disciplines that are broader than, and even subversive of, any putative core practices to which architecture wishes to lay claim. Many educational institutions and practices embrace in their architectural curricula and activity profiles themes that could be thought to reside within engineering, health, social geography, landscape, film, cultural and media studies, music, sound, graphic design, computer interaction, politics, and of course, philosophy. This is not to say architects handle such themes expertly, or even adequately. At this stage in my case it is enough to note architecture's disciplinary profligacy. Architecture's mastery 'of none' need provide no impediment to its security as a discipline.

One clear illustration of architecture's openness to other disciplines in the humanities comes from Tschumi's explanation for his Parc de la Villette project in the 1990s. His vision for the park was to bring together artists and writers as well as designers in a cultural exchange. 'Bringing together various disciplines and establishing crossovers was a key concept of the park, in the same way as in my earlier activity as a teacher at the Architectural Association and at Princeton University in the mid-1970s, I would give my students texts by Kafka, Calvino, Hegel, Poe, Joyce and other authors as programs for architectural projects.'[4] Of course, this particular list omits texts on microclimate, servicing, planning, structures, history, and graphic novels. However, it indicates architecture's claim as a 'synthetic' discipline that brings anything and everything to bear on a design task, even literature.

What does this architectural inclusivity say about research? Such permissiveness has implications for defining architectural research, that is, research carried out by scholars and R&D personnel connected with architecture departments in universities, research institutes, government departments, museums, and private practice. It suggests a fluid approach to research. In the United Kingdom, the issue of what constitutes architectural research is decided pragmatically by who is prepared to fund its projects (if funding is required), which journals or other venues will it be published in, which category does it come under in the UK-wide research assessment system (for example through the Research Excellence Framework or REF) and whether any particular research project might be eligible for professional recognition, for example the annual RIBA Research Awards. Pragmatic institutional pressures that have little to do with architecture and its putative core come into play in the definition of architectural research.

KEYWORD RESEARCH

The instant availability of resources online, particularly through institutional access to digital repositories of research publications, as well as to various other kinds of archive material, also contributes to the permissiveness of architectural research, affecting other disciplines as well. Web searching is highly sympathetic to the practices of design. Whereas once a designer would browse magazines for pictures offering ideas and inspiration, images are available in profusion online, and from a wealth of sources. The same applies to texts. The examiner of any undergraduate student essay or design project is now unlikely to be surprised by references to articles from psychology, education, geography, health and philosophy journals that are off the reading list, and could only have been identified and accessed online. Citation data is available at a glance through tools such as Google Scholar, which in turn provides opportunities for researchers to thread their way through both mainstream and marginal literature on a subject, and establish new connections.

Some critics think that we have just entered an era of shallow, superficial browsing and reading. After all Amazon and Google Books provide facilities for searching and extracting quotations from books without having to read them.[5] Other commentators think of the advantages of gathering information in an instant, synthesising it into something new, and conflating the process of reading with that of writing. For commentators such as Don Tapscott, habituated web users do not rely on the linear narratives provided by texts as presented by their authors, but instead, through instant and broadcastable media such as weblogs and Twitter feeds, construct their own narratives.[6] Here reading converges with design. Reading becomes active, synthetic, shared and creative.

Though some seminal texts still require financial outlay, the researcher has instant access to peer-reviewed articles, many of which are oblique to someone steeped in the disciplines of architecture. In fact, my recent search on 'sustainability' and

'cladding' on Edinburgh University's own text search engine yielded 33 full text articles from journals specialising in nuclear reactors, energy management, contracts, risk, as well as to building-related journals, any of which could be relevant to an architectural research project. They are available at the click of a button for browsing, selecting, reading, quoting and citing.

Then there's the more ludic opportunities provided by web search. What happens when you enter 'sustainability' and 'Piranesi' into a search engine? Something synthetic emerges. If it is not the answer to a research problem, then as a stimulus to the interpretive capabilities of the design researcher, it is a bit like contemplating a hat stand in proximity to an anvil in a Surrealist artwork.[7]

Keyword (re)search looms large in the contemporary researcher's repertoire. An early foray into a potential research venture can begin

with web search. Has anyone thought of relating sustainability, architecture and music? The search engine that I use reveals that Mario Bellini Architects designed a pop music centre for Taipei that does just that. The search engine produced 66 articles. Only a few are about concert halls. Keyword search at first blush appears superficial and even trivial as means of developing a research trajectory. In working with research students I have learned that the use of search terms is a skill requiring fluency in the language of the search medium. Whether or not search engine research will aid productive and efficient research, encourage deep understanding of a topic, instil clarity, or beget confusion and casual scholarship, it increases exposure to an extravagance of sources, more than architecture.

It is also possible that this access to online resources will enhance architecture's contact with its own assets. I commonly review articles and books on

10.1   A typical research-oriented weblog using Word Press

10.2   Search engine as association machine, revealing a pictorial collage from the unlikely combination of search terms 'sustainability' and 'Piranesi' urbanism that reference key sources, as they should (for example texts by Manuell Castells, Michel de Certeau, Henri Lefebvre), but seem unaware of the contribution in these areas of other researchers from within architecture, other than those within the researcher's close knit peer community. The increasingly noisy context of international Internet scholarship may yet render research cultures in architecture more critical and even more robust, and demand advanced skills in discriminating and filtering source material.

Internet-savvy researchers combine online research repositories with social media, weblogs, micro-blogging and other online practices as media in which to develop research: for gaining evidence, receiving feedback, rehearsing, reviewing, and supplementing research, as well as building research communities and enhancing confidence and esteem. Building on the kinds of databases and algorithms used in anti-plagiarism software for checking student work, we may soon see software that takes a researcher's draft text and recommends books and articles as yet uncited. This promiscuous research milieu is inevitably noisy and no doubt prone to difficulties and unpredicted misuse. The risk in avoiding the noise is that there are now fewer pretexts for ignoring the research of others. We researchers are exposed, including to those outside the discipline.

THE QUANTIFICATION OF THE INTELLECT

The Internet also exposes the reputations of researchers in certain ways, not least by online metrics of followers, hit and citation counts and the controversial publication of individual citation indices, each likely to influence research trajectories. Architectural research has a relatively small audience, producing modest metrics. In so far as numbers have any kind of influence, then architectural researchers may start to skew their outputs to appeal to an even wider audience. That scholars from other disciplines can stumble across architectural research online may increase pressure to expand its appeal, reach and impact.

The economic and social impact of research is a qualitative matter that easily elides into a consideration of quantities, influencing the boundaries of a discipline. The impact of a research project is often indicated by audience figures: book sales, footfall at exhibitions, demonstrably large numbers of readers, visitors, users, consumers and beneficiaries. With its propensity towards counting, currently available online media seem to be drawing the communication of research in the direction of the mass media. For example, the British government's new-found emphasis on public accountability under the rubric of impact, combined with the growth of the Internet as a powerful broadcast medium, brings otherwise niche research themes into collision with the idea of a mass audience. Important research into allergy-free living environments resides cheek-by-jowl with pop videos of piano-playing cats and homespun advice on dating. Scholarly research is typically a narrow-cast activity, but the channels in which research is developed and disseminated are becoming broader. The Internet pressures the architectural researcher to think about and construct an 'online presence', and orchestrate their own publicity in the noisy context of online broadcasting.

Internet tools are available for researchers to publish and promote their research, via messages, comments, articles, images and volumes for anyone

Architecture etc Like 0

Pictures appearing in richardcoyne.com blog posts with links to specific posts. All photos are by the author (except where indicated, the BookAdopter logo and book covers).

Richard Coyne   Edit Board   17 followers, 141 pins

10.3   Pictorial information in Pinterest,
        referenced to weblog posts

Country	Views
United Kingdom	13,489
United States	2,375
Australia	758
Canada	419
Netherlands	339
Greece	317
India	290
Germany	264
Italy	258
Portugal	243
France	208
Philippines	203
New Zealand	193
Malaysia	177
Brazil	177
Malta	176
Spain	164
Ireland	153
Turkey	151
Denmark	150
Republic of Korea	148
Singapore	135

10.4 Information on website visits to the author's own blog site according to country

to see, to garner feedback and construct networks of followers, readers and 'fans' through social media, all under the reign of numbers: page views, hits, visitors, friends, followers, citations, subscribers. As a broadcast medium, quantities are conspicuously present on the Internet – to be viewed, compared, gloated over, embarrassed about, and provide evidence for influence, reputation and impact, or its lack.

It is sobering to compare mass media statistics readily available online, such as those provided by the Broadcasters Audience Research Board (BARB) in the UK, with research citations. At the end of last year I looked up the BARB figures for the popular ITV programme *The X Factor*. Over 10.8 million viewers were entertained by the show on the last night of the series. Around that time the most viewed video on YouTube was *Evolution of Dance* by Judson Laipply, with over 180 million cumulative hits. *The Guardian* newspaper was averaging 232,566 sales per daily issue (although falling). The top-selling book

series was the *Harry Potter* stories (over 45 million according to a recent Wikipedia entry). Compare these figures with research citations. According to an academic article on citation indices, the average paper in the life sciences is cited about 6 times.[8] The publication of download figures from paper repositories such as academic.edu, when available, are unlikely to reveal numbers comparable to those of the reception of mass media content.

These media channels and content types do not of course have comparable intellectual impact or influence. The unit of measure is not the same in each case. But increasingly researchers have to make choices about the time they invest as scholars, opposed to online citizen reporters and popularisers. The latter restricts research communications to bite-sized chunks, simplification, sensationalism, topicality and migrating across topics without settling on outcomes. In any case, the new online contexts in which research takes place, pose challenges for researchers, expanding the boundaries of their disciplines and exposing them to wider audiences.

Add to this permissiveness the online fascination with user-generated content (for example YouTube and Vimeo) and concepts of co-creation.[9] The Internet promotes the rhetoric of democratised creativity, knowledge and information. There are online methods for gathering data (for example online surveys and quizzes), and means of harnessing skills distributed in the community, such as crowd sourcing used in some data-processing activity that requires uniquely human capability to solve – deploying the problem-solving skills of online volunteers to identify three-dimensional protein structures, or discover new stellar objects from images of the night sky. The Internet amplifies the promise of small elements contributing to the creation of a complex whole that exceeds the sum of its parts. In this case it is done through the combined agency of hundreds of interconnected individual computer users. Crowd-sourcing implies that we are all in it together, irrespective of expertise or training, and is indicative of an abrogation of traditional disciplinary boundaries as sites of expertise.

Such digital tactics resonate with the social-orientation of much architectural thinking. Consider the case of Hannes Meyer (1889–1954) and the social ambitions of the Bauhaus, and the user-participation social housing projects of the architect Ralph Erskine (1914–2005), among others, including more recent activist practice. According to some observers, participatory and community-oriented design projects seek to challenge 'academic, professional, artistic, and political practice' by addressing 'the creativity and criticality of a new approach to the city'. This approach is necessarily heterogeneous, and 'reflects a multiplicity of viewpoints and ways of doing'.[10] Crowd-sourced architecture is gaining currency – and is introducing new terms and methods for old ideas.

THE LEGACY OF SYSTEMS THEORY

I have not yet indicated any relationship between architecture's permissiveness in research and the identification of need – in other words, what needs to be researched? Surely researchers have to identify some problem in need of a solution. The means to that end is research. I think that embarking on a programme of research on the basis of problem identification has given way to a more pragmatic recognition that research is problem-defining as well as problem-solving.[11] But even the problem-oriented view speaks of leakages across disciplinary boundaries.

The field of research known as 'systems theory' from the late 1940s onwards, with its promise of aiding post-war reconstruction and ensuring supremacy in engineering, warfare and the space race, was founded on the authority of 'exact formulation' in all the sciences.[12] It built on the conviction that there must be a trajectory from need to research project to solution, also part of the legacy of the earlier scientific Enlightenment. Logical Positivism in the twentieth century sought the certainty that comes from verification, following the lead of mathematics and logic in offering a basis in certainties, and a range of numerical and calculative methods.[13]

Ludwig von Bertalanffy laid out the principles of systems theory in his 1950 paper on 'An outline of general system theory', in which he characterised it as a 'logico-mathematical' field that had priority as a way of thinking about knowledge and understanding.[14] Systems theory has its home within the hard natural sciences, but extends to the 'biological and social realms'. 'General System Theory is a new scientific doctrine of "wholeness" – a notion which has been hitherto considered vague, muddled and metaphysical.'[15] It is the mathematical and logical exactness of the disciplines that signals their common basis in reason. Systems theory seeks to generalise across diverse problem domains, from biology to engineering design. One of its aims is:

> Developing unifying principles running 'vertically' through the universe of the individual sciences, this theory brings us nearer to the goal of the unity of science.[16]

The ideas in systems theory spawned the Design Methods movement which had substantial influence in the field of architectural research.[17] The history of this movement, its controversies, and architecture's debt to it have been well-documented. The 1958 RIBA Conference on Architectural Education held in Oxford secured architecture as a university-based discipline, and spelled out the need for 'fundamental' research on which to build the discipline.[18] The architect Leslie Martin chaired the event, which occurred during his tenure as head at Cambridge University from 1956 to 1964. His summary statement at the Oxford Conference reinforced the interdisciplinary nature of architectural research.

If architecture was to take its proper place in British universities, he argued, and if the knowledge which it entails is to be taught at the highest standard, it will be necessary to establish a bridge between faculties: between the Arts and the Sciences, the Engineering Sciences, Sociology and Economics. Furthermore, the universities would require something more than a study of techniques and parcels of this or that form of knowledge. They should expect and have a right to expect that knowledge will be guided and developed by principles: that is, by theory. 'Theory', as one speaker at the conference said, 'is the body of principles that explains and inter-relates all the facts of a subject'. Research is the tool by which theory is advanced. Without it, teaching can have no direction and thought no cutting edge.[19]

In this light, the purpose of research is to build up to a principled framework, auguring the unity of all knowledge, and architecture's place in it. Early design research, within architecture and outside, drew heavily on systems theory, which defined itself as operating across disciplines. Pivotal in this synthetic ambition was therefore the idea that design also crosses many disciplines.[20] Design has aspects common to all domains: products, graphics, buildings, cities, computers and computer programs. Study one and you are studying them all, a theme expanded by the management theorist, Herbert Simon, in his advocacy of a 'science of design'.[21] The legacy of such 'architectural science' differs from that of the arts and humanities traditions in architecture. At times each may have ignored the other, or been at loggerheads, but both have endorsed the open-ended and cross-disciplinary nature of architectural research.

WHY ARCHITECTS WRITE SUCH GOOD BOOKS

As I have already indicated, technologies provide further opportunities for the interaction between disciplines, no less so than in the development and application of the computer. It is now a commonplace for researchers from all disciplines to have something to say about computers, digital media, social media, and the Internet. This was not always the case, but from a very early stage in the development of the technology (1960s–70s) the main areas of professional application were office automation, scientific data analysis, engineering calculations and with the advent of computer graphics, architectural drafting and modelling. Architecture was among the first disciplines with credibility in the arts, humanities and social sciences to be interested in the possibilities afforded by computers. Architectural researchers and educators were amongst the pioneers of computer applications. In many cases, computer applications researchers had more in common with each other than they did with colleagues in their own disciplines. They attended each other's conferences and shared networks.

Such architects were also highly visionary and had influence beyond architecture. Nicolas Negroponte researched an 'intelligent' design system that offered advice while constructing building plans and sections. In 1973 he published his research as a book entitled *The Architecture Machine*.[22] He later came to found the MIT Media Lab, and wrote regular editorials for *Wired* magazine. Today he is perhaps best known for his book, *Being Digital*.[23] He was followed in the role of Head of MIT's Media Lab by William J. Mitchell, whose early book on *Computer-Aided Architectural Design* provided a snapshot of the breadth and sophistication of research by architects that ultimately impacted on the graphics, modelling and CAD systems commercially available now.[24] Mitchell went on to write about the social and cultural impacts of computer networks on cities.

In my own department, under the leadership of another architect, Aart Bijl, in the 1980s, the Edinburgh Computer Aided Architectural Design (EdCAAD) unit championed artificial intelligence research and held a license for a version of the logic programming language known as Prolog. Architects have also had an impact in the development of computer art, notably under pioneering advocacy from John Lansdown, who in 1988 became Professor and Head of the Centre for Computer Aided Art and Design at Middlesex University.[25] Other early architectural influences stem from research groups in Cambridge, Sheffield, Strathclyde and Liverpool Universities, along with other scholars at University College London, University of East London and University of Sydney. This is just a small snapshot of the field, and from my personal UK and Australian perspective. Technologically-oriented architects influence disciplines even more than architecture.

Systems theory looms large in the history of these disciplines. Artificial intelligence, computer-aided design, and computer art came out of Design Methods, and computer art had a close connection with cybernetics, a further offshoot of systems theory.[26] These are early examples, and the open-ended design research trajectory continues with much innovative research into parametric modelling, virtual environments, collaborative systems, social media applications, community based projects, and engagement in the so-called 'Internet of Things', within the orbit of architecture.[27]

The title of this section references the name Derrida gave to one of his papers, 'Why Peter Eisenman Writes Such Good Books', which in turn echoed Friedrich Nietzsche's conceited chapter title on 'Why I Write Such Good Books'. A similar bravado impels architects to be visionary writers, with a tendency towards utopian speculation. Design is a skill that transfers to other areas of speculation, including the literary. Architecture's acceptance of technologies, questing for the new, orientation towards practical application, and grounding in the humanities, combine with its interdisciplinary ethos to promote speculative talent, encouraging certain individuals at least to write good books about computers.

DISRUPTION AS A RESEARCH METHOD

I have alluded several times to architecture's affinity with computers, and with the Internet. The Internet is strongly based around the culture of the text. Key word search exemplifies this linguistic reductionism. But I have also indicated that online media support images, videos and audio repositories, an expansion that applies to research outputs other than those published as texts. The Internet provides a rich medium in support of design.

Research that is design led provides another channel of support for architecture's courtship of other disciplines.[28] Design-led research seeks to understand the world through direct intervention by the researcher, rather than through detached observation. Ethnographic study also encourages participation by the researcher, getting involved, seeing what life is like from the point of view of the subject, and accepting that the presence of the researcher has an effect on the material under study.[29] Design-led research accepts these tenets of involvement, but actively deploys intervention as a research tool. This is arguably the strategy of the Surrealist artist in placing an object from one context into another in order to provoke a response or to reveal something new: a hat stand with an anvil, a violin in a shipwreck, a fish in a desert. As I've indicated, basic Internet search provides a tool for such opportunistic juxtapositions.

The design approach is comparable to the deliberate introduction by an anthropologist of a refrigerator, a mobile phone or a video camera into a community that had never before seen such devices, in order to elicit responses, reflections or evidence about family relations, the use of language, and attitudes to hygiene. The intervention can serve as a catalyst or an inhibitor that brings current practices into sharp relief and provides a focus for reflection and discussion. So the inhabitants of a remote village under study may not be forthcoming on the role of the visual image in their community until they see a video image of themselves. Anthropology is arguably inhibited from pursuing such approaches by a reluctance to impose change, and an ethical commitment to certain research practices. Not so design. Colleagues and I have developed an argument elsewhere of the value of devices and artifacts as a means of research, and for revealing something new about the environment into which they are placed.[30] Subjecting participants to scenarios outside their usual experience reveals insights that could not easily be obtained by observation and interview alone.

Contemporary architecture can provoke in this way, through the clashing of forms and traditions in ways that are subtle as well as obvious. Nowhere is the capacity for technologies to expose new understandings of space more apparent than with the prosaic pastime of digital photography, by which any tourist can approach architecture from new perspectives.

10.5   Difference and incongruity as
architectural motif: The Military History
Museum in Dresden, Germany,
by Studio Daniel Libeskind

10.6   Interior of the Military History
Museum in Dresden

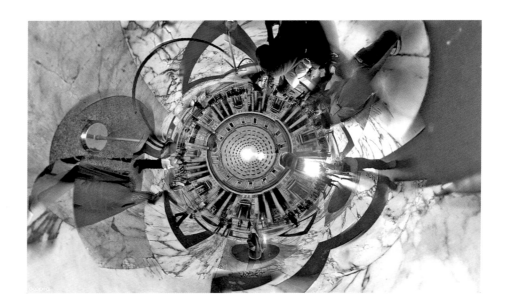

10.7 Looking at space differently: the interior of the Pantheon in Rome photographed by the author on an iPhone using the '360' app by Occipital

10.8 The same image data but inverted by Occipital software

Design-led research develops related research strategies that are activity-based, requiring subjects to undertake a task which becomes an object of reflection, a familiar strategy in education, team-building, problem-solving, attempts to induce creative responses to issues and even entertainment.[31] There are advantages to including design activity as part of a multimodal (triangulated) research strategy. This might involve asking human subjects to design, configure, and arrange objects and elements. The strategy here is to provide a medium in which people can be articulate without having initially to put matters into words. It also provides an environment for reflection and discussion.

A further design strategy familiar to those engaged in practice-led research is that afforded by design activity itself, as undertaken by the researcher, documented, and subjected to critique. In this case the creative output is integral to the research process, and may even constitute the main mode of communication within the research discourse. The strong claim of practice-led research is that all research is practice-led. According to one commentator, 'Research is a practice, writing is practice, doing science is practice, doing design is practice, making art is a practice'.[32] I could add that all research is a 'creative practice'. In this light, therefore, we might be keen to consider practice-led research as integral to research programmes rather than a mode of research that is exceptional.

As a further illustration of how design and cross disciplinary practice can work, myself and some colleagues are in the last year of a three-year project supported by the Scottish Funding Council, entitled 'Moving Targets'. The project also involves researchers from Abertay University in Dundee who specialise in computer gaming. The project is focused on the way that media consumption practices are changing, and how companies need to adapt to this new climate – one where new generations of media consumers are not content to wait for television programmes to be scheduled, but want to download on demand, and where people watch streamed programmes and listen to audio podcasts and music while on the move and have more than one media channel open at once (for example watching television while browsing the Internet on their tablet computer). The roles of producers and consumers of online entertainment and information dissemination are blurring. If consumers are not actively involved in generating their own new YouTube content, they at least expect to be engaged intelligently as active consumers. Terms such as 'content delivery' are giving way to notions of 'audience engagement', 'user-generated content', and even 'prosumerism'. Working on the 'Moving Targets' project has certainly informed my own thinking about how architecture interfaces with online media, as I have outlined in this chapter.

The project also deploys an innovative approach to research. The three researchers employed on the project are regarded as 'knowledge exchange associates' (KEAs). They undergo short placement periods in firms, such as games designers, broadcasters, theatre companies and design firms, and do an actual job of work there. They also report back at various workshops and disseminate the challenges and opportunities faced by the firms under study. This is an active form of 'ethnography', geared to the challenges faced by industry. The KEAs act as catalysts in defining research

10.9 'Moving Targets' workshop prototyping a system for interfacing social media with streamed media content

questions. In a way the KEAs also constitute outputs of the research, as they will continue to contribute to the development and dissemination of new knowledge as they resume their role in the workforce after the project. There are many indirect spin-offs from the project. Not least is the design thread which runs through it. At the moment the team is developing an online tool to assist businesses to establish who their audience is, and how best to engage them.

The need for this tool, and its prototyping, emerged through practice placements, workshops and much discussion amongst the team. The tool will be a product of the project, but in any case, such a task provides a focus and elicits insights such as those outlined in this chapter. If you think that a project focused on media and audiences is somewhat removed from architecture, then think again about the clients and users of architectural services, and the users and occupants of buildings, who can usefully be thought of as audiences, especially if we adopt an understanding of audiences as active and engaged.

We have learned that audiences are not simply out there to be found and gathered up. Like friends, audiences have to be 'made'. The cultivation of audiences is also a bit like education. An audience is the result of an educative process. To educate is to edify. To educate is to bring up or rear, and to edify is to build up. You have to educate an audience, which is to bring it into existence through education. Perhaps this is what successful media providers, teachers, politicians, authors and architects are able to do. They don't just put their produce on show and lure customers, audiences and clients, like wasps to a pile of toffee. They make their audiences. There's something about creativity and design here – the art of making (*poiesis*), about which more has been written elsewhere.[33] Making an audience is also about building community. I have already sought to establish that design is of necessity interdisciplinary: how much more then is design-led research the recognition of the openness of architecture to other disciplines.

ENCOUNTERING THE OTHER

Architectural research draws on common interests, and architects can argue that their research is constructed on grounds that are common to those with whom they collaborate. But the most compelling case for architectural research that is even more than architecture resides not in the similarities between disciplines but in their differences.

Design-led research champions this argument. The idea of a design intervention is to expose something about the context in which it is placed. If this is true of physical and propositional interventions, as a stimulus to and constituent of, research then it is also the case with exposure to other 'others', such as other disciplines, even cultures and histories. Technologies also have the capacity to disrupt disciplinary relationships, and expose differences rather than similarities.[34] I often think that computer-graphics imagery, of the kind demonstrated in architectural renderings and film effects, depends less on representational similarity with some external state of affairs, than with exposing or revealing some new aspect of reality, or unreality.[35] In any case, new developments in digital technologies – including mobile and locational media, social media, crowd-sourcing, user-generated content – prompt us to re-examine social, economic and spatial relationships.[36] The prominence of the human voice in mobile phone communications also has the potential to lead architecture in the direction of an awareness of the sonic aspects of environment.[37]

Otherness is a strong theme in postcolonial studies.[38] It also emerges from the philosophy of science. Thomas Kuhn, for example, has identified the issue of incommensurabilities between scientific paradigms.[39] We can translate his analysis to the encounter between disciplines. There are many possible outcomes when one discipline, school of thought, culture, set of ideas, or frame of reference, encounters another. There's the possibility of a harmonious fusion, the recognition that they are not so different after all. More usually, in the case of academic disciplines, the participants in a friendly encounter fall into a mode of polite filtering based on preconceptions about each other. One discipline may not recognise the weight and importance of certain terms used by the other. Concepts that appear incomprehensible will likely be ignored. Think of how a computer scientist might receive architecturally current terms such as 'place making', 'poetics', 'procurement', 'disjunction' or 'deconstruction', and what might an architect make of 'computability', 'recursion' and 'error control'. Either party might adopt a simplified language for explaining themselves to lay people, easily interpreted as condescension. The power relationships between the parties may also be uneven, or be perceived as such by the disciplines, and that colours the encounter. There might also be an assumption that the other is a homogeneous group, when in fact there are factions and disagreements among them. After all, there are many schools of thought within architecture that others fail to recognise, or that we forget to broadcast.

I am here focussing on good-will encounters, where there is personal engagement and a genuine desire to discover opportunities to work together.[40] In other contexts, such as the anonymous assessment of grant applications, peer assessment of a paper that seems to have found its way into the review process of the wrong journal, or political arguments about university resources, such differences and their attendant prejudices can expose substantial consequences, even resulting in the obliteration of disciplines from a university's profile. Encountering the other hence requires intellectual work. The hermeneutical philosopher Hans-Georg Gadamer describes this work as the 'fusion of horizons', which operates at many scales of interpretation, from a conversation between two friendly colleagues to the clash of cultures on the political and national stage, with disciplinary encounters somewhere within that spectrum.

It is tempting to think that the means to effective communication, interaction and collaboration is to bury differences and to focus on commonalities, or even to build bridges as suggested at the 1958 Oxford Conference. But often it is more productive and helpful

to admit to a lack of comprehension, and let difference do its work – a subtle and deliberative process. The result of the encounter is an alteration in thinking, a shift in the grounding of our prejudices. Productive encounters can be personally transforming, and transforming of a discipline. The result is indeterminate and not easily described on a Venn diagram. Such is the nature of human interaction and interpretation, a consummate and significant benefit of research that is even more than architecture.

ACKNOWLEDGEMENTS

This chapter references the 'Moving Targets' project supported by the Scottish Funding Council. The project brings together Scottish universities, industries, agencies and audiences to develop new models for new audiences in the creative media industries. The research team includes Simon Biggs, Mariza Dima, Angela Fernandez Orviz, Dayna Galloway, Beverly Hood, Brent MacGregor, Nicola Searle, Gregor White (project leader) and Mark Wright, with input from Paul Harris.

Notes

1 Dana Cuff, *Architecture: The Story of Practice* (Cambridge, Mass.: MIT Press, 1991); Frank Duffy, 'Strategic Overview', *Strategic Study of the Profession: Phase 1 – Strategic Overview* (London: Royal Institute of British Architects, 1992), pp. 1–11.

2 Jacques Derrida, 'Point de Folie: Maintenant l'architecture', in Neil Leach (ed.) *Rethinking Architecture: A Reader in Cultural Theory* (London: Routledge, 1986), pp. 305–17; Richard Coyne, *Derrida for Architects* (Abingdon, Oxon: Routledge, 2011).

3 Bernard Tschumi, 'Introduction', in Jeffrey Kipnis & Thomas Leeser (eds) *Chora L Works* (New York: Monacelli Press, 1997), p. 125.

4 Ibid.

5 Nicholas Carr, *The Shallows: What the Internet Is Doing to Our Brains* (New York: WW Norton, 2011).

6 Don Tapscott, *Grown Up Digital: How the Net Generation is Changing Your World* (New York: McGraw Hill, 2009).

7   André Breton, *Manifestoes of Surrealism* (Ann Arbor, Michigan: University of Michigan Press, 1969).

8   Sergei Maslov & Sidney Redner, 'Promise and pitfalls of Extending Google's PageRank Algorithm to Citation Networks', *The Journal of Neuroscience*, vol .28 no. 44 (2008), pp. 11103–5; Television viewing figures are taken from the Broadcasters Audience Research Board (BARB) website, http://www.barb.co.uk/ (accessed 28 February 2013); Newspaper circulation figures are taken from the Audit Bureau of Circulations (ABC) website, http://www.abc.org.uk (accessed 28 February 2013).

9   James Surowiecki, *The Wisdom of Crowds: Why the Many are Smarter Than the Few* (New York: Anchor Books, 2005).

10   PEPRAV, *Urban Act: A Handbook for Alternative Practice* (Paris: European Platform for Alternative Practice and Research on the City/ Atelier d'Architecture Autogérée, 2008).

11   Horst Rittel & Melvin Weber, 'Dilemmas in a General Theory of Planning', *Policy Sciences*, vol. 4 (1973), pp. 155–69; Herbert Simon, 'The Structure of Ill-Structured Problems', *Artificial Intelligence*, vol. 4 (1973), pp. 181–201; Donald A. Schön, *Reflective Practitioner: How Professionals Think in Action* (London: Temple Smith, 1983).

12   Donald Schön, *Displacement of Concepts* (London: Tavistock, 1963).

13   Alfred J. Ayer, *Language, Truth and Logic* (London: Penguin, 1990).

14   Ludwig Bertalanffy, *General System Theory: Foundations, Development, Applications* (New York: George Braziller, 1969).

15   Ibid., p. 112.

16   Ibid., p. 38.

17   Christopher Alexander, *Notes on the Synthesis of Form* (Cambridge, Mass: Harvard University Press, 1964); John Christopher Jones, *Design Methods: Seeds of Human Futures* (London: Wiley, 1970).

18   Dean Hawkes, 'The Centre and the Periphery: Some reflections on the Nature and Conduct of Architectural Research', *Architectural Research Quarterly*, vol. 1 (1995), pp. 8–11.

19   Leslie Martin, 'Report by the Chairman', RIBA Conference on Architectural Education, Oxford, UK, 1985, p. 5, viewable at the 2008 Oxford Conference on Architectural Education website, http://www.oxfordconference2008.co.uk/1958conference.htm (accessed 28 February 2013).

20   Tom Inns (ed.), *Designing for the 21st Century: Interdisciplinary Questions andiInsights* (Aldershot: Gower, 2007).

21   Herbert Simon, *The Sciences of the Artificial: Karl Taylor Compton Lectures, 1968* (Cambridge, Mass: MIT Press, 1969).

22   Nicholas Negroponte, *The Architecture Machine* (Cambridge, Mass: MIT Press, 1973).

23   Nicholas Negroponte, *Being Digital* (London: Hodder & Stoughton, 1995).

24   William J. Mitchell, *Computer-Aided Architectural Design* (New York: John Wiley, 1977).

25   Paul Brown, Charlie Gere, Nicholas Lambert & Catherine Mason, *White Heat Cold Logic: British Computer Art, 1960–1980* (Cambridge, Mass: MIT Press, 2008).

26   Norbert Weiner, *The Human Use of Human Beings* (Cambridge, Mass: Da Capo Press, 1950); Ranulph Glanville, 'Try Again, Fail Again, Fail Better: The Cybernetics in Design and the Design in Cybernetics', *Kybernetes*, vol. 36 no. 9/10 (2007), pp. 1173–1206.

27   Chris Speed, 'An Internet of Old Things', *Digital Creativity*, vol. 21 no. 4 (2010), pp. 239–46.

28   Chris Rust, Judith Mottram & Jeremy Till, *AHRC Research Review: Practice-led Research in Art, Design Aand Architecture* (Bristol: Arts and Humanities Research Council, 2007).

29   Harold Garfinkel, *Studies in Ethnomethodology* (Cambridge: Polity Press, 1967).

30   Richard Coyne, Hoon Park & Dorian Wiszniewski, 'Design Devices: What They Reveal and Conceal', *Kritische Berichte: Zeitschrift für Kunst- und Kulturwissenschaften*, vol. 3 (2000), pp. 55–69.

31   Linda Groat & David Wang, *Architectural Research Methods* (New York: Wiley, 2002).

32   Christopher Frayling, 'Research in Art and Design', *Royal College of Art Research Papers*, vol. 1 no. 1 (1993/94), p. 4.

33   Adrian Snodgrass & Richard Coyne, *Interpretation in Architecture: Design as a Way of Thinking* (London: Routledge, 2006).

34   Clayton M. Christensen, *The Innovator's Dilemma: When New Technologies Cause Great Firms to Fail* (Boston: Harvard Business School Press, 1997).

35   Richard Coyne, 'The Digital Uncanny', in Phil Turner & Elisabeth Davenport (eds), *Spaces, Spatiality and Technology* (Dordrecht: Springer, 2005), pp. 5–18.

36   Richard Coyne, *The Tuning of Place: Sociable Spaces and Pervasive Digital Media* (Cambridge, Mass: MIT Press, 2010).

37   Barry Blesser & Linda-Ruth Salter, *Spaces Speak, Are You Listening? Experiencing Aural Architecture* (Cambridge, Mass: MIT Press, 2006); Richard Coyne, 'Creativity and Sound: The Agony of the Senses', in Tudor Rickards, Mark A. Runco & Susan Moger (eds) *The Routledge Companion to Creativity* (Routledge: London, 2009), pp. 25–36; Richard Coyne & Martin Parker, 'Voice and Space: The Agency of the Acousmêtre in Spatial Design', in Phil Turner, Susan Turner & Elisabeth Davenport (eds), *Exploration of Space, Technology and Spatiality: Interdisciplinary Perspectives* (Hershey, Penn: Information Science Reference, 2009), pp. 102–12.

38   H.K. Bhabha, *The Location of Culture* (London: Routledge, 1994); Felipe Hernández, *Bhabha for Architects* (London: Routledge, 2010); Hans-Georg Gadamer, *Truth and Method* (New York: Seabury Press, 1975); Snodgrass & Coyne, *Interpretation in Architecture*.

39   Thomas Kuhn, *The Structure of Scientific Revolutions* (Chicago: University of Chicago Press, 1970).

40   Jacques Derrida, 'Three Questions to Hans-Georg Gadamer', in Diane P. Michelfelder & Richard E. Palmer (eds), *Dialogue and Deconstruction: The Gadamer-Derrida Encounter* (Albany, New York: State University of New York Press, 1989), pp. 52–4.

Plate 17   Spaces of conflict and marginality on the US/Mexican border: the Political Equator 3 meeting in June 2011

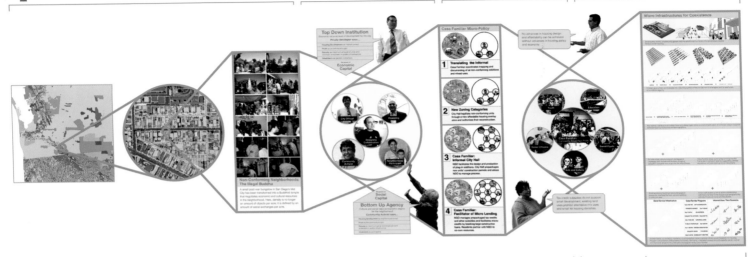

1 An Urbanism of Retrofit:
The urban future depends on the pixelation of the large with the small.

2 Expanded Models of Practice:
Architects as mediators of top down economic development and bottom up social agency.

3 Constructing the Political:
Designing a micro-policy and new conceptions of ownership for the border neighborhood of San Ysidro.

4 The Neighborhood as Developer:
Housing cannot be sustainable on its own. It needs to be plugged with socio-economic support systems.

The multi-color 'confetti' of Tijuana's compacted land uses seeps into San Diego, altering the homogeneity of this large exclusionary colors of Southern California's zoning.

A migrant urbanism deposits itself in many older California neighborhoods, where mono-use parcels are transformed into complex micro socio-economic systems.

Citizenship is a creative act that transforms and reorganizes existing spacial and institutional protocols.

While the global city became the privileged site of consumption and display, the immigrant local neighborhood remains a site of production, of new cultural and socio-economic relations.

Besides designing buildings, architects can also collaborate in constructing new political and economic processes.

The future of urbanism will not be led by buildings but by the reorganization of socio-economic relations.

We need to move from the neutral notion of the public to the specific rights of the neighborhood.

Casa Familiar in San Ysidro: Neighborhood based community non-profit organization becomes micro-developer, translating invisible socio-economic value.

"Not everyone can own a unit": New social contracts between Casa Familiar and neighborhood participants

The tactical distribution of diverse housing building types within a small infrastructure of collective spaces allows the choreography of temporal socio-educational and economic community programming.

Plate 18   Diagram showing Teddy Cruz's vision of an urbanisation of retrofit linked into community participation

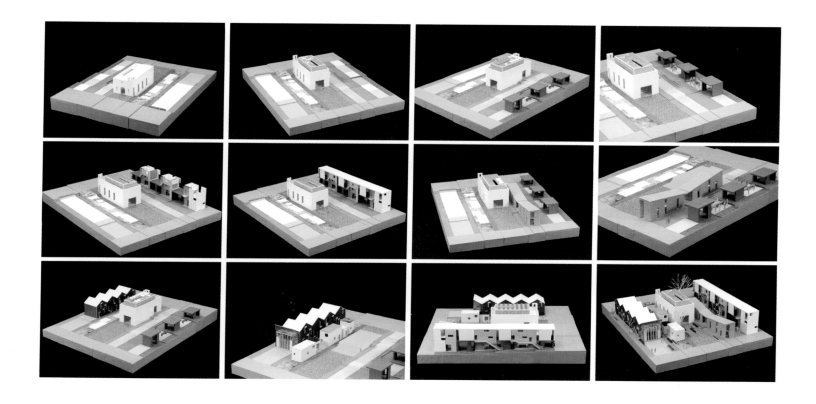

Plate 19　Estudio Teddy Cruz, *Casa Familiar: Living Rooms at the Border*, San Ysidro in southern California (2001 onwards)

Plate 20   Interior photograph of the model
by Shigeru Ban for the 'temporary' cardboard
cathedral in Christchurch, New Zealand (2012–13)

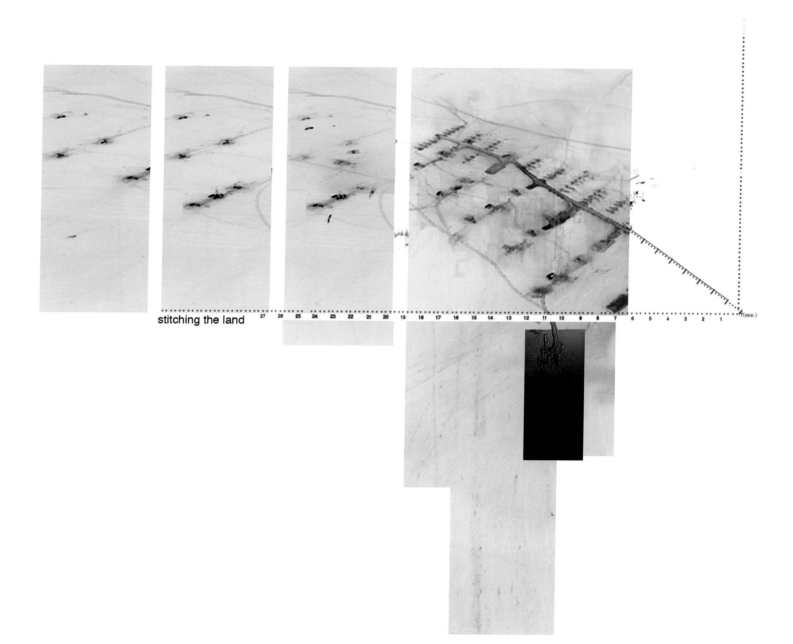

stitching the land

Plate 21   Conceptual drawing by Yara Sharif for stitching the divided landscape of Palestine/Israel

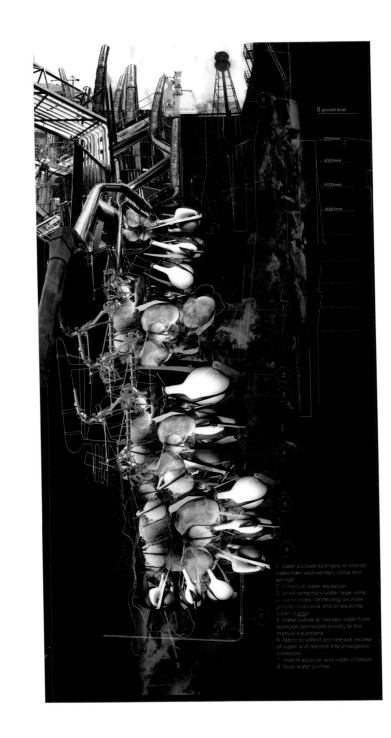

Plate 22   Clusters of sponge elements
to absorb rainfall and ground water in
the reoccupied stone quarries in the
Palestinian West Bank, as one project
for Yara Sharif's PhD by Design at the
University of Westminster, London

Plate 23   Lebbeus Woods, *Manifesto* (1993)

Plate 24   Lebbeus Woods, *Injection Parasite, Sarajevo* (1992)

RETURNING DUCHAMP'S URINAL TO THE BATHROOM? ON THE RECONNECTION BETWEEN ARTISTIC EXPERIMENTATION, SOCIAL RESPONSIBILITY AND INSTITUTIONAL TRANSFORMATION

Teddy Cruz

It is obvious by now that the celebrated metropolitan explosion of the last years of economic boom also produced in tandem a dramatic project of marginalisation, resulting in the unprecedented growth of slums surrounding major urban centres, exacerbating the socio-economic and demographic conflicts of an uneven urbanisation – an urban asymmetry which is at the centre of today's crises. In the context of these shifts, our design professions are paralysed, silently witnessing the consolidation of the most blatant politics of unaccountability, the shrinkage of social and public institutions, and not one single proposal or action that can suggest a different approach, different arrangements. So, before economic and environmental, ours is primarily a cultural crisis resulting in the inability of institutions to question their ways of thinking, their exclusionary policies, the rigidity of their own protocols and silos. It is within this radical context that we must question the role of architecture research and design today.

In fact, one primary site of artistic intervention today for research and design is the gap itself that has been produced between cultural institutions and the public, instigating a new civic imagination and collective political will. It is not enough only to give art the task of metaphorically revealing the very socio-economic histories and injustices that have produced these crises, but it is essential that it also becomes an instrument to construct specific procedures to transcend them, a more *functional* set of operations that can reconnect art and architecture to the urgency of the everyday and the re-thinking of its institutions. The formation of new platforms of engagement in our creative fields can only be made possible with a sense of urgency, pushing us to rethink our very procedures. The need for expanded modes of artistic practice, alternative sites of research and pedagogy, new conceptions of cultural and economic production, and the re-organisation of social relations seem more urgent than ever.

EXPANDING ARTISTIC PRACTICES: FROM CRITICAL DISTANCE TO CRITICAL PROXIMITY

The revision of our own artistic procedures is essential today. The same ideological divide permeating politics today, we also find in art and architecture's current implicit debate. On one hand we find those who continue to defend art and architecture as a self-referential project of apolitical formalism, made of hyper-aesthetics for the sake of aesthetics, which continues to press the notion of the avant-garde as an autonomous project, 'needing' a *critical distance* from the institutions to operate critically in the research of experimental form. On the other hand, we find those who need to step out of this autonomy in order to engage the socio-political and economic domains that have remained peripheral to the specialisations of art and architecture, questioning our profession's powerlessness in the context of the world's most pressing current crises.

These latter emerging practices seek, instead, for a project of *radical proximity* to the institutions, encroaching into them to transform them from the inside out in order to produce new aesthetic categories that can problematise the relationship of the social, the political, and the formal – thereby questioning our creative field's unconditional love affair, in the last years, with a system of economic excess that was needed to legitimise artistic autonomy. How to reconnect artistic experimentation and social responsibility, a major aspiration of the historic avant-garde, must be the central question in today's debate.

What is being sought, then, is an expanded mode of practice, where architects are responsible for imagining counter spatial procedures, political and economic structures that can produce new modes of sociability and encounter. Without altering the exclusionary policies that have produced the current crises in the first place, our professions will continue to be subordinated to the visionless and homogeneous environments defined by the bottom-line urbanism of the developer's spreadsheet and the neo-conservative politics and economics of a hyper-individualistic ownership society. In essence, then, the autonomous role of artists needs to be coupled with the role of the activist. I do not see one as more important than the other because both are necessary today.

RE-THINKING THE SITES OF EXPERIMENTATION: NEW PARADIGMS IN RESEARCH AND DESIGN WILL EMERGE FROM THE MARGINS

The world's architectural intelligentsia – supported by the glamorous economy of the last few years – flocked *en masse* to the United Arab Emirates and China to help build the dream castles that would catapult these enclaves of wealth into global epicentres of urban development. Other than a few isolated protagonist architectural interventions whose images have been disseminated widely, many of these high-profile projects produced in those cities have in fact only perpetuated the exhausted recipes of an oil-hungry globalisation. In other words, no major ideas were advanced there to transform existing paradigms of housing, infrastructure and density, or to resolve the major problems of urbanisation today which are grounded in the inability of institutions of urban development to engage informality, socio-economic inequity and lack of affordable housing and infrastructure. So, while the attention of the world had been focused on those enclaves of economic power in the last years, the most radical ideas advancing new models of urban development were produced in the margins, across Latin American cities. Challenging entrenched neo-liberal urban logics of development founded on top down privatisation, homogeneity and exclusion, visionary mayors in cities such as Porto Alegre, Curitiba, Bogota and Medellin began to enable new institutional protocols by enabling public participation, civic culture and unorthodox cross-institutional collaborations – rethinking the very meaning of infrastructure, housing and density and mediating top down development and bottom up social organisation. I cannot think of any other continental region in the world where we can find this type of collective effort led by municipal and federal governments seeking a new brand of progressive politics to produce an urbanism of inclusion.

This suggests the urgency to reorient our focus to other sites of research and design intervention, arguing that some of the most relevant practices and projects forwarding socio-economic sustainability will not emerge from sites of economic abundance but from sites of scarcity. New experimental practices of research and intervention will emerge from zones of conflict. It is in the periphery where conditions of social emergency are transforming our ways of thinking about urban matters, and the matters of concern about the city.

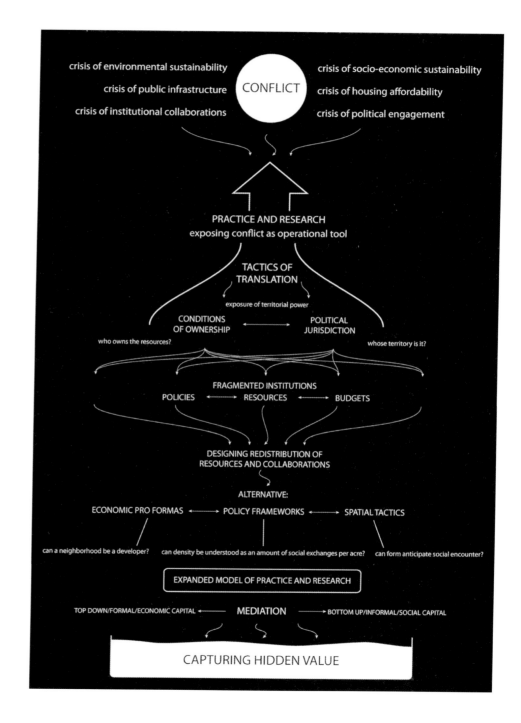

11.1   Practice diagram for Estudio Teddy Cruz

11.2 Reconnecting the masses to the politics and processes of urban development

RADICALISING THE PARTICULAR: MOVING FROM THE AMBIGUITY OF THE PUBLIC TO THE SPECIFICITY OF RIGHTS

We need to move beyond the abstraction of the 'global' in order to 'hit the ground' and engage the particularities of the political inscribed within local geographies of conflict. It is within the specificity of conflict where contemporary artistic practice needs to reposition itself in order to expose the particularity of hidden institutional histories, revealing the missing information that can allow us to piece together a more accurate, anticipatory urban research and design intervention. To be political in our field means a commitment to revealing the particular conditions of conflict inscribed in the territory and the institutional mechanisms that have perpetuated such conflicts. What produced the crisis in the first place? Only the knowledge informing us of the specific conditions that produced it can enable us to think politically. In other words, the only way to produce a truly experimental architecture in our time involves the specific re-organisation of the political and economic 'ground', the very conditions that continue to produce conflict between top-down forces of urbanisation and bottom-up social and ecological networks. In this way, enclaves of mega-wealth and sectors of marginalisation can become the material for design.

What is needed is a more critical role for design to encroach into the fragmented and discriminatory policies and economics that have that have produced these collisions in the first place. At this moment, it is not buildings, but the fundamental re-organisation of socio-economic relations that is the necessary ground for producing new paradigms of democratisation and urbanisation. Artists and architects have a role in the conceptualisation of such new protocols. In other words, it is the construction of the political itself what is at stake here not just political art or architecture.

It has been said that the post-war Civil Rights movement in the United States began in a bus. At least that is the image that consolidated the argument that detonated the unfolding of such constitutional transformation. It was a small act trickling up into the collective's awareness. While public transport at that time was labelled 'PUBLIC', it was not accessible to all. It is necessary to move from the neutrality of the term 'public' in our political debate at this moment in order to arrive to the specificity of rights, as in the rights to the city, to the neighbourhood. This opens up the idea that architects and artists, besides being researchers and designers of form, buildings and objects, can be designers of political processes, alternative economic models and collaborations across institutions and jurisdictions.

This can be in the form of small, incremental acts of retrofit of existing urban fabrics, or of regulation, encroaching into the privatisation of public domain and infrastructure, as well as attacking the rigidity of institutional thinking. The most radical interventions in our time can emerge from specific, bottom-up urban and regulatory alterations, modest in nature, but with enough resolution and assurance to trickle up to transform top-down institutional structures.

COMMUNITIES OF CULTURAL PRODUCTION: THE INFORMAL AS PRAXIS

So, while in the last years the 'global city' became the privileged site of an urbanisation of *consumption* and display, local informal neighbourhoods in the margins of such centres of economic power remained sites of cultural *production*. These are peripheral communities where emergent economic configurations continue to take place through the tactical adaptation and retrofit of existing discriminating zoning and exclusionary economic development. It produces a different notion of the 'political', at the intersection between formal and informal urbanisations and the conflicts between top-down policy and bottom up social contingency. It is from these informal settlements worldwide where a new politics of urban growth for the contemporary city can be shaped, taking into account bottom-up socio-cultural productivity in the re-structuring of top-down unsustainable urban policies.

But as we return to these informal settlements for clues, their stealth urban praxis also needs artistic interpretation and political representation, and so this should be the space of intervention of contemporary architecture practice, engaging the specificity of the political within the performativity of the informal as the main creative tool to expand notions of design. In other words, as architects

11.3   Spaces of conflict and marginality on the US–Mexican border. In June 2011, Teddy Cruz organized the Political Equator 3 meeting in collaboration with two community-based NGOs from both sides of the Tijuana–San Diego border. After negotiating with US Homeland Security and the Mexican Immigration Agency, a recently built border drain was transformed into a 24-hour official port of entry, enabling a crowd of activists, scholars, artists and politicians, with passports on hand, to cross the border as a public performance that exposed the collisions between the environmental zone, the infrastructure of surveillance, and informal settlements

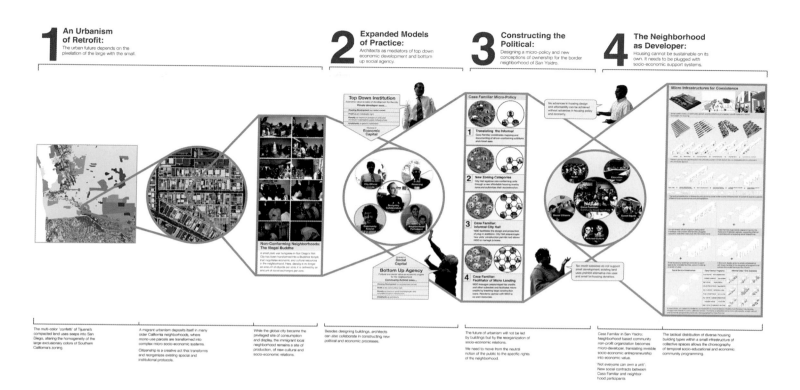

11.4 An urbanisation of retrofit linked into community participation

we continue being seduced with the 'image' of the informal, seeing it as an aesthetic category only and we are not translating its operative dimension, its actual socio-economic and political procedures. The informal is not just an image of precariousness; it is a compendium of practices, a set of functional urban operations that counter and transgress imposed political boundaries and top-down economic models. These hidden urban operations of the most compelling cases of informal urbanisation across Latin America and around the world, need to be translated into a new political language with particular spatial consequences, from which to produce new interpretations of housing, infrastructure, property and citizenship, and inspiring 'other' modes of intervention in the contemporary city. The aims should be:

1. To challenge normative notions of architecture, conceiving itself as an autonomous, self-referential system that freezes and spatialises time. How to engage instead with the temporalisation of space found in informal urbanisation's management of time, people, spaces and resources? Within this new paradigm, conventional *zoning* ceases to be the punitive tool that prevents socialisation, becoming instead a generative

tool that organises and anticipates social and economic activity; and *density* is no longer measured as an abstract amount of objects per acre, but as an amount of socio-economic exchanges per acre. This suggests that the future of the city will be small. In conditions of socio-economic and environmental crisis, urban growth will depend on the pixellation of the large by the small, as an 'urbanisation of retrofit'. The micro-socio-economic contingencies of the informal will transform the homogeneous largeness of official urbanisation into more sustainable, plural and complex environments.

2. To question the identity of the global city based on the dominance of private development and economic value alone, which, through budgets and profits, sponsors a fixed image of progress. How to engage social value as the catalyst for an incremental low-cost layering of urban development found in informal urbanisation? This suggests the need to rethink existing models of property by redefining affordability and the value of social participation, enhancing the role of communities in co-producing housing and enabling a more inclusive idea of ownership.

3. To re-imagine existing logics of jurisdiction, as conventional government protocols give primacy to the abstraction of administrative boundaries over the social and environmental boundaries that informality negotiates as devices to construct community. In other words, how to enable more meaningful systems of political and jurisdictional representation at the scale of neighbourhoods that can tactically calibrate individual and collective interests? This suggests the need for mediating agencies that can produce new forms of local governance, and the social contracts that can enable guarantees of protection for these communities to share the profits of urbanisation and prevent gentrification.

4. To critically intervene in the gap that divides institutions and communities. How to produce a more meaningful role for local non-profit community-based organisations, empowering them to co-own and co-manage – with their communities – the resources of development and become the long-term choreographers of social and cultural programming for housing? These agencies can be the urban curators, enabling the reorganisation of social systems and economic resources at local scales and amplifying and enforcing the critical interface between top-down, government infrastructural support and the creative bottom-up intelligence and sweat equity of communities and activists.

5. To denounce the consolidation of the economic and political power that has installed an anti-tax, anti-immigration, and anti-public spending culture today, cementing the final erosion of civic participation from the political process and a culture of impunity in the upper echelons of institutional structures everywhere.

In other words, at a time when the longevity of the 'welfare state' seems no longer possible, we must remember that social and environmental justice

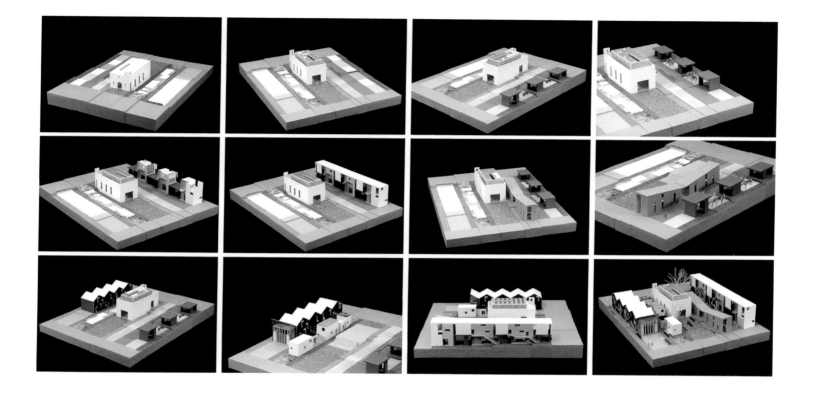

11.5 Estudio Teddy Cruz, *Casa Familiar: Living Rooms at the Border*, San Ysidro in Southern California (2001 onwards). Model photographs showing the sequence of constructing the different block typologies to form a new neighbourhood next to the US–Mexican border

is not only about the redistribution of resources but about the redistribution of knowledges, the rights of marginal communities to have access to education. The common conceptual threads and lessons that run along the many exemplary projects in Latin America mentioned in the beginning of these reflections elevate the need for an urgent collective imagination, an investment in an urban pedagogy – that is, the transfer of knowledge across governments and communities – and the pursuit of a civic culture as the basis for an inclusive urbanisation. It is within the informal where other conceptions of the 'public' and of citizenship will be found.

TOWARDS AN URBAN PEDAGOGY: THE VISUALISATION OF A NEW CIVIC IMAGINATION

Fundamental to the rethinking of exclusionary political and economic frameworks that defined the logics of uneven urban development in the last years is the translation and visualisation of the socio-cultural and economic entrepreneurial intelligence embedded in many marginal immigrant neighbourhoods. While the 'global city' has become the privileged site of consumption and display, marginal neighbourhoods across the world have remained sites of production. But the hidden value (cultural, social and economic) of the informal transactions in these communities

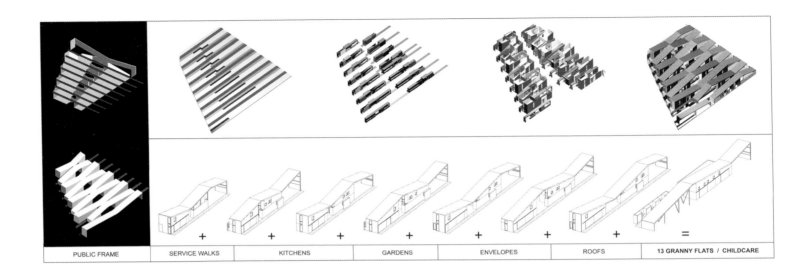

| PUBLIC FRAME | SERVICE WALKS | KITCHENS | GARDENS | ENVELOPES | ROOFS | 13 GRANNY FLATS / CHILDCARE |

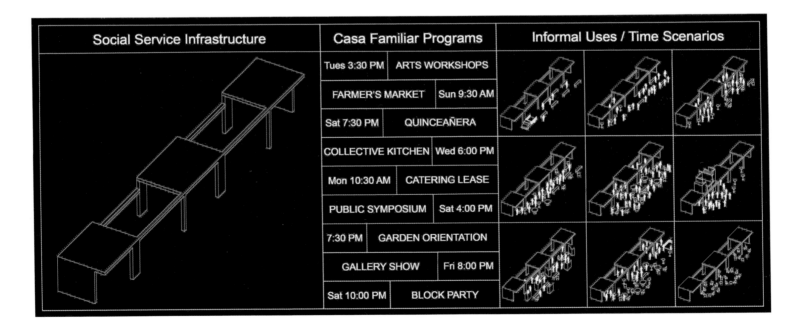

Social Service Infrastructure	Casa Familiar Programs		Informal Uses / Time Scenarios
	Tues 3:30 PM	ARTS WORKSHOPS	
	FARMER'S MARKET	Sun 9:30 AM	
	Sat 7:30 PM	QUINCEAÑERA	
	COLLECTIVE KITCHEN	Wed 6:00 PM	
	Mon 10:30 AM	CATERING LEASE	
	PUBLIC SYMPOSIUM	Sat 4:00 PM	
	7:30 PM	GARDEN ORIENTATION	
	GALLERY SHOW	Fri 8:00 PM	
	Sat 10:00 PM	BLOCK PARTY	

11.6   Various applications of the multi-use frames for the San Ysidro project over time

11.7   Composition diagram of a San Ysidro block combining senior citizens' housing with childcare

across bottom-up cultural activism, economies and densities continues to be off the radar of conventional top-down planning institutions.

If we consider citizenship as a primarily creative act, enabling the transformation of institutional protocols and the spaces of the city, it is within these marginal communities of practice where a new conception of civic culture can emerge. In this context, I see informal urbanisation as the site of a new interpretation of community, citizenship and praxis, where emergent urban configurations produced out of social emergency suggest the performative role of individuals constructing their own spaces. The invisible urban praxis of these communities needs interpretation and representation, and this is the space of intervention institutions of art, culture and governance need to engage. How to design the conditions that can mobilise this activism into new spatial and economic infrastructures that benefits these communities of practice in the long term, beyond the short-term problem solving of private developers or the institutions of charity?

But, often, these communities lack the conceptual devices to understand their own everyday procedures, and how their neighbourhood agency can trickle up to produce new institutional transformations, shaping alternative politics and economies at the scale of their own daily needs. It is in the context of these conditions where a different role for art, architecture, environmental and community activist practices can emerge – one that goes beyond the metaphorical representation of people, where only the community's symbolic image is amplified, instead of its operative dimension.

Because of this, the questioning new forms of *urban pedagogy* is one of the most critical sites for artistic investigation and practice today, rethinking the gap that currently exists between cultural institutions and the public. How, then, can we produce new interfaces with the public to raise awareness of the conditions that have produced our environmental, economic and social crises? The conventional structures and protocols of academic institutions may be seen to be at odds with activist-practices, which are, by their very nature, organic and extra-academic. Should activist-practices challenge the nature and structure of pedagogy within the institution? Are new modes of teaching and learning called for?

Today, it is essential to reorient our gaze towards the drama embedded in the reality of the everyday, and in so doing engage the shifting socio-political and economic domains that have been ungraspable by art and design. Or as the artist Tania Bruguera said to me recently: 'It is time to restore Duchamp's urinal back to the bathroom' – thereby suggesting the urgency of a more functional relationship between research, design and the production of the city, restoring the ethical imperative between individuals, collectives and institutions. Bruguera's recent installation for the Queens Museum of Art in New York City did precisely that.

In my own research-based practice and teaching, over the last ten years, the Tijuana–San Diego border has served as a laboratory for researching the current politics of surveillance, immigration and labour, the polarisation of informal and formal systems of urbanisation, and the expanded gap between wealth and poverty. This has led me to understand that we need to rethink our very practices themselves, seeing them as the main site of intervention, not only to enable bottom-up creative intelligence to

scale up, but to also participate more meaningfully in the retrofitting of existing political and economic systems.

Ultimately, it is irrelevant whether architecture and urban development is wrapped in the latest morphogenetic skins, or neo-classical props, or Leadership in Energy and Environmental Design (LEED)-certified photovoltaic panels, if all such approaches continue to camouflage the most pressing problems of urbanisation today. As mentioned above, if we don't alter the socially exclusionary policies and economics which have created our current crises, then cities around the globe city will continue to be subordinated to the exploitation inherent in neo-liberal politics and economics. I have been thinking lately about what Bernard Tschumi wrote many years ago, when he reminded us that as architects we continue to be obsessed with the *conditions of design*; instead, he suggested, we must engage the *design of conditions*. This is the task of design research today, designing the conditions for socio-economic and environmental justice from which a more experimental architecture can emerge.

11.8   Tania Bruguera, Useful Art (2010). Medium: sculpture installed in bathroom. Materials: ceramic, water supply tube, flange bolts, silicone caulk, black paint

'A TWO-FOLD MOVEMENT': DESIGN RESEARCH AS DIALECTICAL CRITICAL PRACTICE

Murray Fraser

This final chapter looks at design research as a critical practice which can partake more directly with the socio-economic and professional realities in whichever country or context it is in. A particular concern is the implications for the potential methodology of design research in its task of interweaving projects (design) with texts or books (writing). One of the themes running throughout this book has been the range and diversity of approaches to design research. No-one can possibly claim to own the territory, nor are the different approaches necessarily mutually exclusive. Instead, it is always important to show the spread of the field. How then can we say something more general about design research? Here I will put forward a more socially engaged mode of investigation for design research, and will then suggest how this could shape how we conceive of it as an intellectual activity, and what the methods should be to enact it in practice.

Above all, it seems evident that design research can never be treated as a simple linear process, even if one tries to conceive things more creatively such as by viewing the process of research as a spiral form (as Le Corbusier suggested) or a sequence of iterative loops (as per Donald Schön). What I will do instead is to adapt, and hopefully update, a remarkably innovative conception of 'two-fold movement' which was set out by Eliel Saarinen in his book, *The City*, published in America in 1943. Taking my cue from Saarinen's insights, this chapter is written in reverse chronology.[1] It therefore starts out with a brief discussion of some contemporary practitioners who are engaged in critically engaged design investigations, linking their ideas back to Lebbeus Woods, who sadly died on the very day after Hurricane Sandy's devastating storm surge

had hit New York City on 29 October 2012. In turn, I will link the approach taken by Woods back to Rem Koolhaas's seminal book, *Delirious New York*, which first came out in 1978, and also ask how that book has influenced, or perhaps not, the work of Koolhaas as a theoretician and practitioner. Adding to the theme of reverse chronology, the brilliant central conceit of *Delirious New York* was Koolhaas's portrayal of himself as a ghostwriter hired to write what he termed 'a retroactive' manifesto for that city. Tellingly, however, Koolhaas also included some fascinating speculative projects at the end of the book which showed his awareness of the need to be looking both forwards and backwards at the same time. This stance can be directly likened, further back, to the idea of 'two-fold movement' – which oscillates in both directions and simultaneously between the past and present and future – which was described so vividly in Eliel Saarinen's text. What this mean for our understanding of design research and its possible methodology forms the conclusion to the chapter.

Along with this idea of a 'two-fold movement' within design research, the other central contention of this chapter is that design research can best engender speculative thinking and experimentation through an conscious engagement with the normative practices of everyday life in the contemporary city. The lineage of thinking about design research I will discuss is therefore deeply embedded in urban analysis, being specifically interested in understanding the commonplace, quotidian elements that make up cities – as opposed to the official, privileged, monumental spaces inhabited by elite groups. By definition, this attitude to design research brings into play a broad spectrum of social, economic, political and cultural issues. And in doing so, it deliberately turns itself away from a more internalised form of discourse about architecture (for example theory/representation/meaning) in favour of analysing the social and cultural inequalities and clashes found everywhere in present-day or future cities. In turn this shifts the locus of agency within design research from the particular architect's own individual contribution to the collective processes and urban spaces of our metropolitan life. Typically, kind of comment leads tends to lead automatically to mentions of pivotal contributions about the modern metropolis by the likes of Walter Benjamin, Michel de Certeau, Henri Lefebvre, Gilles Deleuze and Felix Guattari and such like. Benjamin is of course pertinent also to references to chronology given his much-quoted interpretation of Paul Klee's etching of the *Angelus Novus*:

> A Klee painting named 'Angelus Novus' shows an angel looking as though he is about to move away from something he is fixedly contemplating. His eyes are staring, his mouth is open, his wings are spread. This is how one pictures the angel of history. His face is turned toward the past. Where we perceive a chain of events, he sees one single catastrophe which keeps piling wreckage upon wreckage and hurls it in front of his feet. The angel would like to stay, awaken the dead, and make whole what has been smashed. But a storm is blowing from Paradise; it has got caught in his wings with such violence that the angel can no longer close them. The storm irresistibly propels him into the future to which his back is turned, while the pile of debris before him grows skyward. This storm is what we call progress.[2]

Likewise, the problematising of our usual patterns of chronology recurs in the multiple writings of

Deleuze and Guattari, such as via their conceptual figure of the 'rhizome', as taken from the Greek word for the mass of roots that certain plants can grow horizontally underground. Of this they wrote: 'A rhizome has no beginning or end; it is always in the middle, between things, interbeing, *intermezzo*.'[3] Ideas of exactitude about what is past or present or future have to slip accordingly – which is not to say, however, that chronology does not still perform a necessary role in our thinking, such as in being able to invert it. Elsewhere in *A Thousand Plateaus*, Deleuze and Guattari made reference to 'reverse causality', describing this as a set of relations 'which are without finality but testify nonetheless to an action of the future on the present'.[4] Yet before I embark on telling a reverse history here, it is useful first to map out the need for critical practice as the basis for action in design research.

THE NEED FOR CRITICAL PRACTICE

An ongoing dilemma for any architectural practice is how it views itself in relation to the context it operates in. What, indeed, are the conditions under which architecture can be produced, not least in light of the urban systems and structure within which it is almost invariably created? This was the great challenge thrown down by Manfredo Tafuri in the 1960s and 70s when pointing out the failings of modernist architects. The latter believed they were transforming the post-war world through welfare building programmes and urban development, thus finally achieving the 1920s myths of social improvement and economic redistribution by architectural means, but Tafuri showed that the realities were anything but that.[5] If anything the pendulum has swung even further in the other direction since Tafuri's attack. 'Architects are pretty much high-class whores' was Philip Johnson's infamous quote from the 1980s, and a similar cynicism pervaded the flurry of so-called 'post-critical' thinking in US East Coast schools of architecture around the turn of the millennium, for whom the mantra was 'just get the job'.[6] The onset of a major global recession in 2008 and the first signs of the ending of American hegemony, given the ongoing shift of capital and power to Asia, soon ended any pretence of having entered a period of 'post-critical' practice. Furthermore, as Jane Rendell, Jonathan Hill, Mark Dorrian and I argued in our edited book on *Critical Architecture* (2007), the thorny relationship of architects to conditions of production and reproduction remains a pressing concern.[7] The issue simply cannot be ignored if one claims to have any level of self-reflective practice. In our book we reasserted the continual need for architecture to conceive of itself as a critical discourse – something which is also essential given the persistence of a line of thought, based around Fredric Jameson's adaptation of the questions posed by Tafuri, which believes the only response is to retreat from the problems of architectural ideology.[8] This represents a position of withdrawal from practice, even renunciation, and is not particularly appealing to those engaged in thinking about and producing architecture.

Design research in architecture thus needs to see itself as being entirely framed by socio-economic and cultural factors, with, as noted, these largely located within urban practices and processes. In many ways the contemporary city represents the testing ground of design research as it too consists of ideas and histories and systems and structures which are in search of a revealed meaning. Aldo Rossi wrote of his own personal growth as someone involved in design research:

> I believed that the Renaissance treatise had to be become an apparatus which could be translated into objects. I scorned memories, and at the same time, I made use of urban impressions: behind feelings I searched for fixed laws of a timeless typology. I saw courts and galleries, the elements of urban morphology, distributed in the city with a purity of mineralogy. I read books on urban geography, topography and history, like a general who wishes to know every battlefield – the high grounds, the passages, the woods. I walked the cities of Europe to understand their plans and classify them according to type. Like a lover sustained by my egotism, I often ignored the secret feelings I had for these cities: it was enough to know the systems that governed them. Perhaps I simply wanted to free myself of the city. Actually, I was discovering my own architecture. …
>
> I searched for it in history, and I translated it into my own history. Thus typological and functional certainty were extended, or brought back, to the world of objects: the house I designed at Borgo Ticino rediscovered the cabins of fishermen, the world of the lake and the river, a typology without history.[9]

Given such social and cultural aspirations, especially in terms of helping construct the meaning of a city, the question this is how they might ever be achieved. Obviously there is no simple or definitive reading of how architects ought to interact with the rest of society, nor can architecture ever be used instrumentally to 'deliver' a specific social or political transformation. Michel Foucault once observed, when asked whether Le Corbusier's work should be seen as a form of liberation or oppression:

Perhaps the means that he [Corbusier] proposed were in the end less liberating than he thought, but, once again, I think that it can never be inherent in the structure of things to guarantee the exercise of freedom. The guarantee of freedom is freedom.[10]

Hence, just as one cannot simply enact legal structures to ensure the condition of freedom, so too only the practice of architectural creativity can ever guarantee the required conditions for those wishing to innovate in design terms. Intellectual and material factors will also need to be arranged in such a manner as to make this possible. It is a crucial point, for it means therefore that design research in architecture has to form its operations around a dialectical engagement between ideas and practices. Nothing can be prefigured. All has to be questioned. But what architecture is certainly able to do is to examine, and experiment, with the conditions under which it is conceived and produced, which means that a very real task for design research is to act as a mechanism for a wider critique of architecture itself.

Leading architectural exponents who take this more radical view of design research, and who base their work on a position of critique, include Teddy Cruz, who writes so passionately on the topic elsewhere in this book. Others from around the world include Doina Petrescu in the UK, Lacaton and Vassal in France, Elemental in Chile and Hsieh Ying-chun (*The Anarchist Gardener*) in Taiwan. Much of this terrain has been superbly collated by Nishat Awan, Tatjana Schneider and Jeremy Till in their book, *Spatial Agency* (2011), and its associated website.[11] One of the fish that the

Spatial Agency book let slip, and probably should not have, is Shigeru Ban, an architect currently spending a great deal of time on post-tsunami reconstruction work in Japan. This builds upon previous temporary structures he designed and constructed out of paper and cardboard tubing in wake of humanitarian disasters like the Rwandan genocide in 1994 or the Kobe earthquake the following year. As a designer whose avowed aim is to use cheap and plentiful materials, and therefore eschew waste in all senses – and yet still arrive at glorious architectural refinement through a systematic process of construction-led research – his is an overtly critical position. Shigeru Ban has said he is disappointed that more architects are not doing work for social benefit rather than for wealthy clients, noting: 'For privileged people the money and power is invisible, so they need an architect to visualise their power and money to the public. So that's what our profession is about.'[12] Ban wants to do things rather differently.

Perhaps most emblematic of Shigeru Ban's current projects is for a 'transitional' cardboard cathedral in Christchurch in New Zealand. As a relatively prosperous city that was rocked by a deadly earthquake in February 2011, Christchurch has insufficient funds to rebuild itself as it once was, plus it has already lost about 10 per cent of its population. At the moment, the city remains uncertain as to whether it will ever regain its hitherto economic status. There have also been a series of subsequent aftershocks, adding to the neuroses of inhabitants. In such a situation there might only be despair, but instead the local priest engaged Shigeru Ban to design a new cathedral for 700 people that could be erected in just a few months,

12.1 Design sketches by Shigeru Ban for the 'temporary' cardboard cathedral in Christchurch, New Zealand

12.2 Interior photograph of the model for the
cardboard cathedral

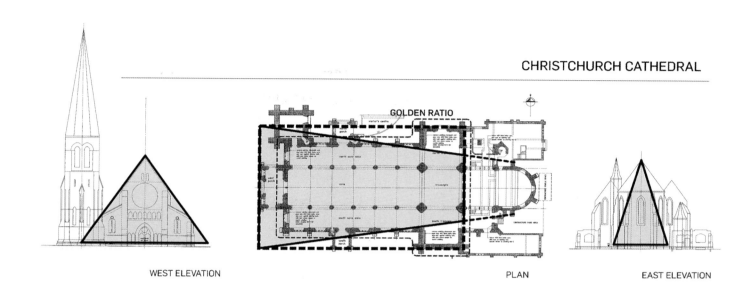

CHRISTCHURCH CATHEDRAL

GOLDEN RATIO

WEST ELEVATION   PLAN   EAST ELEVATION

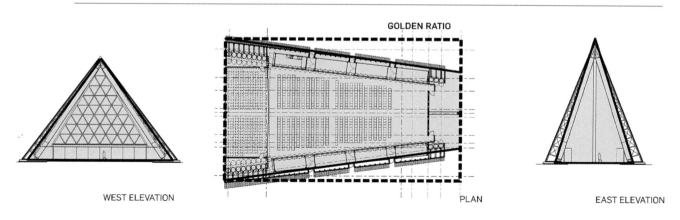

CARDBOARD CATHEDRAL

GOLDEN RATIO

WEST ELEVATION   PLAN   EAST ELEVATION

12.3   Analytical comparison between the old collapsed Christchurch Cathedral and the new 'temporary' cardboard one

12.4   Shigeru Ban's cardboard cathedral
under construction

and which was 'only' intended to last for a 20–30 year lifespan. The result is a work of genuine beauty, drawing upon Ban's long-standing design research into the responsive yet aesthetic use of cheap ordinary materials. In this case the church's structure is made from reinforced cardboard tubes, and the design is backed up by ritualised visual devices such as coloured glass to provide a suitably religious sensibility. True to its aims, the project is literally about to be completed on site.[13]

SPACES OF POSSIBILITY IN PALESTINE

Asserting an even more explicitly political slant, perhaps here I can mention briefly my own work with the Palestine Regeneration Team (PART): this is a group that I jointly set up in 2008 with Yara Sharif and Nasser Golzari.[14] Our conscious strategy is to involve ourselves in a series of intertwined projects in Palestine, both of the 'real world' constructed variety – such as in helping design the restored historic centre of Birzeit for Riwaq: Centre for Architectural Conservation, an ambitious Palestinian NGO – and other schemes which are far more open-ended and speculative. We also engage in writing and making exhibitions about the issues involved. PART is keen to use all types of design research and architectural projects that contain the potential to enact spatial changes, and thus open up new spatial possibilities, despite the ongoing Palestinian/Israeli conflict. The aspiration is to repair some of the violent fractures caused by many years of Israeli occupation, and above all to help to empower Palestinian communities. In this bitter confrontation between Palestine and Israel, where the map on the ground is daily becoming ever more disconnected and fragmented, it is even more crucial for architects to define their role within such a complex context. Between existence and co-existence there is a thin line that has managed to separate not only Palestinians from the Israelis, but also Palestinians from themselves. The worrying question, of course, is whether the current spatial fractures can ever be mended again? While stating this worry, however, the echoes of the last moments of apartheid in South Africa ring a bell in our minds. There is always the possibility of change even in what appears the most unwelcome of situations, as will be mentioned again when talking about Lebbeus Woods.

In terms of design research being created by someone from Palestine, a rich and challenging body of texts and projects was devised by Yara Sharif for her PhD by Design at the University of Westminster in London, for which I was the supervisor. She always unflinchingly asked deep ethical questions of herself, and as such was open about the contradictions and shortcomings in her approach. Yet most of all she embarked on a fertile process of testing, mapping, designing, building and reflecting. Sharif defines her intentions in this way:

> Looking at the dialogue of daily resistance also shows that within the current Israeli policies of hardening the border zones, the quest for a counter-space is carving out new cultural and urban realities against the forces of power. Perhaps the most outstanding outcomes of this reality are the everyday forms of Palestinian spatial resistance, which is recasting the geo-political map of Palestine by displaying creative tools that architecture and planning have so far failed to match. The emergence of small-scale Palestinian networks seems to be able to overcome and adapt to the situation, and as a result they can redefine the meaning of the built environment around them. These collective and informal networks/events are now also drawing their own lines for a new kind of thinking within architecture. Ostensibly, their task is to subvert spaces of pure oppression and change them into spaces of play and creativity so that social life can be recuperated.[15]

Discussion of these kinds of issues with a broad spectrum of Palestinian groups, including those running the clandestine networks which secretly move illegal workers in and out of Israel every day, gave Sharif the insights she needed to identify the pressure points of tension and opportunity.

12.5   View of the old town centre in Birzeit, close to Ramallah, in the Palestinian West Bank

Many are located near to the notorious 'Separation Wall' being erected by the Israeli government. Having thereby defined what was undoubtedly an original and hard-hitting agenda for her design research to operate with, and upon, Sharif worked on a series of architectural and landscape proposals for the 'spaces of possibility' she had so carefully identified. As she explains:

My design interventions – or more correctly the moments of possibility I have proposed in this thesis – may not hold the full answer or the solution for the Palestinian/Israeli conflict. However, they do illustrate how one could begin to pick up on a very simple detail from daily life and celebrate it, and then turn what might seem a very normal observation into a subversive concept, and then after that turn this concept into a tool, and that tool into a design proposal. Indeed, my wish

226

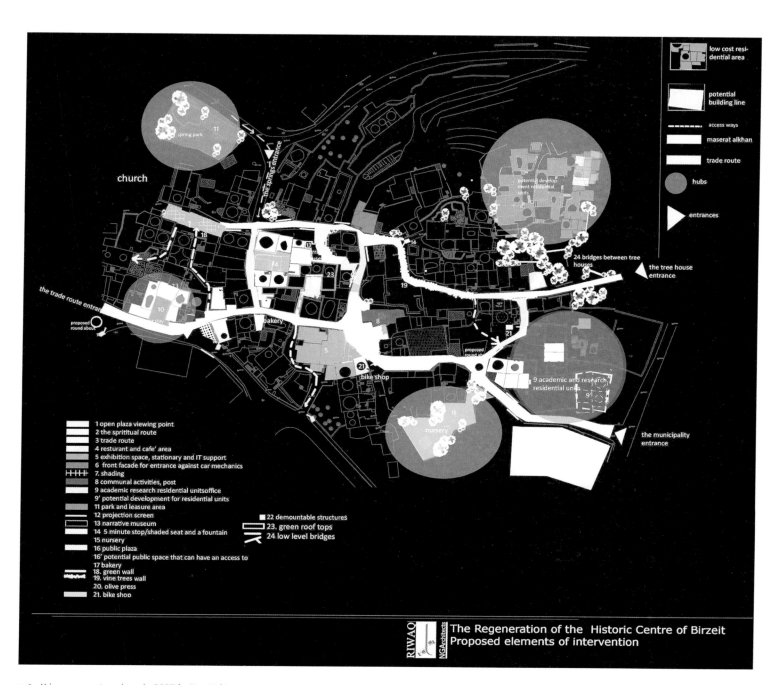

The legend/labels within the figure:

low cost resi-
dential area

potential
building line

access ways

maserat alkhan

trade route

hubs

entrances

24 bridges between tree
houses

the tree house
entrance

the municipality
entrance

church

the spring entrance

the trade route entrance

proposed round about

spring park

potential development residential units

bakery

bike shop

9 academic and research residential units

nursery

proposed round about

1 open plaza viewing point
2 the sprititual route
3 trade route
4 resturant and cafe' area
5 exhibition space, stationary and IT support
6 front facade for entrance against car mechanics
7. shading
8 communal activities, post
9 academic research residential unitsoffice
9' potential development for residential units
11 park and leasure area
12 projection screen
13 narrative museum
14 5 minute stop/shaded seat and a fountain
15 nursery
16 public plaza
16' potential public space that can have an access to
17 bakery
18. green wall
19. vine trees wall
20. olive press
21. bike shop

22 demountable structures
23. green roof tops
24 low level bridges

RIWAQ NGArchitects
The Regeneration of the Historic Centre of Birzeit
Proposed elements of intervention

12.6   Urban regeneration scheme by PART for Birzeit's historic centre

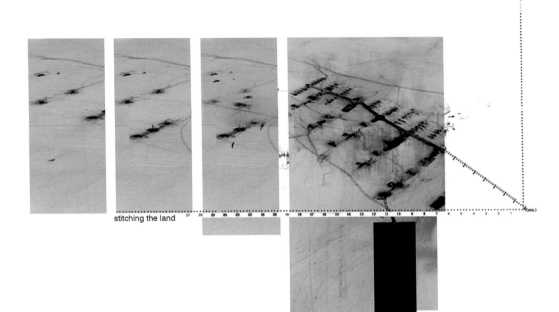

stitching the land

12.7   Palestinians daily having to traverse the 'Separation Wall'

12.8   Conceptual drawing by Yara Sharif for stitching the divided landscape of Palestine/Israel

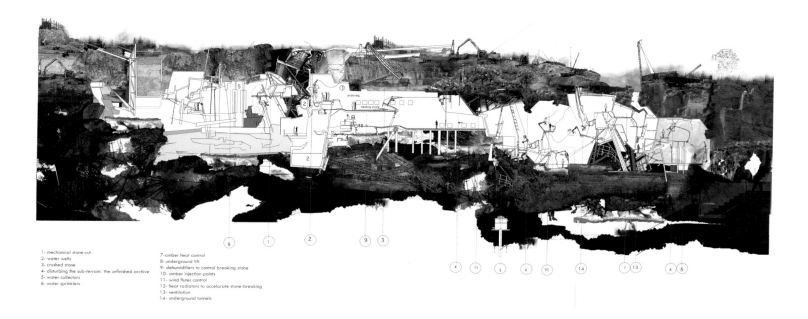

1- mechanical stone-cut
2- water wells
3- crushed stone
4- disturbing the sub-terrain: the unfinished archive
5- water collectors
6- water sprinklers

7- amber heat control
8- underground lift
9- dehumidifiers to control breaking stone
10- amber injection points
11- wind flutes control
12- heat radiators to accelerate stone-breaking
13- ventilation
14- underground tunnels

12.9 Inserted structures which reoccupy the abandoned stone quarries of the Palestinian West Bank, as part of Yara Sharif's PhD by Design

is to argue that resilience as a way of life is not necessarily a form of giving up or accepting facts on the ground, as many might argue. Instead, it can be a creative tool of resistance when backed up with a clear strategy, such as can be provided – as shown here – by innovative architectural design proposals.[16]

To touch upon just one of these design research projects, Sharif through her investigations uncovered the destruction of a great deal of the West Bank's land surface by stone quarries – some of these are owned by Israeli companies but mostly by Palestinian entrepreneurs. So lucrative is this trade that the stone is being nicknamed 'white gold' or 'white oil'. Whoever gets the profit from these quarries, the brute reality is that the stone is mostly being extracted (an estimated 75 per cent of it) to build illegal Israeli settlements in the West Bank, or else to aggrandise Jerusalem into a monocultural Jewish capital by turning ever more into the proverbial 'city of stone'. In parallel, the monopolisation of access to water resources in the West Bank by Israeli companies, with piped water then being sold to Palestinian citizens at a far higher cost than to Israeli settlers, is exacerbating the real danger of water shortages (especially clean drinking water) for West Bank Palestinians. Sharif therefore imagined a future for the abandoned stone quarries in which they can be re-occupied by Palestinian groups who then install networks of absorbent sponge bags to capture the rainfall and ground water before it filters down to the aquifer (whereupon it would only be tapped off by Israeli water companies). As a secret act of re-colonisation, these clusters of bags and reused underground spaces suggest, through the visceral drawings for

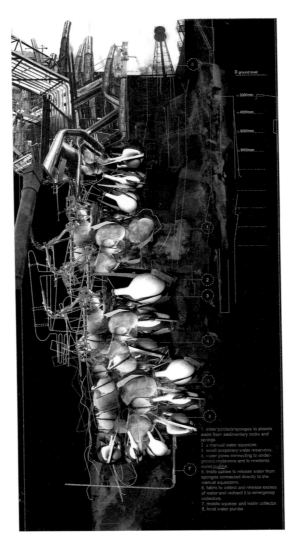

1. water pockets/sponges to absorb water from sedimentary rocks and springs
2. a manual water squeezer.
3. small temporary water reservoirs.
4. water pipes connecting to underground reservoirs and to residents water pumps.
5. trails cables to release water from sponges connected directly to the manual squeezers.
6. fabric to collect and release excess of water and redirect it to emergency collectors.
7. mobile squeezer and water collector.
8. local water pumps.

0 ground level

— 2000mm

— 4000mm

— 6000mm

— 8000mm

disasters has of course a definite lineage, perhaps none quite as direct as Lebbeus Woods. As a critical and oppositional thinker, Woods also sought spatial possibilities that might lead to more inclusive and democratic social formations, and he realised only too well that to do this required proactive research inquiry:

> Architecture is, first and foremost, a process of creating (and not merely an expression of) knowledge. Because of this, the making of architecture is a major coalescing activity in society, bringing together many flows into a single complex stream.[17]

Tellingly, he came to regard the spaces of war as offering the best creative opportunities, offering a sort of hope in destruction. Woods produced an abundance of powerfully provocative projects and texts over the years, but perhaps none were more evocative than those in his 1997 book on *Radical Reconstruction*. In that book, his text was full of things like 'scabs', 'scars' and potential 'transforming walls' within damaged cities – albeit each of these linguistic terms intended in a positive and constructive sense. It was accompanied by designs for strange amorphous structures that could appear on existing buildings, almost as living organisms – indeed viruses – which could grow and take on their own programmatic purposes. Hence the old and the new were treated as working symbiotically together. In *Radical Reconstruction*, Woods focussed on three cities that were fraught with different kinds of tension and disruption within their built fabric: Sarajevo after the destruction of the terrible Balkan wars in the early 1990s, Havana in its state of decay and misery as a consequence of the slow economic

Sharif's design doctorate, a new suite of sumptuous and subversive counter-spaces.

'CREATE THE VERNACULAR, NOT MONUMENTS'

The focus of architects like Shigeru Ban and Yara Sharif on responding to natural or man-made

12.10 Clusters of sponge elements to absorb rainfall and ground water in the reoccupied stone quarries

230

strangulation of Cuba by the far mightier USA, for purely ideological reasons; and the need to find new concepts for dwellings that might withstand the earthquake threat in San Francisco along the San Andreas Fault. The latter condition, for instance, saw Woods devise a range of housing types with suitably explicit names: 'shard houses', 'wave houses', slip houses', 'fault houses' and 'wheel houses'.

Typical of Woods's ethos, *Radical Reconstruction* was a bold attempt to imagine radical avant-garde design but in a socially committed manner. Its texts and projects played off each other as vehicles for a thoroughly dialectical design research method. Together they were used to suggest counteractive tactics and strategies that could create, on behalf of ordinary citizens, greater opportunities of choice, openness and equality. The narrow mindset of existing social hierarchies needed to be replaced, according to Woods, by more inclusive heterarchies. His underlying thrust involved a full-frontal critique of official architecture and the power relations it aims to produce and reproduce. 'Create the vernacular, not monuments', declared Woods defiantly, in a contrary mode.[18] Thus, despite the free license that Lebbeus Woods might appear to have allowed himself, in terms of what he could then chose to imagine and draw, there was always a clear systematic argument being developed through his design research process. The astonishing image making of his drawings was never done for its own sake, but acted to place his research ideas into the mind of the reader and invite them to become complicit in the design process by association. For more than anything in *Radical Reconstruction*, it was the poignant renderings of new additions and extensions that could grow, weed-like or parasite-like, within the bombed-out buildings of Sarajevo that hit so many people's imaginations at the time. If the famous *Carceri* sketches by Piranesi seemed ambivalent to the power wielded by the early-modern state, even appearing to fetishise it, here in contrast were expressive images for our age that warned against all social inequalities. Woods, for instance, was amongst those concerned in the 1990s by the potential social consequences of the introduction of digitalised communication technology, as he explained:

> Now it is possible to create complex, fluid and multilayered societies, rich with diversity and choice. For the moment these [digital] technologies are controlled by public and private hierarchies who use them as a means of domination from above, frustrating the emergence of a more inclusive human society. But that will change, and has already started to change. The building of new urban tissues where the old ones have been torn to pieces by war is one crisis point – beyond the immediate provenance of hierarchies – where the struggle to form new, heterarchical societies will be engaged.[19]

The 'vernacular' neighbourhood-level projects imagined by Lebbeus Woods also chimed in well with interest during the early 1990s in the pervasive hybridity of what Henri Lefebvre had termed 'planetary urbanism': that is, in distinction to the outdated notion of regarding cities as if they were singular entities. Lefebvre and Woods also shared an interest in the awkward patterns and rhythms of everyday life, and the power to change reality at an intimate level via spatial appropriation by disadvantaged social groups. Woods through his architectural projects also played with one's sense of time. The programme-free 'scabs' and 'scars'

12.11   Lebbeus Woods, *Manifesto* (1993)

12.12   Lebbeus Woods, *Havana, Radically Reconstructed* (1994)

12.13 Lebbeus Woods, *Injection
Parasite, Sarajevo* (1992)

being added to devastated cities were initially without any purpose, but as such their forms would then have to be lived with, and in time transformed into some kind of productive space. It was a sort of functionalism in reverse. But what he was attempting most of all was to switch who held the power over what kinds of spaces were built in cities, who could use them, and for what: this was to be removed from official governments and design professionals. Instead it was to be ordinary people who would make these spaces at a local and incidental level within the city. To make this point was not so much an Ernst Schumacher-esque argument that 'small is beautiful', but rather the recognition of the complex intricacy of contemporary urban conditions even at the tiniest scale. If anything, the design research of Woods was not that far from what Nabeel Hamdi has been arguing for (in a different way) in terms of the ability of 'small change' to effect bigger social transformations, especially among those social groups who are generally excluded anyway from mainstream initiatives.[20]

As mentioned before, the intellectual approach of Lebbeus Woods was one that was rooted explicitly in everyday urbanism, and by implication was extremely critical of the forms of spatial power enacted by social elites in their efforts to maintain privilege. What one got the sense of with Woods, as indeed with Shigeru Ban and Yara Sharif, is a heightened sense of the importance of ordinary people, the inhabiting subjects of our cities, in the shaping of architectural projects. For them, hence, the populace is the mainstay of their design research processes. The obvious fascination of Woods with all aspects of urban life, and specifically of the conditions in the city where he lived and

worked – New York – was ever present in the popular blogsite he kept up almost to his death. Among the various musings on his blogsite, he expressed an acute understanding of Rem Koolhaas, that most famous chronicler of the urban qualities known as 'Manhattanism'. In a short post on 24 October 2009, Woods chose to reminisce upon one of the 'lost' unbuilt Koolhaas/OMA projects from the 1980s, the second-placed entry for the Parc de la Villette competition in Paris:

> We might call this park a proto- or supra-urban landscape, in that its experience evokes the qualities we would want a city to have, foremost among them the ingredients of our personally selected self-invention. It is very much a people's park, not because it caters to the lowest common denominators of expectations, but playfully challenges people to make of it what they can, each in their own way. This project reminds us that there was once a Rem Koolhaas quite different from the corporate starchitect we see today. His work in the 70s and early 80s was radical and innovative, but did not get built. Often he didn't seem to care – it was the ideas that mattered. However, his scheme for the Parc de la Villette begs to have been built and we can only regret that it never was.[21]

THE RETROACTIVE MANIFESTO

There is of course a sense of disappointment behind these comments of Lebbeus Woods about Koolhaas's career trajectory, but equally there is praise in that Koolhaas had previously identified many of the social and urban qualities needed by cities if they were to meet public expectations. It is worth examining this more, by now tracing the story back to *Delirious New York*. Up till the mid-1970s, it has been the case that an aspect left out of virtually all writings about architecture and cities was the experience of people as individual subjects within the urban realm. This refers not to the narrow official definitions of what subjective experience might be, but one that includes the full gamut of human life in the contemporary metropolis – whether these activities are purportedly 'high' or 'low', or whether this means things like artistic culture, sexual preference, emotional feelings (fear, aggression and so on). A sea-change in thinking about subjectivity (as it tends to be termed today) undoubtedly came from feminist thought, notably the branch of Marxist feminism that during the 1970s started to break away from the orthodoxies of Soviet or Maoist Communism. In France, writers such as Simone de Beauvoir now began to be linked to post-structuralist feminist philosophers like Helene Cixous, Luce Irigaray and Julia Kristeva, who, given their keen interest also in psychoanalysis and anthropology, addressed issues around the body, sexuality and identity. The impact on architectural discourse was not that immediate or dynamic, yet it did gradually filter through.

It was Madelon Vriesendorp who provided the haunting, dream-like drawings of famous Manhattan skyscrapers in bed together, including *Flagrant Delit* on the front cover, for the shockingly original book by her husband, Rem Koolhaas.[22] *Delirious New York* was the first major text within architectural discourse to situate subjective experience of architecture and urban design in a non-linear and non-deterministic manner. The book is also noteworthy in that – certainly in my view – it was the first sustained and conscious example of design research as a systematic field of application. By this I mean that it was deliberately composed

out of innovative historical and theoretical research, much of it from obscure archives, which then fed into, and also took inspiration from, a parallel set of architectural projects. In all this, there was no doubt a conscious echo of Le Corbusier's declamatory style in texts such as *Vers Une Architecture* and *Urbanisme*, but the tone and the aims of Koolhaas were very different.

In terms of the narrative construction in *Delirious New York*, it was in effect a case of looking back at history in reverse to explain how a particular city, New York, had come to be designed and built: the author even described it as 'a retroactive manifesto'. Koolhaas has since noted that one of his main intentions was to place people and their messy urban lives at the heart of architectural discourse.[23] The background to the book is also relevant. After finishing his training at the Architectural Association in central London, Koolhaas took up a Harkness scholarship at Cornell University from 1972–4 so that he could carry out the research for *Delirious New York*, while also being closely involved in the Institute for Architecture and Urban Studies in New York. At that time in thrall to Roland Barthes, Koolhaas reinterpreted Manhattan like a detective or an archaeologist, seeking out forensic evidence of those forces which had come to transform New York, through its pioneering forms of architectural and urban development, into the 'Capital of Capitalism' during the course of the twentieth century.

Delirious New York, like much of that which emerged at the Architectural Association in the 1960s and 70s, was at heart a glorious student project, and as such it served to launch a new mode of thinking and writing about cities. It was also the outcome of yet another anguished twentieth-century European intellectual who visited America in order to discover, and sort out, their own beliefs. Koolhaas cast himself as the ghostwriter in the story: the unseen outsider who could be brought in from outside to find a purpose and structure in what was otherwise a marvellously complex tale. New York was condensed into Manhattan, even in the title of the book, and Manhattan therefore became all of New York. The city was portrayed as 'a culture of congestion' – a dizzying blur of activity, electricity and desire – in which the horizontal dimension of the planning grid suggested a possible sense of order, and was then crossed by the rampant variety of the vertical, the dimension of the ego.

Koolhaas's starkest revelation was that New York was in fact foreshadowed by Coney Island, which had hitherto been regarded, wrongly, merely as Manhattan's playground. Coney Island during its heyday before the First World War, we were told, was actually a mini-laboratory for urbanism, a testing ground for the giant city it served. Both relied on each other. Coney was a displaced Manhattan, and one that showed to us that cities are in fact largely products of our subconscious dreams and desires. It was thus no accident that the Coney theme park which Koolhaas described in most detail was called 'Dreamland'. Rationalist European intellectuals such Maxim Gorky did not really get this point when they visited New York, recoiling in disgust. Le Corbusier came over more in a mood to conquer, with Koolhaas describing him as 'pregnant' with ideas he wished to deliver. But in *Delirious New York*, Le Corbusier is shown as struggling in his efforts to tame and organise the child he wished to create, the rationalised high-rise skyscraper, and ended

up returning to France only cradling his vision for the Ville Radieuse – the other of the 'Siamese twins' which had to be cut off from its American sibling, as a puny sanitised version of the high-rise city without any of New York's vitality and congestion of activities. The Surrealist artist, Salvador Dali, who memorably described Manhattan as 'the Atlantis of the subconscious', was seen as much more on track; he simply dived headlong into the libidinous pleasures the city offered.

In terms of the designs which Koolhaas included in the last part of the book ('Appendix'), as an accompaniment to his startling historical insights, these featured projects – some designed by Elia and Zoe Zenghelis, and with Vriesendorp – for 'The City of the Captive Globe', 'Hotel Sphinx' and such like. In the description for 'The Story of the Pool', a Russian architectural student in 1923 designs a giant floating swimming pool which he and his classmates construct out of steel frame and metal panels. By the 1930s, with Stalinist repression setting in, they decide to swim in synchronised fashion so they can use the floating pool to escape the USSR, having realised that if they all swim in one direction, then the pool is pushed the other way. It however takes 40 years to get to New York, during which time the pool has to be altered to suit changing conditions. On arrival the Russian architects/swimmers are less than enamoured with what New York has become in the meantime, while the locals deride the floating structure as a rusting piece of outdated modernism. As an allegory of the essayed transportation of neo-Constructivist architecture by Koolhaas and others to an America in the mid-1970s which was then in thrall to post-modernism, it forms a fitting epilogue to the book in terms of the (literal) exhaustion of its subject. More pertinent here, it also represents another metaphor of design which pushes forwards and backwards at the same moment. Having uncovered the psychological urges which had created Manhattan, Koolhaas wanted to test out notions of cultural congestion and subconscious desire in his own designs, such that they could be introduced to architectural discourse and practice elsewhere in the world. In his own words, the final design-based part of his book was to be regarded:

> … as a *fictional conclusion*, an interpretation of the same material, not through words, but in a series of architectural projects. These proposals are the provisional product of Manhattanism as a conscious doctrine whose pertinence is no longer limited to the island of its invention.[24]

After the publication of *Delirious New York*, Rem Koolhaas and his Office for Metropolitan Architecture began to enjoy a glittering reputation but had relatively little work. Gradually their workload increased, forcing them to take on issues of urban and architectural scale. Koolhaas appeared to be desperate to remove any trace of humanism and idealism, particularly of the Dutch structuralist variety, from the architectural agenda. This was to be achieved by two strategies: on one hand, an unsentimental rehabilitation of 1920s modernist visions of 'the city without qualities'; and on the other, a celebration of the way in which dreams and desires are given urban form. Planning and pleasure; profit and pornography. What was deliberately left out was the safe, cosy middle-ground of architectural conformity. During the late 1970s and early 80s, the spread of post-structuralist theory gave Koolhaas a critical edge, but as early examples of a developing

approach to design research, the initial OMA projects never really reached beyond awkward propaganda. The cartoon-like ethos of, say, the Netherlands Dance Centre in The Hague (1984–7) managed to squash any spatial innovations it was trying to impart.

Thus by the late 1980s there was a growing disillusionment within OMA about their trajectory. In Koolhaas's view, post-structuralism worked well as the basis for critical opposition in the 1970s, but it was inadequate for when an architect started to deal with the realities of architectural production within the capitalist system. Modernism could well be criticised as flawed formalism, but the participation of architects in the process of modernist urbanisation remained inescapable. As such, 'honesty' and 'realism' became the new mantras for Koolhaas. As he noted:

> After *Delirious New York*, it was convenient to treat the book – the transformation of architecture it implied – as an isolated incident. OMA's European beginnings in the early eighties offered no pretexts for its relevance. We were involved in our own on-the-job training, staring the best of architecture in the face for the first time. The additional weight of proving the book's combined revisions would have been a theoretical millstone. As in cryogenics, this body of work was frozen.[25]

Gradually, however, OMA's projects began to fit better with the research inquiries that inspire them, as exemplified by the Rotterdam Kunsthal (1989–92), in which the subtle nuances of designing a museum in the guise of an inhabited ramp led to what is probably still Koolhaas's best building. The change in approach was also the result of a conscious policy to work only with the best professional consultants available. Again, as Koolhaas explained:

> In 1985 we began to collaborate with Cecil Balmond, a Ceylonese engineer, and his structure and services unit at Ove Arup. He was patient with our unreasonable demands, and sometimes took our amateurism seriously. Our growing intimacy with each other's disciplines – in fact, a mutual invasion of territory – and the corresponding blurring of specific professional identities (not always painless) allowed us, at the end of the eighties – when, to our consternation, Bigness emerged like an iceberg from the midst of deconstructivist discourse and imposed itself as a political, economic, artistic necessity – to defrost earlier ambitions and to explore the redesign and mystification of architecture, this time experimenting on ourselves.[26]

The clearest expression of OMA's dilemma over which direction it ought to take was the publication of *S,M,L,XL* in 1995. At the front of this book were a set of graphics describing the political economy of architectural practice: turnover, profits, expenses, labour supply and similar aspects. What these graphics also revealed was an economic downturn for OMA after an earnings peak in 1992; hence the need to publish a book. At well over 1,000 pages, *S,M,L,XL* represented the huge monument that the ego of Koolhaas added to the grid of architectural publishing. It played around with the ordering and categorisation of architectural projects by adopting the commercialised code for sizes used by the fashion industry, Yet, at the same time there was for many of us something profoundly disappointing about it as a book. Instead of offering a new model for design research, thereby updating and transcending *Delirious New York*, it came across as a practice brochure fattened up and hiding itself behind Bruce Mau's dazzling graphic design. The book's most telling contribution was the hint given in the two best essays, 'Singapore Songlines' and 'The Generic City' – that the future of cities, and of architecture, would be decided in Asia, thereby ending centuries of western domination under which Europeans, and then Americans, got to determine what architecture was about, and what it could achieve. This 'Asian turn' in *S,M,L,XL* also reflected the move by Koolhaas over to his Harvard Project on the City, with its subsequent edited volumes on issues like the Pearl River Delta or shopping malls.[27] Yet if anything, these later books – and as demonstrated even more clearly by Koolhaas setting up AMO as the 'mirror' research wing of OMA -were just going further off the mark, in that they acted to sever (and thus negate) the necessary continuities of design research between text and project. This dichotomy is expressed in the project for the China Central Television headquarters in Beijing's main business district, where the architect's affectation of there being a socially inclusive public route through the building is destroyed entirely by the policies of the building owners, not least the fact that the building is still more or less unoccupied and is surrounded by a gated 'park' which denies access. Lebbeus Woods, showing that he was not at all convinced, wrote of Koolhaas's project:

> The CCTV building is certainly a symbol of the power of the Chinese Communist Party and perhaps ... a metaphor of China's headlong rush into the future, but its almost suburban isolation from the city around it, as well as the pathetic 'park' at its base and the brutal way the slick glass-cladded masses cut into the ground without a hint of

12.14 China Central Television Building
(CCTV) by Rem Koolhaas/OMA as
another chess-piece in Beijing's CBD

approach or entry, broadcasts its anti-urban spirit better than any TV propaganda produced within it. To the knowing, this is supposed to be read as 'irony,' or 'a critique'. To regular people it is just business as usual in an authoritarian state.[28]

'A TWO-FOLD MOVEMENT'

In retrospect, perhaps the most striking innovation of *Delirious New York* was its conception of the 'retroactive manifesto' – in other words, the drawing out of the meaning behind buildings and urban spaces which otherwise seem to defy explanation, and the use of designs and written texts to uncover this meaning. As a literary conceit within the sphere of architecture and urbanism, the only real precedent I can think of – which Koolhaas possibly never read – is in the brief but fascinating mention of design research by Eliel Saarinen in the last few pages of his now largely-forgotten 1943 book, *The City: Its Growth, its Decay, its Future*.[29] Published during the uncertainties of the USA in the Second World War, the book offered a link between pre-war hopes and post-war anxieties.

Saarinen was of course a notable figure in twentieth-century architectural history. Born in Finland, and widely regarded as that country's best exponent in the 1900s and 1910s of what is usually called 'national romanticism' – a culturally specific Nordic variant of freestyle Arts and Crafts – Saarinen emigrated along with his family to America in 1923, after being given second place in the international design competition for the Chicago Tribune Tower.[30] Among the many triumphs of Eliel Saarinen in the USA was his appointment as head of the Cranbrook Academy of Art in Bloomfield Hills, located in the northern suburbs of Detroit, Michigan, and for which he designed a number of buildings. He also

created a series of elegantly inflected modernist gems such as the Kleinhans Music Hall in Buffalo, New York (1939–40) and the First Christian Church in Columbus, Indiana (1939–42). Most famously of all, he nurtured the career of his famous son, Eero Saarinen, who joined the family practice in the late 1930s. Together they worked on the initial designs for the General Motors Research Center in North Detroit (built from 1950–56). Eero Saarinen inherited this latter project after his father's death in July 1950, and went on – during a creatively intense period in the 1950s – to become one of the best architects in the world, before dying tragically early, just 51 years old, from a brain haemorrhage in 1961.

Returning to Eliel Saarinen's 1943 book on *The City*, it was notable for the complex range of themes it covered. For a start, Saarinen tapped into his Arts and Crafts sensibilities, especially the concept of informally composed 'street pictures' which Raymond Unwin had brazenly adapted for the Garden City movement after reading Camillo Sitte's classic study, *City Building According to Artistic Principles* (1889). Eliel Saarinen likewise cited Sitte's text as a foundation stone for his own thinking: he included a lengthy section summarising Sitte's ideas, while also noting Unwin's invaluable role in introducing these principles to Britain.[31] Urban theory was hardly new territory for Eliel Saarinen, as prior to emigrating he had enjoyed extensive town planning experience in places like Helsinki, Budapest and Tallinn (then Reval). His book also contained some echoes of Steen Eiler Rasmussen's lyrical rhapsody in 1934 to Georgian London's bounteous parks and squares.[32] But above all, Saarinen's book embraced the humanistic and civic ethos of the great Scottish polymath and cultural geographer, Patrick Geddes,

12.15   Eliel Saarinen's First Christian Church,
Columbus, Indiana (1939–42)

who is widely credited as the inventor of regional planning. America's leading apostle of Geddes in the 1920s and 30s was the architectural critic and urban theorist, Lewis Mumford, someone whom Eliel Saarinen came to know well. Mumford's own contributions of that era included *The Culture of Cities* (1938) and the commentary he wrote for a documentary film, simply titled *The City*, which was shown at the 1939 New York World's Fair.[33] In turn, this Geddesian influence from Mumford, along with the writings of Eliel Saarinen, fed into later critiques of modernist urbanism such as Jane Jacobs' *The Death and Life of Great American Cities* (1961).[34]

Yet Eliel Saarinen was also sensitive to the new ideals of modernism, and the two most publicised town planning visions of this kind in the 1930s scene were obviously Frank Lloyd Wright's 'Broadacre City' and Le Corbusier's 'Ville Radieuse'. Both of those figures had shown early signs of interest in Garden City ideals yet soon moved off in very different ways. Le Corbusier was also of importance here for his ready acceptance of the need for research in architecture: his comment on carrying out research as a 'step by step' process was cited in this book's introductory chapter, and certainly when he was planning to set up his own foundation and archive, prior to his death, he declared: 'After my time, the Fondation Le Corbusier will prolong the research I have devoted myself to ....'[35] Corbusier appears to have conceived of research as happening along a spiralling path, and his dedicated search to discover successful patents from his ideas demonstrated his wide-ranging research approach.

If this was the lineage that Eliel Saarinen's book fitted into, what is directly relevant to this chapter is that it is the first text – certainly that I am aware of, although there could be previous examples – which consciously refers to the idea of design research in architecture. This is not to say that design research hadn't existed in various forms for at least 500 years already – as Jonathan Hill points out elsewhere in this book – or indeed for even longer than that, if one takes things back to Vitruvius. However, never had the term been used in an explicit way before. The actual phrase used by Eliel Saarinen in the epilogue of his 1943 book was 'research design', but his meaning – at least in certain vital regards – was the same as we might understand it now. How, then, did Saarinen build up his argument in the book? In essence, *The City* consists a sequence of historical and contemporary examples through which Saarinen argued for the superiority of what he called 'town-design', a fully three-dimensional and spatialised artistic practice, over the dominant yet less useful preference for two-dimensional, diagrammatic thinking within 'town-planning'. His epilogue was duly titled 'Town-Design', and in it Saarinen set out his views on how architects should make cities in future. Architectural schools needed to train their students about the social aspects which made up the collective city, and likewise architects in practice could only ever hope to succeed in town-design if they engaged upon fundamental research processes. He wrote (with the author's emphasis in bold):

As Caesar crossed the Rubicon, he discerned beyond its banks his real problems to come. So must the town-designer of today stretch far beyond the boundaries of present possibilities, for his real work lies way out there in the future. **The character of his actions, therefore, is that of the 'pioneer', and the means and methods of his work are those of 'research'.**

Saarinen went on to explain:

> When we speak about research, however, we do not mean mere digging through statistical material pertaining to the city's past. This kind of research does not belong to realm of actual design, it merely is that material from which actual design must grow. We mean [instead].. 'planning research' dealing solely with the city's organisation henceforth. Such work aims to outline the city's future by producing a number of tentative schemes through which to survey all the various possibilities of future organisation and growth. This is the kind of progressive planning research from which future realities can and must emerge.[36]

Passing on to observe that every modern industrial company of any repute now possessed its own research wing, Saarinen suggested the establishment of research institutions at the urban level:

> In the city's case, therefore, research must be the pioneer of design. This kind of pioneering planning research must stretch the feelers of prehension far beyond existing conditions: it must find new ways and means to forward far-sighted design toward better order in the city; and it must open-mindedly discern future possibilities in present impossibilities. In this manner the new possibilities, when the city is ripe for their application, will from time to time be graduated from the research stage to the actuality of final design. By this kind of procedure, the city's physical development will keep pace with the progress of life. On the other hand, in case this kind of a research-toward-design process is ignored, the city is doomed to continue its road toward increasing compactness and disorder.[37]

Saarinen then went on to discuss the creative nature of research required in differing disciplines:

> Research in science is a matter of vision. Thanks to this vision, countless discoveries have been made, often surpassing even the boldest imagination … Similarly, town-design must be much a matter of vision, for it must span a long bridge toward that unknown future. The designer must visualize his city as it might develop over a tentatively estimated period of time. This period of time constitutes the designer's field of action, within which his imagination must evolve the tentative lay-out, intended to show the most appropriate direction of the city's development toward the future.[38]

Hence a flexible, rather than fixed, vision was needed for any 'dream scheme' for a city so that the project could be continuously adapted in its course, as if one was sailing a ship on the seas. 'The outlining of the future dream scheme, however, is only the first step in the process of research design', he declared.[39] Remarkably, Saarinen went on to outline a novel way of looking at the problem. If one was able to envisage a bold future city design that could be realised after a period of (say) 50 years' time, then equally one could trace back the relevant level of urban transformation after periods of 40 years/30 years/20 years/10 years, and use this to draw up a phased implementation strategy. He wrote, intriguingly:

> In accordance with this kind of a calculus, the research design would go on step-by-step backward in time, approaching gradually – and perhaps with reduced time intervals – the existing realities. Likewise, this step-by-step, backward in time, research design must happen in a flexible manner as a matter of suggestive thought. The more such a scheming approaches existing conditions, the more real the suggestive thought must be. And when the scheming coincides with the very present time, this backward-in-time-scheming will be

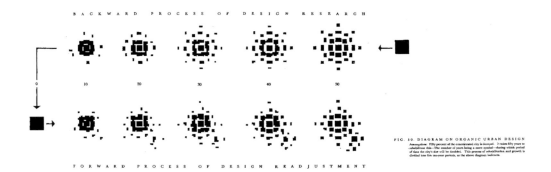

FIG. 50. DIAGRAM ON ORGANIC URBAN DESIGN

FORWARD   PROCESS   OF   DESIGN   READJUSTMENT

changed into town-design of actual conditions. From then on, the design work will run forward in time, parallel and in close co-operation with actual town-building.[40]

This ingenious rationale gave Eliel Saarinen the necessary head of steam to deliver his final *coup-de-grace* (again with the author's own emphasis):

> The imaginative research design, as we see, moves in a direction opposite to that taken by actual design. **We have also a two-fold movement with opposite orientation: first, we have town-design from the future toward the present; and second, we have town-design from the present toward the future. Both are indispensable.**[41]

It was a brilliant insight, in that it conceived of building projects as moving in a linear process from the present into the future, as we conventionally tend to do, yet of design research operating in the opposite direction – that is, from the eventual vision back in time to inform the present design thinking of the architect. In a diagram to explain this concept, Saarinen explicitly referred to the 'backward process of design research' as being indispensable for conceiving buildings and especially larger entities

12.16   Eliel Saarinen's diagram from *The City* (1943) showing the 'Backward Process of Design Research' and the 'Forward Process of Urban Readjustment'

like cities. So in this regard he can plausibly be claimed as one of the first architects – if not even *the* first – to have coined the phrase 'design research'. We have arrived at the start of our tale.

A POTENTIAL METHODOLOGY FOR DESIGN RESEARCH

Despite the undoubted novelty of his ideas about design research, which of course were never properly recognised at the time, there is little need to overplay the contribution of Eliel Saarinen's *The City*. His book remained old-fashioned in terms of its high-handed, patrician tone, the product of a quintessentially pre-war cultural attitude. Saarinen was above all trying to conceive of how one might design a whole city which would take decades to realise, and thinking of how one might possibly be able to do that. And of course he did not quite comprehend design research as we do today, with the design itself as the central, inherent driver of the process throughout: he tended to regard research, like other modernists at the time, as the precursor to design. But in his two-fold conception he undoubtedly made a creative leap, and showed how this idea of two layers working in different directions, and temporalities, meant there was a dialectic operation at work there as well. The description of 'research toward design' is also evocative, suggesting that with the idea of design in mind, the actual research might be conducted in a different manner. His was an extremely interesting take, and in this sense an example of Deleuzian 'reverse causality' – not treated as anything final as such, but a recognition of how future projections can affect the present – which forces us to problematise our view of design research and its particular methodology.

We can find, therefore, a double-dialectic at work – the first is between the constituent processes of projects (design) and texts and books (writing), and the other is between the 'two-fold movement' of projecting ideas and research forwards and at the same time of projecting ideas and research backwards (that is, from present to the future, and future to the present). If this all implies almost rhizomic condition in which there is no clear starting point or ending point, then that is appropriate for a form of investigation – design research – which above all seeks to raise questions than offer simple solutions to 'problems'. Such a realisation, therefore, might lie at the core of design research in architecture. We need of course to be very careful in stating such things, as there are obviously many different types of design research, just as there are different types of scientific research, or social science research, or historical research. One would never want to stereotype. Yet the inclusion of 'reverse causality' implied by Saarinen can help us to see design research in architecture as an intensely two-fold activity in which a part of the research involved plots its path forward from the start of the process while, simultaneously, another

part maps itself back from an imagined end result, or series of results, to analyse and influence the design process as it is happening. Hence, rather than a linear activity, it becomes a far more complex crossover of forward-looking aspects and backward-looking aspects, with its own internal verifications and checks, and making its own explanations and causal connections as required. In this regard it could perhaps be seen as a happy hybrid of the dominant methodological approaches of, say, science and history, but on the basis that it is the design investigations which constitute the core of the process.

It is also significant to note here that Saarinen regarded the locus for design research as that of the urban level. Therefore his insights are married to the earlier contention in this chapter that design research needs to look beyond the specifics of the individual architect's contribution to address the broader realities of urban life – as was also demonstrated so well by *Delirious New York* or the projects of Lebbeus Woods. Both of these precedents showed the way in which design research can be thoroughly informed by an awareness of conditions of practice. This was achieved by pushing the forward-looking agenda of architectural design while also allowing the design research process to become even more potent and impactful by detaching itself in part from practice realities, and then using this constructed distance to look at the conditions of practice from outside and backwards, at the same time. This is of course not simply something which applies to architectural academics or those producing imaginary 'paper' architecture. Design research can thus be posited as revealing what is *not* yet there in a project design or in an architectural practice, but which has the potential to be. In this sense design research is anticipatory, and necessary, for any architectural practice which wants to develop its ideas and its projects. Design research acts on these designs and unpicks them in reverse to show what could be.

Having travelled back in time to rediscover Eliel Saarinen's writings from the early 1940s, it is time to conclude this essay, and indeed this book as a whole. Design research offers a rich approach for architects and academics to develop ever more their own particular kind of knowledge, and establish their own approaches and methodologies. Given the open and speculative nature of design, a whole range of topics are able to be drawn into the act of design research, as the essays in this book show. These include for example: spatial morphology, building typology, architectural history and theory, philosophy, performance and perfomativity, drawn/modelled representations, building materials, construction techniques, sustainability, sociology, psychology, subjective experience, gender relationships, architectural practice, digital social media and such like. Perhaps the key thing to hold onto is the inventiveness and suppleness of design research, which in turn echoes the sheer fluidity of social and economic relations across the world, especially within the new networked conditions we usually refer to as globalisation. Just as socio-economic systems, or indeed the very patterns of human life, are never written fully in advance, so too does design research offer a breath-taking openness.

To some this might smack of a lack of rigour, but for that we only need to remember the role of creativity and chance and contingency in even the most supposedly 'rational' scientific research. Accepting the freedom of design research offers plenty of opportunities for creative interventions in cities, semi-urban or rural areas that could then act as the catalysts for the kind of 'creative vernacular' envisaged by Teddy Cruz, Shigeru Ban, Yara Sharif or Lebbeus Woods, or indeed the processes of 'small change' in society as spoken of by Nabeel Hamdi. It is an incredible challenge for architectural practice and academia, yet cumulatively the effect could be substantial. If there is to be an underlying intent for design research in architecture, let it be the aim of examining and potentially redressing (at least in part) some of the most profound economic, social and cultural inequalities that exist around the world.

Notes

1 I am especially grateful to Hugh Campbell for his brilliant suggestion to organise this chapter in the mode of reverse chronology, after he read an earlier draft sent to him. I can only hope I have achieved something of what he imagined.

2 Walter Benjamin, 'Theses on the Philosophy of History', in Hannah Arendt (ed.), *Walter Benjamin: Illuminations* (London: Fontana Press, 1955/68/92), p. 249.

3 Gilles Deleuze & Felix Guattari, *A Thousand Plateaus* (London/ New York: Continuum Book, 1980/2002), p. 25.

4 Ibid., p. 431.

5 Manfredo Tafuri, *Architecture & Utopia: Design and Capitalist Development* (Cambridge, Mass/London: MIT Press, 1973/76); Manfredo Tafuri, *Theories and History of Architecture* (London: Granada, 1968/80). For an overview of Tafuri's general intellectual contribution, see Andrew Leach, *Manfredo Tafuri: Choosing History* (Ghent, Belgium: A&S Books, 2009).

6 For a snapshot of supposedly 'post-critical' thought, and its critics, see: Robert Somol & Sarah Whiting, 'Notes Around the Doppler Effect and Other Moods of Modernism', *Perspecta*, vol. 33 (2002), pp. 75-7; George Baird, '"Criticality" and its Discontents', *Harvard Design Magazine*, no .21 (Fall-Winter 2004), pp. 16-21.

7 Jane Rendell, Jonathan Hill, Murray Fraser & Mark Dorrian (eds), *Critical Architecture* (London/New York: Routledge, 2007).

8 Fredric Jameson, *Postmodernism, or the Cultural Logic of Late-capitalism* (London: Verso, 1991); Fredric Jameson, 'Architecture and the Critique of Ideology', in *The Ideologies of Theory: Essays 1971-1986* (Vol.2; Minneapolis: University of Minnesota, 1988), pp. 35-60.

For updated versions of Jameson's approach, see a number of the essays in Nadir Lahiji (ed.), *The Political Unconscious of Architecture* (Farnham, Surrey/Burlington, Vermont: Ashgate, 2013).

9   Aldo Rossi, *A Scientific Autobiography* (Cambridge, Mass/London: MIT Press/Graham Foundation for Advanced Studies in the Fine Arts, 1981), pp. 15–16.

10   'An Interview with Paul Rabinow', *Skyline*, March 1982 (trans. Christian Hubert), in Michel Foucault, *Power/Knowledge: Selected Interviews and Other Writings, 1972-77* (New York: Pantheon, 1980), viewable online at The Funambulist: Architectural Narratives website, http://thefunambulist.net/2012/06/20/foucault-episode-1-michel-foucaults-architectural-underestimation/ (accessed 10 March 2013).

11   Nishat Awan, Tatjana Schneider & Jeremy Till (eds.), *Spatial Agency: Other Ways of Doing Architecture* (London/New York: Routledge, 2011). See also the Spatial Agency website, http://www.spatialagency.net/ (accessed 24 March 2013).

12   Quote from Shigeru Ban in 'This Week's Ups and Downs', *Building Design*, 7 October 2011, p. 24.

13   'Cardboard Cathedral being Built in Earthquake-hit Christchurch', BBC News website, 27 December 2012, http://www.bbc.co.uk/news/world-asia-pacific-20852410 (accessed 10 March 2013); Mary Frances Schonberg, '"Cardboard Cathedral" Rises in Christchurch, NZ', Episcopal News Service website, 22 February 2013, http://episcopaldigitalnetwork.com/ens/2013/02/22/video-feature-cardboard-cathedral-rises-in-christchurch-nz/ (accessed 10 March 2013); 'Cardboard Cathedral – Christchurch, New Zealand), Shigeru Ban Architects website, http://www.shigerubanarchitects.com/SBA_WORKS/SBA_PROJECTS/SBA_PROJECTS_26/SBA_Projects_26.html (accessed 10 March 2013).

14   Much of the work of the Palestine Regeneration Team (PART) can be seen on our Palestine Regeneration Project Forum website, http://www.palestineregenerationproject.com/ (accessed 12 March 2013). See also the essay by Nasser Golzari & Yara Sharif, 'Reclaiming Space and Identity: Heritage-led regeneration in Palestine', *The Journal of Architecture*, vol. 16 no. 1 (2011), pp.121–44.

15   Yara Sharif, 'Spaces of Possibility and Imagination within the Palestinian/Israeli Conflict: Healing Fractures Through the Dialogues of Everyday Behaviour', Unpublished PhD Thesis, University of Westminster, London, UK (2012), p. 1

16   Ibid., p. 293.

17   Lebbeus Woods, *Radical Reconstruction* (New York: Princeton Architectural Press, 1997), p. 14.

18   Ibid., p. 30.

19   Ibid., p. 14.

20   Ernst Friedrich Schumacher, *Small is Beautiful: Economics as if People Mattered* (London: Bond and Briggs, 1973); Nabeel Hamdi,

Small Change: The Art of Practice and the Limits of Planning in Cities (London: Earthscan, 2004).

21   Lebbeus Woods, 'Another Rem', post on the Lebbeus Woods blogsite, 24 October 2009, http://lebbeuswoods.wordpress.com/2009/10/24/another-rem/ (accessed 24 March 2013).

22   Rem Koolhaas, *Delirious New York: Towards a Retroactive Manifesto* (New York: Monacelli Press, 1978).

23   Ibid., p. 293.

24   Comment made by Rem Koolhaas at 'Supercrit 5: Rem Koolhaas's *Delirious New York*', 5 May 2006, Department of Architecture, University of Westminster, London, UK. For a more biographical account of the background to the book, see Roberto Gargiani, *Rem Koolhaas/OMA: The Construction of Merveilles* (Lausanne/Abingdon, Oxon: EPFL Press/Routledge, 2008), pp. 3–75.

25   Rem Koolhaas & Bruce Mau. *S,M,L,XL* (Rotterdam/New York: 010 Publishers/Monacelli Press, 1995), p. 666.

26   Ibid., pp. 666–7.

27   Chuihua Judy Chung, Rem Koolhaas et al (eds), *The Harvard Project on the City: Vol.1. The Great Leap Forward* (Koln: Taschen, 2001); Chuihua Judy Chung et al (eds), *Harvard Design School Guide to Shopping: Project on the City, Vol. 2* (Koln: Taschen, 2001).

28   Footnote added by Lebbeus Woods to a post by Cheng Feng Lau, 'Report from Beijing 1: CCTV', on the Lebbeus Woods blogsite, 8 July 2011, http://lebbeuswoods.wordpress.com/2011/07/08/report-from-beijing-1-2/ (accessed 24 March 2013). For an almost identical interpretation, albeit in different words, see Murray Fraser, 'Beyond Koolhaas', in Jane Rendell et al (eds), *Critical Architecture* (London/New York: Routledge, 2007), pp. 332–9.

29   Eliel Saarinen, *The City: Its Growth, its Decay, its Future* (New York: Reinhold Publishing, 1943).

30   The clearest account of the Saarinen family's emigration to the USA is given in Jayne Merkel, *Eero Saarinen* (London: Phaidon, 2005), pp. 11–53.

31   Saarinen, *The City*, pp. 114–33, 362–4. See also: George R. Collins & Christiane C. Collins, *Camillo Sitte: The Birth of Modern City Planning* (New York: Rizzoli, 1986); Raymond Unwin, *Town Planning in Practice: An Introduction to the Art of Designing Cities and Suburbs* (London: T. Fisher Unwin, 1909).

32   Steen Eiler Rasmussen, *London: The Unique City* (Cambridge, Mass; MIT Press, 1934/82).

33   Lewis Mumford, The Culture of Cities (New York: Harcourt Brace, 1938); R. Wojtowicz, *Lewis Mumford and American Modernism: Eutopian Theories for Architecture and Urban Planning* (Cambridge/New York: Cambridge University Press, 1996), pp. 142–4; '"The City" – A World's Fair Film', *Architectural Review*, vol. 86 no. 513 (August 1939), pp. 93–4.

34   Jane Jacobs, *The Death and Life of Great American Cities* (New York/London: Random House/Cape, 1961/94).

35   Letter from Le Corbusier to Raoul La Roche, as cited in the entry on 'Fondation: History, Early Projects', Fondation Le Corbusier website, http://www.fondationlecorbusier.fr/corbuweb/morpheus. aspx?sysId=51&sysLanguage=en-en&itemPos=1&sysParentId=51&clear Query=1 (accessed 25 January 2013). The quote about step-by-step research is taken from Le Corbusier, *Precisions: On the Present State of Architecture and City Planning* (Cambridge, Mass: MIT Press, 1930/91), p. 25.

36   Saarinen, *The City*, p. 372.

37   Ibid., p. 373.

38   Ibid., p. 374.

39   Ibid., p. 373.

40   Ibid., p. 376.

41   Ibid., p. 374.

Indicative Bibliography

The purposes of including an Indicative Bibliography seemed relatively simple: firstly, to show there has been a long lineage of design research which is unique to architecture, and secondly to affirm its sheer diversity and vibrancy. Then the doubts started. Would it be seen as trying to establish a 'canon' of approved works, even though one was aiming for the absolute opposite? Also, given that the history of architecture is not best known for equality in terms of gender, geography or ethnicity, would a list such as this be too white, male and western (I exhibit symptoms of all three conditions) in light of current social values? But on balance, I still felt that it was worth including. Indeed, if anything, the list through its more recent items shows there is a change now towards a more inclusive condition in terms of gender, geography and ethnicity; this will hopefully increase as architecture (and design research) becomes more thoroughly gender balanced and globalised. Parallel exercises covering other parts of the world would undoubtedly help.

What follows, then, is a list of around 125 books which represent either significant examples of design research with a combination of design investigation and written analysis in a symbiotic manner, so as to create innovative knowledge, or else they are texts with especial pertinence to wider issues about design research in architecture. Since the aim of this Indicative Bibliography is to demonstrate the dialectical relationships between designing, thinking and writing, I decided against including actual buildings as such. The only exceptions to this rule are a few longer-term speculative 'paper projects' in which the depth of investigation constitutes an exemplar of design research. I realise that this absence of buildings might look like I am trying to steer the path of design research in architecture towards books rather than built designs. That however is not the case, and I would repeat my introductory point that the parallel Ashgate book series seems to me the more ideal medium for investigating in detail how buildings are and can be shaped through design research. Again, a parallel list of buildings which exemplify the purpose of design research could be an interesting future exercise.

Hence the present intention is not to offer a definitive list of the best books on design research, or indeed on the subject of architecture more generally. Instead it is merely meant for debate, and readers will no doubt disagree with some choices and could probably suggest far better items that have been inadvertently omitted. These exercises always tend to be like that, and what follows is certainly meant to be provisional. All said, the list is laid out chronologically, rather than alphabetically by surname or according to different classifications, to offer a sense of how the passage of time has impacted on design research in architecture. The sample is also deliberately weighted towards contemporary examples to reflect the fact that this is the era in which design research in architecture has truly come of age.

Marcus Vitruvius Pollo, *The Ten Books on Architecture* (trans. Ingrid Rowland, commentary by Thomas N. Howe; Cambridge: Cambridge University Press, 1st century BC/1999).

Leon Batista Alberti, *On the Art of Building in Ten Books* (trans. Joseph Rykwert, Neil Leach & Robert Tavernor; Cambridge, Mass/London: MIT Press, 1485/1988).

Francesco Colonna, *Hypnerotomachia Poliphili* (trans. Joscelyn Godwin; London, Thames & Hudson, 1499/1999).

Sebastiano Serlio, *On Architecture – Vol.1. Books I-V of 'Tutte L'Opera d'architettura et prospetiva' by Sebastiano Serlio* (trans. Vaughan Hart & Peter Hicks; New Haven/London: Yale University Press, 1537/1611/1996).

Andrea Palladio, *The Four Books of Architecture* (prepared by Isaac Ware; New York: Dover Publications, 1570/1738/1965).

Giovanni Battista Piranesi, *The Prisons (Le Carceri): The Complete First and Second States* (New York/London: Dover Publications/Constable, 1750/1973).

Abbe Marc-Antoine Laugier, *Essay on Architecture* (trans. Wolfgang & Anni Herrmann; Los Angeles: Hennessey & Ingalls, 1753/1977).

Claude Nicolas Ledoux, 'Chaux', project from 1775 et seq.

Nicolas Le Camus de Mézières, *The Genius of Architecture, or: The Analogy of that Art with our Sensations* (trans. Daniel Brott; Los Angeles: Getty Centre for History of Art and the Humanities, 1780/1992).

Jean Francois Bastide, *The Little House: An Architectural Seduction* (trans. Rodophe el-Kihoury; New York: Princeton Architectural Press, 1789/1996).

Karl Friedrich Schinkel, *The English Journey: Journal of a Visit to France and Britain in 1826* (trans. F. Gayna Walls; New Haven/London: Yale University Press, 1827/1993).

John Soane, *Description of the House and Museum on the North Side of Lincoln's-Inn-Fields, the Residence of John Soane* (London, 1830/32/35).

John Claudius Loudon, *Encyclopaedia of Cottage, Farm and Villa Architecture and Furniture* (Shaftesbury: Donhead, 1839/2000).

Augustus Pugin, *The True Principles of Pointed or Christian Architecture* (Reading: Spire Books, 1841/2011).

Andrew Jackson Downing & Alexander Jackson Davis, *Cottage Residences: Or, a Series of Designs for Rural Cottages and Cottage Villas, and their Gardens and Grounds, Adapted to North America* (New York: Wiley & Putnam, 1842).

Gottfried Semper, *Style in the Technical and Tectonic Arts, or, Practical Aesthetics: A Handbook for Technicians, Artists and Friends of the Arts* (trans. Harry F. Mallgrave & Michael Robinson; Los Angeles: Getty Research Institute Publications Program, 1851/2004).

George Edmund Street, *Brick and Marble in the Middle Ages: Notes of a Tour in the North of Italy* (London: John Murray, 1855).

William Lethaby, *Architecture, Mysticism and Myth* (London: Architectural Press, 1891/1974).

Tony Garnier, 'City Industrielle', project from 1901 et seq.

Le Corbusier, *Journey to the East* (trans. Ivan Zaknić with Nicole Pertuiset; Cambridge, Mass/London: MIT Press, 1911/87).

D'Arcy Wentworth Thompson, *On Growth and Form* (Cambridge: Cambridge University Press, 1917/42).

Louis Sullivan, *Kindergarten Chats and Other Writings* (New York: Dover Publications, 1918/79).

Le Corbusier, *Towards a New Architecture* (trans. Frederick Etchells; London: Architectural Press, 1923/27/82).

Walter Gropius, *The New Architecture and the Bauhaus* (trans. P. Morton Shand; London: Faber & Faber, 1925/35).

Erich Mendelsohn, *Amerika: Bilderbuch eines Architekten* (Berlin/New York: Rudolph Mosse/Dover Publications, 1926/93).

László Moholy-Nagy, *The New Vision: Fundamentals of Design, Painting, Sculpture, Architecture* (New York: W.W. Norton, 1928/38).

Hugh Ferriss, *The Metropolis of Tomorrow* (New York/Princeton, NJ: Ives Washington/Princeton Architectural Press, 1929/86).

Richard Buckminster Fuller, *Nine Chains to the Moon* (London: Jonathan Cape, 1938/73).

Frank Lloyd Wright, *An Organic Architecture* (London: Lund Humphries, 1939).

Arthur Korn & Felix Samuely (Modern Architecture Research Group), 'A Master Plan for London', *Architectural Review*, vol. 91 no. 1, January 1942, pp. 143–50.

Eliel Saarinen, *The City: Its Growth, its Decay, its Future* (New York: Reinhold Publishing, 1943).

Patrick Abercrombie & John Henry Forshaw, *County of London Plan* (London: Macmillan, 1943).

Ludwig Hilberseimer, *The New City: Principles of Planning* (Chicago: Paul Theobald, 1944).

Le Corbusier, *The Modulor* (trans. Peter de Francia and Anna Bostock; London: Faber & Faber, 1951/61).

Constant Nieuwenhuys, 'New Babylon', project from 1956 et seq.

Yona Friedman, *L'Architecture Mobile: Vers une cite concue par ses habitants* (Paris: Casterman, 1958/70).

Victor Gruen, *Shopping Towns, USA: The Planning of Shopping Centers* (New York: Reinhold Publishing, 1960).

Ezra Ehrenkrantz, 'School Construction System Development (SCSD)', project from 1961 et seq.

Archigram, *Archigram* magazines, as published from 1961 et seq.

Robert Venturi, *Complexity and Contradiction in Architecture* (London/New York: Architectural Press/ Museum of Modern Art, 1966/77).

Aldo Rossi, *The Architecture of the City* (New York/Cambridge, Mass: Graham Foundation/MIT Press, 1966/82).

Alison Smithson (ed.), *Team 10 Primer* (Cambridge, Mass: MIT Press, 1968).

Gordon Pask, 'The Architectural Relevance of Cybernetics', *Architectural Design*, vol. 39 no. 9 (1969), pp. 494–6.

Geoffrey Broadbent & Anthony Ward (eds), *Design Methods in Architecture* (New York: George Wittenborn, 1969).

N. John Habraken, *Supports: An Alternate to Mass Housing* (trans. Ben Valkenburg; London: Architectural Press, 1972/99).

Lionel March & Philip Steadman, *Geometry of Environment* (London: RIBA Publications, 1972).

Robert Venturi, Denise Scott Brown & Steven Izenour, *Learning from Las Vegas: the Forgotten Symbolism of Architectural Form* (Cambridge, Mass: MIT Press, 1972/77).

Alison & Peter Smithson, *Without Rhetoric: An Architectural Aesthetic* (London: Latimer New Dimensions, 1973).

Frank Duffy, Colin Cave & John Worthington, *Planning Office Space* (London: Architectural Press, 1976).

Christopher Alexander et al, *A Pattern Language* (Oxford/New York: Oxford University Press, 1977).

Colin Rowe & Fred Koetter, *Collage City* (Cambridge, Mass/London: MIT Press, 1978).

Rem Koolhaas, *Delirious New York: A Retroactive Manifesto for Manhattan* (New York: Monacelli Press, 1978/94).

Charles Moore, Gerald Allen & Donlyn Lyndon, *The Place of Houses* (Berkeley/London: University of California Press, 1974/2000).

Ranulph Glanville, 'Why Design Research' (1980), in Robin Jacques & James A. Powell (eds), *Design, Science, Method: Proceedings of the 1980 Design Research Society Conference* (Guildford: Westbury House, 1981).

Aldo Rossi, *A Scientific Autobiography* (Cambridge, Mass/London: MIT Press/Graham Foundation for Advanced Studies in the Fine Arts, 1981).

Bernard Tschumi, *The Manhattan Transcripts* (London: Academy Editions, 1981/94).

Reyner Banham, *Scenes in American Deserta* (Cambridge, Mass/London: MIT Press, 1982/89).

Donald A. Schön, *The Reflective Practitioner: How Professionals Think in Action* (New York/London: Basic Books, 1983).

Alison Smithson, *AS in DS: An Eye on the Road* (Delft: Delft University Press, 1983).

Cedric Price, *The Square Book* (London: Wiley-Academy, 1984/2003).

John Hejduk, *The Mask of Medusa: Works 1947–1983* (New York: Rizzoli, 1985).

Kisho Kurokawa, *Architecture of Symbiosis* (Los Angeles: California Museum of Science & Industry, 1987).

Michael Webb, *Temple Island* (London: AA Publications, 1987).

Ben Nicholson, *Appliance House* (Cambridge, Mass/London: MIT Press/ Chicago Institute of Architecture & Urbanism, 1990).

Herman Hertzberger, *Lessons for Students in Architecture* (trans. Ina Rike; Rotterdam: 010 Publishers, 1991).

Alessandra Latour (ed.), *Louis I Kahn: Writings, Lectures, Interviews* (New York: Rizzoli, 1991).

Lebbeus Woods, *Anarchitecture: Architecture is a Political Act* (London: Academy Editions, 1992).

Jennifer Bloomer, *Architecture and the Text: The (S)crypts of Joyce and Piranesi* (New Haven/London: Yale University Press, 1993).

Christopher Frayling, 'Research in Art and Design', *Royal College of Art Research Papers*, vol. 1 no. 1 (1993/94), pp. 1–5.

Bernard Tschumi, *Event Cities 1: Praxis* (Cambridge, Mass/London: MIT Press, 1994 – followed by *Event Cities 2*, 2000; *Event Cities 3*, 2004; *Event Cities 4*, 2010).

John Frazer, *An Evolutionary Architecture* (London: Architectural Association, 1995).

Rem Koolhaas, *S,M,L,XL* (New York: Monacelli Press, 1995).

Juhani Pallasmaa, *The Eyes of the Skin: Architecture and the Senses* (Chichester: John Wiley, 1996/2005).

Lebbeus Woods, *Radical Reconstruction* (New York: Princeton Architectural Press, 1997).

Jonathan Hill, *The Illegal Architect* (London: Black Dog, 1998).

MVRDV, *Farmax: Excursions on Density* (Rotterdam: 010 Publishers, 1998).

Jane Rendell, 'Doing it, (Un)Doing it, (Over) Doing it Yourself: Rhetorics of Architectural Abuse', in Jonathan Hill (ed.), *Occupying Architecture: Between the Architect and the User* (London: Routledge, 1998).

Ranulph Glanville, 'Researching Design and Designing Research', *Design Issues*, vol. 15 no. 2 (Summer 1999), pp. 80–91.

Greg Lynn, *Animate Form* (New York: Princeton Architectural Press, 1999).

Steven Holl, *Parallax* (New York: Princeton Architectural Press, 2000).

Lesley Lokko (ed.), *White Paper, Black Marks: Architecture, Race, Culture* (Minneapolis: University of Minnesota Press, 2000).

Atelier Bow Wow, *Pet Architecture Guide Book* (2 vols; Tokyo: World Photo Press, 2001/2).

Katherine Shonfield, *This is What We Do: A MUF Manual* (London: Ellipsis, 2001).

Décosterd & Rahm, *Physiological Architecture* (Basel: Birkhäuser, 2002).

Elizabeth Diller & Ricardo Scofidio, *Blur: The Making of Nothing* (New York/London: Harry N. Abrams, 2002).

Peter Downton, *Design Research* (Melbourne: RMIT Publishing, 2003).

Foreign Office Architects, *Phylogenesis: FOA's ark* (Barcelona: Actar, 2003).

Samantha Hardingham (ed.), *Cedric Price: Opera* (London: Wiley-Academy, 2003).

Jonathan Hill, *Actions of Architecture: Architects and Creative Users* (London/New York: Routledge, 2003).

David Moos & Gail Treschel (eds), *Samuel Mockbee and the Rural Studio: Community Architecture* (Birmingham, Alabama: Birmingham Museum of Art, 2003).

Aurora Fernandez Per (ed.), *As Built: Caruso St John Architects* (Vitoria-Gasteiz: A & T Ediciones, 2005).

Claire Melhuish & Pierre D'Avoine, *Housey Housey: A Pattern Book of Ideal Homes* (London: Black Dog, 2005).

MVRDV, *KM3: Excursions on capacities* (Barcelona: Actar, 2005).

Alison & Peter Smithson, *The Charged Void* (New York: Monacelli Press, 2005).

Leon van Schaik, *Mastering Architecture: Becoming a Creative Innovator in Practice* (Chichester: John Wiley, 2005).

Ben van Berkel & Caroline Bos, *UN Studio – Design Models: Architecture, Urbanism, infrastructure* (London: Thames & Hudson, 2006).

Aldo van Eyck, *Writings* (2 vols; Amsterdam: SUN Publishers, 2006).

Tim Anstey, Katja Grillner & Rolf Hughes (eds), *Architecture and Authorship* (London: Black Dog, 2007).

Mark Burry (ed.), *Gaudi Unseen: Completing the Sagrada Familia* (Berlin: Jovis Verlag, 2007).

Murray Fraser, 'Beyond Koolhaas', in Jane Rendell, Jonathan Hill, Murray Fraser and Mark Dorrian (eds), *Critical Architecture* (London/New York: Routledge, 2007), pp. 332–9.

Frederic Druot, Anne Lacaton & Jean-Philippe Vassal, *Plus: Large Scale Housing Development – An Exceptional Case* (Barcelona: Gustavo Gili, 2007).

Doina Petrescu (ed.), *Altering Practices: Feminist Politics and Poetics of Space* (London: Routledge, 2007).

Gerard Reinmuth & Scott Balmforth (eds), *TERROIR: Cosmopolitan Ground* (Broadway, New South Wales: DAB Documents/Faculty of Design Architecture and Building, University of Technology Sydney, 2007).

Sally Yard with Teddy Cruz, Olivier Debroise & Steve Fagin, *A Dynamic Equilibrium: In Pursuit of Public Terrain* (Tijuana/San Diego: Installation Gallery, inSite05, 2007).

Shigeru Ban, *Shigeru Ban Architects* (Tokyo: Shigeru Ban Architects, 2008).

Dorita Hannah & Olav Harsløf (eds), *Performance Design* (Copenhagen: Museum Tusculanum Press, 2008).

John Tuomey, *Architecture, Craft and Culture* (Dublin: Gandon Editions, 2008).

Ken Yeang, *Ecodesign: A Manual for Ecological Design* (London: John Wiley, 2008).

Carlos Castanheira & Alvaro Siza, *Alvaro Siza: The Function of Beauty* (London: Phaidon, 2009).

Michael Biggs & Henrik Karlsson (eds), *The Routledge Companion to Research in the Arts* (Abingdon, Oxon: Routledge, 2010).

Leslie Kavanaugh, *Meditations on Space* (Amsterdam: studiokav, 2010).

C.J. Lim & Ed Liu, *Smart Cities and Eco-Warriors* (London/New York: Routledge, 2010).

Sheila O'Donnell & John Tuomey, *Ways of Working: O'Donnell and Tuomey* (Buffalo: Buffalo Books/State University of New York Buffalo School of Architecture and Planning, 2010).

Jane Rendell, *Site-Writing* (London: IB Tauris, 2010).

Patrik Schumacher, *The Autopoesis of Architecture* (2 vols; London: John Wiley, 2010/12).

David Adjaye (Peter Allison ed.), *Africa Metropolitan Architecture* (New York: Rizzoli, 2011).

Nishat Awan, Tatjana Schneider & Jeremy Till (eds), *Spatial Agency: Other Ways of Doing Architecture* (London/New York: Routledge, 2011).

Lori A. Brown, *Feminist Practices: Interdisciplinary Approaches to Women in Architecture* (Farnham, Surrey: Ashgate, 2011).

Ruairi Glynn & Bob Sheil (eds), *Fabricate: Making Digital Architecture* (Cambridge, Ontario: Riverside Architectural Press, 2011).

Leon van Schaik & Anna Johnson (eds), *Architecture and Design, By Practice, By Invitation: Design Practice Research at RMIT* (Melbourne: RMIT Publishing, 2011).

Sarah Wigglesworth (ed.), *Around and About Stock Orchard Street* (Abingdon, Oxon/New York: Routledge, 2011).

Elemental (Alejandro Aravena & Andres Iacobelli), *Incremental Housing and Participatory Design Manual* (Ostfilderm, Germany: Hatje Cantz, 2012).

David Leatherbarrow, 'The Project of Design Research', in Michael U. Hensel (ed.), *Design Innovation for the Built Environment: Research by Design and the Renovation of Practice* (London: Routledge, 2012), pp. 5–13.

Halina Dunin-Woyseth & Fredrik Nilsson, 'On the Emergence of Research by Design and Practice-based Research Approaches in Architecture and Urban Design', in Michael U. Hensel (ed.), *Design Innovation for the Built Environment: Research by Design and the Renovation of Practice* (London: Routledge, 2012), pp. 37–52.

Wang Shu, *Wang Shu: Imagining the House* (Zurich: Lars Muller, 2012).

Nigel Bertram, *Furniture, Structure, Infrastructure* (Farnham, Surrey: Ashgate, 2013).

Yeoryia Manolopoulou, *Architectures of Chance* (Farnham, Surrey: Ashgate, 2013).

Index